And the children shall lead them

And the children shall lead them

An NGO Journey into Peace Education

BILL LOWREY, ALLEN HARDER AND VACHEL MILLER

EDITORS

And the Children Shall Lead Them: An NGO Journey into Peace Education

Bill Lowrey, Allen Harder and Vachel Miller, editors

Printed in the United States of America.

Published by World Vision International, 800 West Chestnut Avenue, Monrovia, California 91016 U.S.A.

Editor in chief: Edna Valdez. Senior editor: Rebecca Russell. Copyediting and typesetting: Joan Laflamme. Cover design: Judy Walker. Proofreader: RLou Norquist.

ISBN 1–933785–00–4

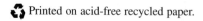 Printed on acid-free recycled paper.

Contents

List of Illustrations   vii

Abbreviations and Acronyms   ix

Acknowledgements   xi

Foreword: Margaret Sinclair   xiii

Introduction: Nurturing cultures of peace for children   xvii
A mandate for peace education
ALLEN HARDER

Part I

Encountering possibilities:
Planting peace education in the soil of humanitarian assistance and community development

1   From conflict resolution training to peace camps   3
World Vision peace education programmes around the world
RANDALL SALM

2   Potential for peace education in international development
programmes   35
*Concepts and strategies from World Vision's area
development programmes*
ROBERT KRECH

Part II

Encountering the core:
Growing a peace education curriculum and teacher/learner concept

3   Where's the peace? What's the education?   81
Part I: A closer look at existing curricula
VACHEL W. MILLER

4   Where's the peace? What's the education?   113
    Part II: Questions asked of peace education curricula
        VACHEL W. MILLER

5   Teaching for peace   131
    Helping people learn to live peacefully
        JAMES OLESEN AND MAVIS OLESEN

Part III

Encountering the edges:
Extending peace education
to embrace child protection and inner beliefs

6   Peace education in the context of family and community   177
    Peace education and child protection
        HEATHER MACLEOD

7   Inner beliefs as foundational to peace education   223
        BILL LOWREY

Appendix 1: Unpacking peace education   269
        VACHEL W. MILLER AND ROBERT KRECH

Appendix 2: Putting peace education to work in the context
    of Cambodia in the shadow of Angkor Wat   275
    A case study
        ALLEN HARDER

Appendix 3: Peace education resource packet   281
        RANDALL SALM

Contributors   307

List of Illustrations

Figure Intro-1.   Conflict transformation   xxvi

Figure Intro-2.   Integrating peace education   xxvii

Figure 1-1.   WV peace education projects   9

Figure 1–2.   Considerations for designing a peace education initiative   30

Figure 2–1.   A tranformational development flow chart   41

Figure 2–2.   The relationship between peacebuilding strategic
                   processes and TD domains of change   42

Figure 2–3.   Levels of conflict experienced by surveyed ADPs   47

Figure 2–4.   A child-focused framework
                   of conflict mapping and peace education   63

Figure 3-1.   Overview of key elements in peace education resources   90

Figure 3-2.   Programmes and learning objectives   93

Figure 3-3.   Distribution of learning objectives (numbers in
                   per cents)   99

Figure 3-4.   Summary distribution of learning objectives (numbers
                   in per cents)   101

Figure 3-5.   Strategies   105

Figure 5–1.   A model of thinking skills   160

Figure 6–1.   A safer world for children   180

Figure 7–1.   A matrix of the twelve affirmations   254

Figure 7–2.   Spheres of conflict and peace   256

Figure 7–3.   Dynamic model: Persons in context   259

Figure A1–1.   Educational initiatives for learning to live together   272

Figure A1-2.   A peace education sector diagram   274

Abbreviations and Acronyms

ADP	area development programme
CBO	community-based organisation
CCPT	Community Council for Peace and Tolerance (Kosovo)
CRC	Convention on the Rights of the Child
CRIN	Children's Rights Information Network
CRS	Catholic Relief Services
IES	impact and events scale
ISPCAN	International Society for the Prevention of Child Abuse and Neglect
LCP	local capacities for peace
LRA	Lord's Resistance Army (Uganda)
LTTE	Liberation Tamil Tigers of Élan
NAEYC	National Association for the Education of Young Children
NGO	non-governmental organisation
OTI	Office of Transition Initiatives (USAID)
PEC	Peace Education Consulation (World Vision, 2003)
PEP	UNHCR Peace Education Programme
PETH	Psycho-Educational Trauma Healing
REFLECT	Regenerated Freirean Literacy through Empowering Community Techniques
SHG	self-help group
SWOT	stengths, weaknesses, opportunities, threats (SWOT is an anlytical tool)

TD	transformational development
UNHCR	U.N. High Commissioner for Refugees
WHO	World Health Organization
WV	World Vision
YRTEP	Youth Reintegration Training and Education for Peace Program

Acknowledgements

In that day the wolf and the lamb will live together; the leopard and the goat will be at peace. Calves and yearlings will be safe among lions, and a little child will lead them all.
— ISAIAH 11:6, THE NEW LIVING TRANSLATION

The sacred writings paint a picture of peace . . . and in that vision a little child leads them. World Vision has experienced a taste of that vision. It has been the children who have led us in the direction of peace and peace education. As a child-focused humanitarian and development agency, we know that there must be peace in community, peace in the homes, peace in the schools, good governance systems, care of the environment, and personal skills, attitudes, and behaviours that contribute toward peace. Peace is birthed in the beliefs about peace and relationships and systems. Therefore, peace education engages these areas. Concern for the children has led us here. Now the children in many places have become primary actors for peace and peace education. They will continue to lead us into new ventures. Our first acknowledgement must be to thank the children of the world who dream of peace and who lead us in that direction.

This publication is the product of a process that began in 2002. One of World Vision's regional peacebuilding and advocacy networks, Asia-Pacific PaxNet, discerned that many peace education programmes were being implemented in conflict areas around the world. A peace education consultation was envisioned which would bring field practitioners, programme and strategic planners, policy and advocacy proponents, and experienced resource people to research, document, assess and develop a peace education strategy for integration into World Vision's community development and humanitarian assistance programmes. Bringing this to fruition required a commitment of time, energy and creativity from a significant number of people. The chapters in this book are the product of these countless contributions, far too many to be named.

Allen Harder, at that time the peacebuilding and reconciliation advisor in World Vision Indonesia, designed the consultation, organized the many parts,

xi

and coordinated the contributors. World Vision Indonesia deserves thanks for releasing Allen Harder when needed to work on this task and for providing organizational support. Bill Lowrey, World Vision International's director for peacebuilding and reconciliation, facilitated the international support, provided invaluable counsel and hosted roundtable discussions with the chapter writers. In 2005, after Allen Harder had left his position in Indonesia, he continued to coordinate and facilitate the final process of bringing this book to the production stage. World Vision Cambodia, particularly through its peacebuilding advisor, Bill Forbes, hosted the consultation and provided personnel and logistical support. Its efforts created an unforgettable experience for participants and helped ground this book in the reality of a country which has experienced the horrors of a genocidal regime. David Kupp, from World Vision Canada, provided expert facilitation which elicited and kept in balance the experience of all the participants – no small task, given their diversity. Margaret Sinclair graciously agreed to write the Foreword to this book. With a whole lifetime of experience and dedication to peace education, most recently in the context of the United Nations, her willingness to contribute to this book is received with gratitude.

The writers of these chapters went far beyond their normal work, giving generously of their time, energy, wisdom and heart. They approached the consultation and the subsequent preparations for bringing their papers to the final publication stage with enthusiasm and dedication. Their papers went through many revisions as they willingly subjected their work to the review of others.

We would also like to commend the efforts of the publishing team in bringing this book to fruition. Our thanks go to Edna Valdez at World Vision International's Partnership Offices, and her editorial and production team: Rebecca Russell, for her encouragement during our writing process and keen eidtorial insight; and Joan Laflamme, Judy Walker and RLou Norquist.

Finally, we acknowledge with thanks all those who contributed their time and efforts through attending the consultation. This book is dedicated to all those who are dreaming up, creating and implementing peace education initiatives in the course of their "regular jobs". We are particularly grateful to those who courageously find ways to help children grow into becoming peacemakers in their communities. This project uncovered numerous places where this is happening.

Blessed are the peacemakers, for they shall be called children of God (Matt. 5:9).

Foreword

Margaret Sinclair

Since the end of the Cold War there has been a proliferation of armed conflicts in many parts of the world. Most have been civil wars and disturbances, often led by people who emphasise differences between ethnic or religious groups rather than the possibilities for their harmonious living together in peace. Often, children and adolescents are taught to use guns and bombs and cannot easily adapt to another way of life. In these circumstances humanitarian and development organisations have seen the need to educate for peace; hence this book, about peace education and its relation to peacebuilding and child protection.

Yet it is not only war-affected people who need to understand conflict and ways of resolving it. There are local and global clashes of cultures and peoples impinging on us all. Tensions are aggravated where people of different ethnicities or religious affiliations live side by side under difficult economic conditions. Worldwide, rapid social change means that conflict is found in the home – between generations, between genders and when step-parents and step-siblings have to live together. Conflict is found in schools and the workplace, where bullying and scapegoating are common experiences, and internally conflicted adolescents experience peer and partner pressures leading to risky health behaviours.

And the Children Shall Lead Them focuses primarily on the ways in which NGOs working with conflict-affected populations can help them build "positive peace" – moving away from the personal and group narratives of past problems and building a more functional society for their children. Post-conflict assistance programmes in different sectors such as shelter, income generation, transport and so on can provide support for this process, if they bring together members of different groups in designing and implementing mutually beneficial or social service activities. It is important that local partners help build peace thinking and commitment into these programmes, so that participants realise each day that they are working to build peace and internalise this concept. Ideally, this can be done through peace education workshops for some or all participants, which can lead to supplemental cultural, sports, social service, health or other activities organised on an inter-group basis by those participants who are strongly oriented towards peace.

Peacebuilding and peace education are not easy. They require a shift of focus away from people remembering and reliving their raw and conflictual emotions relating to the past and towards rational thinking about how to work with all parties to a dispute to improve conditions of life in the future. To make this shift from looking back with anger to looking forward in peace requires cognitive and emotional adjustment. Peace education should promote such adjustment through improving skills for effective communication, including listening to the needs of others; expressing one's own needs with emotional self control, neither aggressively nor inadequately; practising co-operative problem solving; developing negotiation skills; and turning to mediation. Peace education should help develop greater awareness of how emotions such as anger, bias, greed and sorrow lead to damaged perception, a one-sided view of the problems and inappropriate judgements. Peace education should show how empathy, a basic human trait, can be harnessed to lead us towards the values of social peace, justice and good governance.

At the spiritual level, peace education serves as a reminder of the critical and unending task of saying no to self-pity and its more active partners, anger and bitterness, and of saying yes to virtuous states such as compassion, loving kindness, sympathetic joy and even-mindedness (the four houses of the divine spirit in the Buddhist tradition), compassion and mercy (as in the Muslim's constantly repeated names for Allah – the Compassionate, the Merciful), experiencing and responding to God's love and loving all of one's neighbours as oneself (as in the Christian tradition).

Peace education alone cannot stop a recurrence of armed conflict, but it can contribute to multi-sectoral as well as faith-based efforts to nurture the fragile seedling of peace. Formal schooling must play its part – it has the largest outreach of any organised programme – the only question is how. A full-fledged peace education programme of the type described in this book is best, where circumstances permit. Under very difficult conditions, however, the effort might take a simpler form. I remember a preschool in a multiethnic refugee camp in Kenya where the children frequently sang "We are one, we are one; from the north, from the south, from the east, from the west, we are one, we are one." In multifaith situations it would be beneficial if a brief common prayer, song or poem about peace in society, community and homes could be agreed upon among all parties and recited daily in schools.

My own experience in helping develop peace education in schools for refugees and conflict-affected populations in developing countries has shown that the best approach is to have a weekly lesson, taught by specially trained teachers, using specially developed lesson materials; this can be complemented over time by other steps towards a more peaceful school climate and pedagogy. Care should be taken to maximise the benefits of peace education in terms of meeting the psychosocial needs of children and young people affected by trauma and strengthening their resilience in the face of continuing difficulties in their lives.

Multiple channels of peace education should be used to complement formal schooling, with peace education workshops conducted for different groups in society (interethnic and interreligious workshops where possible): adults, women, men, youth, community leaders, religious leaders, health workers, sports clubs, literacy groups, street children, child-headed families, preschools, trainees in vocational and teacher training programmes, participants in income-generation projects and so on – and, of course, for NGO staff and government officials where appropriate. Informal peace education through music, dance, theatre and sports, and, if possible, radio, magazines and other media, should be considered; such activities should be interethnic and interreligious, and could be organised by graduates of peace education workshops as a follow-up which will keep their motivation alive and help them to disseminate what they have learned.

Regarding nomenclature, the learning of the core skills and values for learning to live together in peace, such as active listening, avoiding prejudice, empathy, co-operative problem solving, negotiation and mediation does not have to be called peace education. Rather, it should be called by a title that has local resonance and motivational force. For people recovering from war, the title may well be *education for peace,* which is highly motivational for them. But if there are political objections to the word *peace,* another title may be chosen. For young people facing problems of aggression in the sphere of sexual relations and pressure for unwanted and/or unprotected sex – even in the context of an AIDS epidemic – a better term may be *life skills education.* In another situation the motivational title may be *human rights education. citizenship* (or *civics*) *education,* or *environmental protection.* In each case the same basic skills for peace and conflict resolution are learned and practised, but with an application that reflects local concerns.

The first steps to be undertaken if working with people who have suffered from or are at risk of conflict include talking with local programme staff and community members about possible education regarding peace and conflict prevention, as an education initiative and/or as part of a multi-sectoral peacebuilding activity; creating and supporting a core group of enthusiasts to explore the possibilities; and conducting a series of introductory peace education workshops with educators as well as some young people, and staff concerned with child protection, gender issues, peacebuilding and development. These workshops should preferably draw initially on internationally recognised and field-tested workshop guides such as those of the Inter-agency Network for Education in Emergencies' *Community Manual*, UNICEF's *Education for Conflict Resolution*, Quaker manuals and so forth, and should move on to design locally appropriate initiatives, leading to pilot peace education programmes in selected schools and non-formal settings. Discussions around local values, traditions and ways of seeing the world are important, using "elicitive" methods. Cumulatively, this could enrich the philosophical and spiritual framework for peace education and peacebuilding outlined in the final chapter of this book.

Education for peace, conflict resolution and life skills tends to fall between the cracks of the education process, and World Vision has taken an important step in bringing it to the fore as a policy concern. Following its close involvement in the Local Capacities for Peace project, this NGO has made peacebuilding a cross-cutting issue in the development of its field programmes. The present book does a great service by reviewing a sample of field programmes in areas of conflict and identifying their peace education elements, whether formal, non-formal or informal. It also puts forward a clear analysis of the shared learning objectives and content of peace education at this point in time and identifies some important omissions, such as the concepts of conflict escalation and positive bystandership. It emphasises the need for a thoroughly professional approach, using pedagogically sequenced experiential school activities that progressively build concepts, skills and values according to the age of the children and activities for adults that build on their existing experience but lead them towards peace.

I have long argued that NGOs, who rely on donations and government funds for their work, should "go public" about their programmes, their achievements and difficulties, and lessons learned, even while keeping certain aspects of their programmes confidential. World Vision has set an excellent example in this book, which is based on a global consultation held in 2003. My thanks go to the organisation and the authors for their important contribution to the ongoing development of the field of education for peace or what UNESCO has rightly identified as a key challenge of the coming century – learning to live together.

Introduction

Nurturing cultures of peace for children

A mandate for peace education

Allen Harder

Throughout the world societies are under the duress of social breakdown precipitated by conflict and dysfunctional community structures. Children become its primary victims as they get drawn into its vortex. In war-torn societies war makers exploit children as chattels of war. In consumer societies marketers exploit children by preparing them to be consumers of violence-laden products and perpetrators of violent means to achieve desired ends. In stressed societies children are caught in a self-perpetuating cycle of violence. Many efforts to counteract these directions have been implemented to help families and social institutions, including religious institutions, develop coping mechanisms and strategies to help children, their families and indeed their communities develop values, attitudes and skills to resist violence and to fashion peaceable societies. Peace education initiatives have generated a significant pool of educational resources in support of these initiatives.

In spite of this, the culture of violence is spreading ominously. The U.N. secretary-general's "Study on Violence against Children," commissioned in 2004, covers five areas of violence against children: (1) in the home and family, (2) in schools and education settings, (3) in other institutional settings (including the courts), (4) in the community, and (5) in work situations.[1] That this study has been commissioned at this time indicates that the problem is serious and growing and that it needs special strategies to address it. Questions are being asked about the effectiveness of peace education strategies to stem the tide.

The sources of violence are systemic and relational. The majority of the victims are children and women. Political, economic and social systems rely on coercion, manipulation and force to achieve their goals. Beliefs, practices and habits that foster violence easily become deeply embedded. Restoring them into life-giving ones may take generations. The propensity to regress into a culture of violence, which often occurs subtly and over time, compels a commitment to countervailing change that must also be deeply rooted and patient. Aid agencies are not immune to abetting the subtle slip towards violence when their social analysis does not include analysis of social dynamics which contribute to a culture of violence.

The Rwanda genocide of a decade ago had it roots in systemic conflict embedded in its colonial history, which separated and excluded ethnic Hutu and Tutsi Rwandans. That history formed the backdrop for the escalating groundswell of inter-ethnic hatred which burst in 1994. Between 1990 and 1994 the gradual degeneration towards genocide went largely unnoticed by international development agencies, who considered Rwanda to be the pearl of international development efforts (Uvin 1998). Peter Uvin argues that development agencies contributed to the genocide by being blinkered by the perception that Rwanda was an international development success and by not recognising the escalation of stereotyping and ethnic intolerance even within their own organisations and by not taking countermeasures. In fact, national and international institutions permitted themselves to get drawn into the dynamic by not countering its claims.

In the aftermath these same agencies felt obligated to help Rwandans piece their world back together again. Could peace education have helped avoid the genocide? Possibly not, but it may have contributed to a less catastrophic outcome. Can peace education help Rwandans reconstruct their world? It has already been doing so.

The emergence of "cultures of peace" thinking is empowering efforts to counteract "cultures of violence" with visions of peaceable societies that are able to resolve issues peacefully and to live in ways that are life giving. Indeed, fundamental problems need to be addressed at the systemic and institutional levels. Peace education finds its niche addressing the problems from the perspective of formation, training and capacity building. Concern for the future of our societies drives the impetus for a special focus on the formation of children, their care givers and their supporting communities for peaceable living. Addressing these issues in the less resourced countries, where providing even basic education is a major challenge, requires extraordinary efforts to bring attention to nurturing and mentoring life skills needed for peaceable living. Whereas many organisations are focused on meeting the well-being needs of children, fewer pay special attention to integrating peace and non-violence education as a component of their larger mandates.

PEACE EDUCATION AND THE CULTURE OF PEACE

Peace education's primary goal is to nurture and develop capacity contributing to building a culture of peace. Sustainable development depends on a society's ability to maintain just and compassionate systems and institutions, manage and resolve conflicts, and deal with competing interests and diversity in ways that value life in all its fullness. Above all, it is committed to resolve differences without the use of violence, manipulation and coercion. Building a culture of peace requires nurturing a growing "movement" of many local, small peace education initiatives supported at the macro level by international agencies.

Douglas Roche, a Canadian statesman and peace activist, describes a culture of peace as

> an approach to life that seeks to transform the cultural tendencies toward war and violence into a culture where dialogue, respect and fairness govern social relations. In this way, violence can be prevented through a more tolerant common global ethic. . . . The culture of peace is, at its core, an ethical approach to life. It recognizes that the world is experiencing a fundamental crisis. Though this crisis is often expressed in economic, ecological, or political terms, it is fundamentally a crisis of the human spirit. It is a crisis of all humanity that, in the journey through time, has reached the point where we are capable of destroying all life on earth just at the moment when the recognition of the inherent human rights of everyone is beginning to take hold. It illuminates our choice in how to live and which path we will follow. The culture of peace offers the vision of a global ethic toward life in full vibrancy; the culture of war offers the prospect of misery and annihilation. (Roche 2003, 108)

The U.N.'s Culture of Peace mandate attempts to move the culture of peace into a global movement. In 2003 the U.N. General Assembly passed Resolution A/RES/58/11 launching the "International Decade for a Culture of Peace and Non-Violence for the Children of the World, 2001–2010."[2] This resolution is based on one passed in 1999, "Declaration and Programme of Action on a

Culture of Peace" (A/RES/53/243), which challenges signatories to support and initiate activities in the eight domains-of-change action plan:

- culture of peace through education
- sustainable economic and social development
- respect for all human rights
- equality between women and men
- democratic participation
- understanding tolerance and solidarity
- free flow of information and knowledge
- international peace and security

The culture of peace framework is broad based and all-encompassing. The role of education, and peace education in particular, is key to bringing about a culture of peace because it addresses the "crisis of all humanity," as stated by Roche. A part of that crisis is that the mainstream of society finds the culture of peace threatening. Roche reports that most Western governments are reluctant to support the U.N. Culture of Peace initiative because if it were to take hold, it would undermine their capacity to make war (Roche 2003, 117–18). He further elevates the argument to human rights – the right to peace as the basis for a culture of peace. A number of U.N. resolutions have been tabled to promote the right to peace, based on a 1997 "Draft Oslo Declaration on the Human Right to Peace," but they have been derailed as being too controversial for resource-rich countries. Roche quotes a U.S. delegate as saying that "peace should not be elevated to the category of human right; otherwise it will be very difficult to start a war" (Roche 2003, 129). That peace education is threatening to the status quo is also underscored by Ian M Harris and Mary Lee Morrison in their chapter "Schools as Cultures of War: Overcoming Obstacles" (in Harris and Morrison 2003). They document in detail how finding support for peace education in America's educational institutions is challenging due to outside pressures through threatened withdrawal of funding and outright opposition. Society has an interest in maintaining the capacity to use culture of violence values to achieve its purposes.

The U.N. conventions on the rights for education and for children's rights provide other avenues to access the mandate for peace education. Gow, Vandergrift and Wanduragala, in a document that articulates WV's policy on children's rights and child protection, focus children's rights on the right to peace and identify clarifying details of the U.N. Convention on the Rights of the Child (CRC). They document that between 1985 and 1995, 2 million children were killed, 6 million were left seriously injured or permanently disabled,

12 million were left homeless, 1 million were orphaned or separated from the parents, 10 million suffered from serious psychological trauma as a result of war and 300,000 served as child soldiers (Gow, Vandergrift and Wanduragala 2000, 9). Margaret Sinclair, an advocate of peace education and senior consultant to UNESCO and UNHCR, documents numerous U.N. initiatives linking children's rights and peace education. Her book outlines a broad programme for tackling issues of global violence and conflict under the theme of learning to live together, which pulls together multiple goals in education programmes focusing on "peace and conflict resolution, social cohesion, respect for human rights and humanitarian norms, gender equality, active citizenship, environmental sustainability, and the practice of health-preserving behaviours, including HIV/AIDS" (Sinclair 2004, 9). She promotes a very broad approach to peace education as foundational to addressing numerous problems contributing to the crisis of humanity where the values of tolerance, respect and justice are being eroded.

An implicit approach to nurturing a culture of peace is suggested in this publication. It suggests imbuing conventional humanitarian assistance and community development programming with peace education values and strategies that contribute to fostering a climate where a culture of peace can grow. It also points towards bringing together peace education, peacebuilding and advocacy modalities to enhance conventional programming with a goal and purpose which look beyond meeting basic needs.

PURPOSE

The purpose of this book is to address the need to think broadly about applying peace education strategies to multi-sectoral programming in violence-prone and conflict-sensitive areas when analysis indicates that this is the appropriate response. It invites readers to consider including culture of peace as a valid community development goal and provides a framework for considering peace education strategies. This book is oriented to readers who have a deep concern for addressing the culture of violence in their programming context, whether that is community development, humanitarian assistance, policy and advocacy or specifically education. Each chapter in this book is a paper commissioned for WV's Peace Education Consultation (PEC), a five-day convention held in Siem Riep, Cambodia, in September 2003. This publication is one of the outputs of that consultation. The chapters included in this book have gone through a rigorous peer-review process. They were revised again after the consultation, benefiting from the lessons learned and additional insights gained.

The book does not claim to be comprehensive in addressing the many issues raised by educators, peace education specialists, peacebuilding and development programmers, and child rights and protection advocates. It is an outcome of a unique process in which field workers in community development and humanitarian assistance engaged with programmers, policy analysis, child advocates, academics and peace education specialists to fashion strategic directions for peace education within WV. It is not a technical treatise, even though it addresses technical issues. Instead, a snapshot of various perspectives is presented, which leads to developing a more comprehensive understanding of the world of peace education programming and resources. Finally, it documents WV's journey towards peace education as it seeks to respond to an increasing awareness that extraordinary interventions are required to address the obstacles that cultures of violence place before efforts to provide safe, nurturing environments for child development.

A NOTE ON THE PEACE EDUCATION CONSULTATION

In the last several years a new concern for, and interest in, developing a child-focused peace education strategy began emerging in WV in response to a growing concern for confronting conflict and violence with peacebuilding strategies. A number of national offices were beginning to take the lead in addressing the needs of communities and especially children in the midst of conflict or in post-conflict situations. A precursory overview of project initiatives indicated that many were already incorporating peace education concepts, whether explicitly or implicitly. Their conceptual foundation was often less than coherent. In spite of this, good work was being done and many valuable lessons were being learned that could benefit the WV partnership as a whole. These lessons needed to be documented and shared.

The PEC represented the convergence of the need to document WV's experience with peace education, develop a consensus about what peace education means in the WV context, explore and expand knowledge and experience, and develop strategies for incorporating it into ongoing programming. It also converged with a rising interest in national offices for quality programming resources that link education and peace.

The consultation gathered 40 WV personnel, representing field level, project implementation staff, programmers, managers, administrators, advisors at national/regional offices, senior national and international office staff and external resource people bringing specialised knowledge and experience. Most of the participants were involved in peacebuilding, education and advocacy initiatives in Latin America, Asia, Africa and the Middle East, and in the Support Offices in Australia, Canada, United States and Germany. The opportunity to intermingle interests, approaches and experiences generated a holistic, practical approach to peace education imbued with the disciplines of peace education expertise.

The consultation resulted in developing an understanding of and agreement around:

- key terminology in peace education
- the role of education within the world of peacebuilding, and its character-istics, practices, impact and links to children and other target groups
- links with the spirituality of peace and non-violence within faith and in-digenous traditions
- pedagogies that promote peace and non-violence in different community contexts

The consultation explored seven themes of inquiry, supported by papers presented by expert resource persons.

- Identify universal concepts in current peace education curricula, identify issues unique to WV's mission and vision which need further develop-ment, and develop a means of assessing peace education curricula.
- Develop an understanding of how children learn/are taught at different developmental stages and in diverse cultural contexts and how these is-sues contribute to developing peace education curricula.
- Assess WV's experience with projects incorporating peace education, document them and analyse for emerging themes, practices and lessons.
- Explore the potential for peace education in the WV's community devel-opment context through using the SWOT analytical tool to survey 18 Area Development Programmes (ADPs) from each of the WV regions and draw out priorities, hindrances and potentials they identify.
- Assess strategies for programming peace education based on experience with a school-based peace education magazine project in Indonesia.
- Engage child protection and advocacy issues in peace education through elucidating the context and culture of violence affecting many children in WV programme areas.
- Consider the religious and spiritual context of peace education in the con-text of WV as a faith-based agency focusing on transformational devel-opment and interfaith sensitivities.

WHAT DO WE MEAN? – PROBLEM OF DEFINITIONS AND THE RELATIONSHIP BETWEEN PEACE EDUCATION AND PEACEBUILDING

The meaning of peace education and peacebuilding and their relationship to transformational development, child-focused advocacy and education generated intense debate. Bringing together a broad spectrum of experience, from the academic to the field practitioner, demands continuous stretching and clarifying the key concepts and applying a generous and holistic approach. Rigorously defined "specialist" approaches tend to limit the parameters and be more exclusive; programmatic approaches tend to have broad and inclusive parameters.

The debate around distinguishing peace education and peacebuilding revolves around the effectiveness of peace education and/or peacebuilding strategies to affect meaningful change in situations of conflict and violence. Can peace education address structural violence or effectively mitigate in conflict situations? Can peacebuilding effectively inaugurate a culture of peace which requires the formation of beliefs, habits and practices in violent situations? Are they complementary but separate components, or is one a subset of the other? Can or should peace education incorporate advocacy, child protection, trauma healing? Is peace education most useful in conflict prevention or in post-conflict rehabilitation? Is peace education appropriate while conflict is raging? These questions were raised in the context of WV's experience, as WV works in all of these scenarios. These questions are also addressed at various points in the chapters herein.

The consultation produced a definition of peace education and refined its relationship to peacebuilding, education, advocacy and transformational development:[3]

> Peace education is the learning and teaching that nurtures the knowledge, attitudes, values, skills and habits that enable people to proactively engage with conflict and violence and build a peaceful world for children and adults.

Defining peace education involves first defining concepts around *peace* and *education*:

> WV's concept of *peace* considers *people and communities* valuing
> to resolve conflicts without violence; the presence of a *network of*

relationships at all levels of society that are characterised by being mutually beneficial and that cross all differences; and the existence of an *environment conducive to creating and sustaining institutions* which honour truth and beauty, show mercy, practice justice and contribute to the common good.[4]

Education creates a change in knowledge, attitudes, values, skills, habits and behaviours. It involves *learning* activities, processes and experiences, whether they are formal or informal, and whether intended or not. *Teaching* involves creating, facilitating and guiding the learning process. Education by itself is neutral – it can produce positive or negative results in purpose and outcome. It can support violence when it does not address issues of conflict as well as it can generate capacities for peaceful living when non-violent modalities are taught and demonstrated.

Peace education applies many of the best practices found in quality education in terms of pedagogy and values. Yet it goes beyond that by addressing violence and conflict, and equipping learners to take an active approach to building peace. As an umbrella concept, peace education can embrace a broad scope of initiatives that have in common holistic efforts to nurture the knowledge, attitudes, values, skills and habits that enable people to engage with conflict and violence and build positive relationships and a healthy community for peace.[5] By themselves, activities such as teaching conflict resolution skills, providing psychosocial assistance or conducting an advocacy campaign might not be considered peace education. However, when such activities involve peace-oriented teaching/learning strategies and are combined in an intentional focus on enabling people to build a more peaceful world, peace education is happening.

In the peacebuilding and peace education debate it is helpful to consider two main types of interventions: *structure-oriented* and *actor-oriented* approaches to address causes of violence and conflict and the grievances of the past, promoting long-term stability and justice, and generating peace-enhancing outcomes. These approaches address both the restoration of relationship and the restoration of justice and good governance in human systems. Systems-oriented approaches work at the systemic root causes of conflict and create opportunities by transforming systems. Actor-oriented approaches focus on conflict transformation and social rehabilitation processes.

In this construct, peace education makes a complementary fit with actor-oriented initiatives addressing the knowledge, attitudes, values, skills, habits and capacities that individuals or groups require for more peace-supporting relationships. Whereas peace education could affect attitudes and behaviours of groups in conflict or perpetrators of violence in a society to support change, it would likely not be used to directly intervene in socioeconomic, institutional and political structural changes contributing to their conflict.[6] Peace education, therefore, is considered as one of a number of peacebuilding intervention strategies complementary with other peacebuilding strategies. Peace education contributes to conflict transformation when it is considered as a long-term process aiming to bring positive change affecting relationships, attitudes and behaviours and structures (see Fig. Intro-1).

Figure Intro-1. Conflict transformation

Source: Action for Conflict Transformation (ACTION) Core Group, Nairobi, Kenya.

Peace education lays the groundwork to enable restoring and healing relationships within and between individuals, families, organisations, communities, nations and the environment. Peace education more explicitly influences attitudes and behaviours, and raises awareness about how systems and structures can hinder or support peace.

ALIGNING PEACE EDUCATION
WITH THE ORGANISATIONAL STRUCTURE

WV is a multi-sectoral child-focused agency with an operational mandate for transformational development, policy and advocacy, and emergency response and disaster mitigation. Having established peace education's affinity to education and peacebuilding, further exploring its link to WV's operational mandate is useful to create a niche for peace education. Figure Intro-2 illustrates the intersection of the education, peace education and peacebuilding components with the three main mission thrusts.[7]

Figure Intro-2. Integrating Peace Education

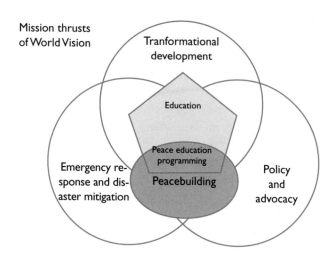

Creating a niche for peace education in the mission structure of a multi-sectoral organisation is essential for sustainability. Whereas in WV's context the education sector is firmly rooted in the transformational development dimension, current WV policies consider peacebuilding a cross-cutting theme integrated into all areas of ministry. Placing peace education into the context of peacebuilding opens up its potential to influence all areas of ministry that are working in areas affected by conflict or the threat of conflict.[8] Peace education is rooted in peacebuilding, using quality educational principles to contribute to conflict transformation and sustainable development.

Link to transformational development

Current transformational development policy integrates peacebuilding into five strategic processes leading towards transformational development:

- creating a culture of good governance
- transforming persons
- working in coalitions beyond commonly recognised boundaries
- developing sustainable livelihoods with just distribution of resources
- enhancing community capacities that generate hope

Peace education is an educational tool supporting strategic process when incorporated as a component in programme designs. More work is required to develop and disseminate the potential for specific peace education links to transformational development, as a distinct component of peacebuilding. Potentials for integrating peace education in related sectors (including HIV/AIDS) could be further explored since the methodologies are very similar. Referring to WV's *Transformational Development Core Documents* (January 2003), in the section "Strategic Processes/Indicators/Tools for Integrating Disaster Mitigation, Peace Building and Response to HIV/AIDS in Transformational Development," the potential for integrating peace education methods and core materials could be explored as one of the means to achieve transformational development goals. Robert Krech includes a more extensive discussion of WV's transformational development policy and strategies (see Chapter 2).

Link to advocacy, child rights and child protection

Bringing advocacy, child protection, and child rights advocacy into the peace education debate challenges the issues of the context/culture of violence in which many of WV's sponsored children live. How does peace education address children's situations when they are desperately trying to survive a violent situation at home or on the streets? The participation of WV child protection and advocacy specialists brought together peace education and advocacy around children. A healthy tension developed around this question: Does peace education contribute to child protection and rights strategies, or is it informed by them? The advocacy debate, in particular, becomes sharpened when considering activities to deal with injustice and structural violence.

Advocacy and justice issues tend to be left out of peace education curricula, and there are still few modules that deal adequately with these broader "peace" questions. Whether peace education should or could be a component of children's advocacy or children's advocacy of peace education did not get resolved. However, the debate underscored a compelling argument that the children's advocacy issues need to be addressed in peace education and that peace education can bring valuable added value to child protection and children's advocacy and initiatives to reduce the context of violence for children. These issues are addressed by Heather MacLeod (see Chapter 6).

Links to spirituality and interfaith bridging: Identifying gaps

The consultation highlighted the need to reconcile WV's core values relating to spiritual formation, transformational development and the formational aspects of peace education. Secularist approaches to peace education tend to ignore the spiritual space of the individual and the community and the spiritual underpinnings of the universal values they promote. Vachel Miller documents a virtual absence of faith-based and spirituality concerns in the non-religion-specific peace education curricula reviewed (see Chapter 3). Virtually all belief systems and world views, whether of the major or the "traditional" religions, teach moral and ethical values relating to peaceable living. The absence of explicit acknowledgement of moral and ethical values that cross faith boundaries is problematic for a holistic approach to peace education. Additionally, the consultation raised the issue of the relationship between violence and religious belief, and conversely, the influence of doing inner spiritual work on challenging cultures of violence. The spiritual formation of children is of special concern, especially in the context of child protection and advocacy. There is a concern that children could become vulnerable to exploitative approaches which could harm their long-term spiritual development.

Exploring inner beliefs and interfaith approaches to peace education spirituality was identified as needing further development. Faith-specific peace education approaches do use the spiritual wisdom of their respective religions. For faith-based agencies working in pluralist contexts, explorations into interfaith models which recognise and value the inner beliefs of participating peoples are called for. Bill Lowrey lays the foundation for embarking on this journey (see Chapter 7).

Link to emergency response and disaster mitigation

Peace education's interventions can play a specialised role in contexts in which an agency responds to emergencies – natural or manmade – where different identity or interest groups experience relational tensions or where significant trauma is involved. Its educational approach lends itself well to situations where there is a need to build awareness, present alternative models of relating and build capacity for collaborative approaches. Additionally, peace education is able to address the need for alternative models of behaviour for children at risk of facing further violence or perpetrating violence themselves. It also has potential to offer support to existing interventions such as emergency education, health, separated children in transit care, agricultural recovery programmes and others where there is a high value placed on bringing people in conflict together.

TOWARDS DEVELOPING A PEACE EDUCATION TOOL KIT

Practitioners and programmers are particularly interested in a convenient peace education tool kit. At the consultation it soon became obvious that it was unrealistic to come up with a core package of peace education strategies and tools, given the broad scope of peace education (and its variants), the large volume of tools available and the need to adapt them to local conditions. Instead, a "road map" leading to processes, resources and available expertise in specialty areas seemed more feasible. A number of specific tool kit components oriented towards programming point towards such a peace education tool kit. Figure 1–2 in Chapter 1 illustrates the various components which contribute to designing and implement a peace education initiative.

Assessment: Conflict-sensitive assessment tools have had a longer period of development and are being used by WV.[9] Conflict-sensitive assessment tools focusing on education are available in organisations specialising in education in emergencies. Additional assessment tools oriented to child protection are also indicated. Heather MacLeod expands on assessing the child's community context (see Chapter 6) and Robert Krech presents a child-focused assessment tool (see Chapter 2). Accurate assessment is necessary to determine whether peace education is the best option, whether it should be combined with other peacebuilding interventions, or if it is not appropriate to achieve a programme's goals and objectives.

Programming: Peace education programming need not be the domain of agencies specialising in education – or peace education. WV's expertise, for example, is in child-focused transformational development, advocacy and relief. Some national offices have developed expertise in peace education based on skills and specialisations introduced by personnel working in integrated, multi-sectoral programmes. Randall Salm describes this development (see Chapter 1). Many national offices of multi-sectoral programmes will not consider starting specialised peace education programmes, but they will consider how to integrate peace education strategies, and even components, into their programmes. The challenge is to provide them with appropriate expertise.

Curriculum: Many peace education curricula are readily available. Vachel Miller provides tools for assessing curricula that will meet the assessed need (see Chapters 3 and 4). A close link among assessment, the nature of the programme and the type of curriculum required for the context is obvious. The assessment would determine whether the need is for formal or informal educational approaches, a child or adult focus – or a student and/or teacher focus – a context-sensitive or more universal approach, or a specialised approach for specific needs such as child protection, advocacy, community development, or whether a special approach needed to be designed. The nature of the need determines the peace education approach. The chapters in this publication all point towards core content that suggests what is universal and applicable to all contexts while building on what is specific to a particular context. This requires involving people in eliciting what is important to them while integrating that into the larger picture of peace education values. Each agency will also have its own core principals and values, important to it, to contribute to designing the curriculum. It is important that these be transparent and articulated in the project's design documents.

Monitoring, evaluation and indicators: Practitioners and programmers are particularly interested in technical issues of assessment, monitoring, evaluation and developing indicators. Being able to articulate them is key to successful fund-raising and quality project management. The difficulty of developing indicators and evaluating peace programmes in general is common knowledge. There are no concrete measures – at least over the lifespan of most projects – that peace, or the numbers of peaceful persons, is increasing or decreasing. Trend and proxy indicators are useful, substituting for outcomes that are not easily quantifiable. Quantitative education indicators are easier to gather, but qualitative indicators tend to be elusive. The experience with transformational development indicators is that it is difficult to get measurable results of the transformation (a very dynamic) process. In the field of peace and peace education, general tool kits for monitoring and evaluation are still in the early stages of development. Existing tool kits tend to have been developed for a specific project.

The chapters in this publication make a significant contribution to this tool kit – in foundational principles, context assessment, curriculum assessment, pedagogy and programming.[10] A sample of developing a context-specific peace education programme is provided in Allen Harder's case study "Putting Peace Education to Work in Cambodia in the Shadow of Angkor Wat" (Appendix 2). The case study came out of a field trip to the ancient Angkor Wat temple complex, where the peace education consultation participants were challenged to absorb the story of genocide under the Khmer Rouge, to hear stories from the current generation of youth living in its shadow and to bring it all together to formulate a peace education strategy.

A PREVIEW OF WHAT IS TO COME

And the Children Shall Lead Them presents peace education as a series of encounters. In Part I we encounter possibilities rooted in WV's experience as a humanitarian assistance and community development agency through the eyes of experienced field practitioners. In Part II the core of peace education – curriculum development and pedagogical formation – is encountered from the perspective of experienced, professional educators. Part III encounters the edges of peace education and challenges readers to extend them to the field of child protection and the disciplines of the formation of inner beliefs. These two themes, presented by senior WV child protection and peacebuilding leaders, bring the book around to areas of central importance to WV as a faith-based organisation – advocacy, justice and holistic development that takes seriously all aspects of children's well-being. These encounters challenge humanitarian assistance and community development NGOs to consider nurturing cultures of peace in their programmes involving children at risk and explore peace education modalities as a reliable means to get there.

Part I: Encountering possibilities: Planting peace education in the soil of humanitarian assistance and community development

The two chapters in this section are rooted in WV's experience with peace education. Randall Salm and Robert Krech document the emergence of peace education initiatives and aspirations as WV responds to contexts of conflict and violence confronting the children in its care. These chapters are programme oriented but are also well rooted in peace and conflict concepts. They demonstrate that the integration of peace education into ongoing programmes is quite feasible and provide valuable pointers to those wishing to explore further peace education strategies.

Randall Salm's chapter, "From Conflict Resolution Curriculum to Peace Camps," documents the development of peace education initiatives in the 14 WV national offices in Asia, Africa, South/Latin America and the Balkans that were identified as having developed programmes with peace education components. Salm posits 7 categories in the peace education typology to assess the projects: school-based curriculum and teacher training, life skills, peace camps, tolerance and diversity, conflict resolution, arts and kids publications, and civic education. This study shows that even though peace education tends not to be clearly articulated, project outcomes reflect peace education outcomes. It also shows that many WV national offices have come to realise that peacebuilding and peace education are necessary for long-term sustainable development. Their paths to arriving at that conclusion and their programming approaches are distinctive, however, and often unique. Access to the many peace education models designed for different contexts provides the flexibility needed to contextualise initiatives. Salm provides guidance to project planners who want to be intentional and deliberate from the first concept development phase through to the monitoring and evaluation phase.

In "Potential for Peace Education in International Development Programmes" Robert Krech documents the results of a survey of 18 WV ADPs from four of its operational regions around the globe. ADPs selected for the SWOT analysis all were experiencing conflict in the areas of operation but not all were implementing peace education or peacebuilding programmes The principal tool used was the SWOT analysis. The practical and theoretical context of the ADPs is described, the possible policy links between WV's transformational development concept and peace education are examined, and the forms of violence reported by participating ADPs are discussed. The report focuses on the potential of WV's ADPs to integrate new peace education projects or activities into existing programmes. Peace education is not portrayed as a "silver bullet" or "cure all." Nevertheless, there is a good fit with peace education through WV's natural links with child rights, its concern with peacebuilding *(shalom)* and transformational development. The chapter concludes with programming recommendations that include the suggested use of a child-centred assessment model in which key institutions affecting children are mapped in terms of conflict and where the SWOTs are clearly identified. Krech then provides guidance for generating a peace education programme design.

Part II: Encountering the core: Growing a peace education curriculum and teacher/learner concept

The three chapters in this section present core curriculum assessment tools and pedagogical concepts which are foundational to developing peace education programming. Vachel Miller and James and Mavis Olesen challenge readers to take a holistic approach to peace education in the context of the community that surrounds the child in addition to the child himself or herself. This section forms the technical, educational core of the book and will be of particular interest to those interested in the philosophy of peace education as well as to practitioners considering selecting or designing a peace education curriculum and designing a delivery strategy.

Vachel Miller's first chapter, Part I of "Where's the Peace? What's the Education?" assesses a "random" selection of nine varying peace education curriculum guidebooks, ranging from a programme focusing on skill-building for violence prevention in an East African refugee community to a training programme for conflict managers in American schools. Miller finds that the curricula tend to converge around central themes. There is a consensus that topics such as co-operation and conflict resolution, appreciation of self and others, communication skills and emotional management should be included in effective peace education curricula and that there is an overall balance of objectives in the acquisition of knowledge, skills, attitudes and values oriented towards peace. On the whole, peace education programmes tend to avoid explicit reference to issues of group identity, preferring to address intergroup relations indirectly. Further, peace education programmes tend to focus on improving students' abilities to manage constructively interpersonal conflict and only tangentially engage students in critical dialogue about other forms of conflict or violence. Miller presents resources for a curriculum developer to select an appropriate curriculum and develop it according to the specific needs of the prospective programme.

Miller's second chapter, Part II of "Where's the Peace? What's the Education?" explores the philosophical side of curriculum selection and design. While it appears that peace educators have been effective in building a solid base of learning activities and pedagogical strategies, it is important to consider what is being left out of peace education. A series of critical questions is posed about the degree to which peace education can be universalised, how peace education can contribute to healing, the role of the inner life and gender in peace education, and the appropriate scope of peace education in light of WV's transformational development agenda. It is argued that while the peace education curricula reviewed can help learners become more skilled in working constructively with conflict and more committed to peace-oriented values, an expanded approach to peace education may contribute to the creation of more peaceful schools and communities.

In "Teaching for Peace" James Olesen and Mavis Olesen present an intercultural philosophy of education to support peace education curriculum development and teacher support. The chapter is rich in learning from their experience in curriculum and pedagogical development in camps for displaced persons in Asia. They see a high degree of congruence between the goals of sound general education and peace education. Peace education is necessary to equip students with those concepts, values and skills that will allow them to invent peaceful ways of living and that will help them to break the cycle of violence which conditions children and to construct a culture of peace. To achieve this, the authors stress that informal learning is as significant as classroom learning. The chapter also stresses the importance of considering stages of development that children go through and of recognising that these stages are universal, regardless of culture. Education strategies must coincide with the internal developmental timetables and needs of children. Education concepts can be cross-cultural, but the predominant values of societies where peace education curricula will be taught need to be defined. The Olesens also address the processes contributing to educational change. Teachers need guidance and permission in determining what changes are needed. They need training in alternative teaching methods that create democratic learning environments. Teachers, parents and community members need to be integral partners in peace education in order to provide holistic support to children's development. This chapter provides valuable inputs for designing the delivery of a peace education initiative.

Part III: Encountering the edges: Extending peace education to embrace child protection and inner beliefs

The two chapters in this section contribute foundational thinking for peace education from the perspective of principles, values, advocacy and spirituality in the WV context. Heather MacLeod and Bill Lowrey explore the two areas that are typically left out of peace education, but are central to WV's vision and mission. They engage issues on the "margins" of peace education raised by authors in the other two sections and propose that the peace education core be extended to incorporate those concerns. They address the need to be holistic, to consider the full context of the child and to take seriously the sources of conflict and violence.

Heather MacLeod's chapter, "Peace Education in the Context of Family and Community," focuses on the family and community contexts in which children live and where they face violence. Writing from the perspective of a child protection advocate, MacLeod unpacks the sources of systemic and cultural violence in the complex web of relationships affecting children. Five fictional children are introduced to readers. They reflect children in many situations in the developing world and will help readers consider the practical realities of peace education for children in the context of their family and community. MacLeod posits three approaches for children: to strengthen a child's resilience, to nurture healing and to help give children a voice. Peace education's role in transforming the context of the community and family surrounding the child is then developed. Particular attention is paid to tradition, gender issues, religion, educational institutions, poverty reduction, the role of NGOs and the making and keeping of law in the construction of a holistic philosophy which takes seriously the whole context of children. Peace education offers a programme with an intentional focus on teaching practical skills for reducing conflict and supporting peaceful living. A proper assessment of the child's environment will determine whether a peace education intervention should be a stand-alone programme or integrated into other existing relief and development programmes. MacLeod sees in peace education one viable modality for supporting social sustainability, emergence of hope and community participation with a focus on the child.

In "Inner Beliefs as Foundational for Peace Education," Bill Lowrey explores an often neglected element of peace education. He delves into the tensions that are generated within each person and community as inner beliefs either support or come into conflict with the values, practices and attitudes that are taught in peace education. He argues for an approach that assists people and communities to draw out and explore those inner beliefs that have a direct impact on peace education. Such an exploratory process is intended to help people consider how their beliefs may either be formed or transformed into values consistent with peace education. Lowrey illustrates the process with his own beliefs, drawn from his religious tradition and life experiences. The resulting personal exploration led him to a set of inner beliefs that have formed his core values. He states this set of beliefs in a series of twelve affirmations that undergird core values. Then he explains the affirmations in a manner that shows how they are rooted in religious, cultural and traditional wisdom as well as being incorporated in international conventions and laws. Because WV is a Christian NGO, particular focus is given to rooting each affirmation in the Judeo-Christian tradition. However, he also links the affirmations to the teachings of Islam, Buddhism, Hinduism, Bahaa'i, Confucianism, and international conventions. Lowrey does not argue that this set of affirmations should be accepted as propositions for all peace education programmes. Rather, he recommends a parallel process of exploration that draws out the beliefs that shape the values within each culture and context. Such community-based processes can lead an NGO to a deeper understanding of the beliefs within the community that are shaping its values, whether they are explicit or implicit. This understanding of inner beliefs related to values of peace and justice is foundational for designing an appropriate peace education curriculum and programme for that community. It would not be surprising to discover a universality to many beliefs and values. But such a universality would grow out of contextualised processes in settings around the world rather than being imposed by some external source. Lowrey's chapter suggests a way to root peace education in the beliefs and values of the local contexts while holding out hope that in time this may lead to affirmation of many universal values that are foundational to peace.

MAKING APPLICATIONS

The chapters in *And the Children Shall Lead Them* may be read in any order. The book does not claim to posit any one coherent methodology or endorse any particular curriculum, and it does not attempt to present a tightly bound philosophy of peace education. The chapters present "snapshots" of issues, methods, techniques, cases, assessments and tools for alert practitioners and planners to fashion a peace education initiative which makes sense in their context. Readers will find this book intellectually stimulating as authors grapple with the philosophical underpinnings of peace education while pushing the edges as they contend with the reality in the field. All the authors write out of their rootedness in and commitment to practical application in the field.

And the Children Shall Lead Them can best be used as a resource for dreaming up, fashioning and implementing a peace education initiative. Appendix 3 presents an annotated peace education resource packet prepared by author Randall Salm, where websites, media and printed resources are introduced.

Readers of *And the Children Shall Lead Them* are challenged to see this book as a living document that stimulates, grows and encounters peace education in ways that will continue to emerge. The challenge to nurture cultures of peace is so enormous that expanding forums for discussion, discernment and creativity are vital to fuel movements for peace. To that end this book is dedicated.

NOTES

[1] The final report will be presented at the U.N. General Assembly in 2006.

[2] Information is available online.

[3] Two consultation resource people, Vachel Miller and Robert Krech, formulated the following discussion, which is based on their paper "Unpacking Peace Education," found in its entirety in Appendix 1. This definition now guides WV policy around peace education.

[4] Condensed from the WV operational definitions.

[5] Refer to Margaret Sinclair's table "Educational initiatives for learning to live together" (Sinclair 2004) and to the "Flower Diagram" in Appendix 1 for a broader perspective on different types of peace education initiatives and their learning goals. This way of defining

peace education also helps draw to the peace education centre the broad scope of programmes implemented by WV (see Chapter 1 herein).

[6] Peace education was discussed as an effective strategy in conflict prevention and post-conflict restoration and transformation. It was seen, however, to be inappropriate for mitigating open and hostile conflict under way.

[7] The diagrams, contributed by Bill Lowrey, were prepared for the PEC.

[8] U.N. agencies often place peace education under the "education in emergencies" umbrella.

[9] See Stephan Jackson, with Siobhan Calthorp, "Making Sense of Turbulent Contexts: Analysis Tools for Humanitarian Actors" (World Vision International, May 2003); World Vision International, "Facilitation Manual for Community-Based LCP Assessment" (January 2005). Do No Harm/Local Capacities for Peace [LCP] is an inter-agency tool created by the Collaborative for Development Action.) Robert Krech's chapter posits a useful child-focused assessment tool.

[10] The simple framework presented in Figure 1–2 in Chapter 1 is helpful for programme designers to develop a peace education initiative. This framework outlines the decisions that need to be made when designing a peace education initiative. This framework will be a useful tool to help map out an approach to peace education programming.

REFERENCES

Gow, Melanie, Kathy Vandergrift and Randini Wanduragala. 2000. "The Right to Peace: Children and Armed Conflict." World Vision Working Paper No. 2. March.

Harris, Ian M., and Mary Lee Morrison. 2003. *Peace Education.* 2nd ed. Jefferson, NC: McFarland and Company.

Roche, Douglas. 2003. *The Human Right to Peace.* Ottawa, Canada: Novalis, Saint Paul University.

Sinclair, Margaret. 2004. *Learning to Live Together: Building Skills, Values and Attitudes for the Twenty First Century.* Geneva: UNESCO International Bureau of Education.

Uvin, Peter. 1998. *Aiding Violence: The Development Enterprise in Rwanda.* Bloomfield, CT: Kumarian Press.

PART 1

ENCOUNTERING POSSIBILITIES

*Planting peace education in the soil
of humanitarian assistance
and community development*

1

From conflict resolution training to peace camps

World Vision peace education programmes around the world

Randall Salm

INTRODUCTION, SCOPE
AND WV PEACE EDUCATION HISTORY

Introduction

Can you envision the impact of 1,100 local development programmes success-fully implementing an effective, comprehensive peace education programme aimed at skill building and character development for both children and adults? If each of those local programmes made significant strides towards peace in the everyday habits and lives of those inhabitants, how much interpersonal and systemic peace would come to pass? This chapter hints at that potential, with the documentation of the development of peace education programmes in over 15 local development programmes by WV.

In recent years WV staff members have become increasingly aware of the need for actions that promote sustainable peace between people in conflict. This need is generated by growing awareness of recurring conflict and vio-lence between some ethnic groups, with attendant social and development prob-lems for those groups and increasing costs for relief and development organisations. As a consequence, several local WV development programmes have included significant peace education activities.[1] Combined with other WV child-focused efforts on such topics as child prostitution, child labour, unaccompanied children and child soldiers, peace education may help rebuild divided communities and prevent future family, community or ethnic violence.

Scope of chapter and key terms

The scope of this chapter is guided by the increased importance in peace education in WV programmes. Its purpose is to survey and assess the peace education work of WV in its various forms in order to gain a clear picture of what has been done and how this fits into an overall "peace education map." The scope was initially defined by identifying those WV projects that concurrently dealt with both education and peace, such as peace camps or school-based peace education curriculum. WV regional project coordinators then identified relevant peace education projects within their regions that fit the pre-identified categories. As the proposals and reports were received, a few were excluded due to a lack of focus on one of those twin concepts, such as a primary school project lacking a noteworthy peace component.

We first define some of the main terms used in this report, briefly document of the history of peace education at WV and describe underlying WV values that support peace education. A conceptual map that cross references countries and programme types is then given, with an explanation of the seven types of peace education programmes.[2] A brief summary of each WV peace education country project that was found is given, followed by conclusions and recommendations.

It is worthwhile to note that most WV programme proposals did not clearly define peace education or identify what indicators could be used to determine success. This observation highlights the need for clarity on what value, attitude or behavioural outcomes are needed for peaceful relationships to occur. It may be possible for universal outcomes to be developed, with additional criteria appropriate for local cultural contexts.

For the purpose of this study, we use Maxwell O'Kane's definition of *peace*: "Positive peace is a pattern of cooperation and integration between major human groups. . . . It is about people interacting in cooperative ways; it is about social organizations of diverse peoples who willingly choose to cooperate for the benefit of all humankind; it calls for a system in which there are no winners and losers – all are winners; it is a state so highly valued that institutions are built around it to protect and promote it" (quoted in Sandy and Perkins 2002, 4)

Peace education requires both inner peace and interpersonal peace. The inner peace comes from having a balanced set of values and goals, loving one's self, understanding faults and strengths, and much more. While difficult to define and see, inner peace is often considered a necessary precursor to interpersonal peace. Interpersonal peace is the harmony that exists when relationships are based on love, respect, empathy, tolerance, concern, consideration and other critical values. This type of peace often requires special "prosocial" attitudes or values, especially respect and tolerance, but it also calls for social skills and abilities for resolving the differences or conflicts that arise normally in all social relationships.[3] Hence, children need adequate human development for building inner peace and appropriate social interaction for gaining interpersonal peace in order to be able to live fully in peace with themselves and others.

Past and present WV programmes use various terms in their peace education work. These include such key words as *peace education, conflict resolution, tolerance, diversity, multicultural awareness, non-violence, media and violence, life skills, counselling, civic education, health education* and *social studies.* These different topics are addressed using such methods as peace camps, arts and theatre, school-based curriculum, teacher training, foreign interchanges, vocational training, community outreach activities, leadership training, religious summits and more. The focus of this chapter is limited to those topics where peace and education come together. Specifically, we have searched for WV experiences that seek to build inner or interpersonal peace in some constituent group using some educational or teaching methods. While this scope is still somewhat ambiguous, it allows all potential peace education programmes at WV to be included.

The move into peace education at WV

As noted in the U.S. Institute for Peace document *Faith Based NGOs and International Peacebuilding*, WV has moved in recent years to promote conflict prevention and peacebuilding. WV recognised that progress on relief and development is often undermined by the renewal of conflicts. For instance, a major development project in Indonesia had to be abandoned because of increased violent conflict. Moreover, WV recognises that relief and development activities have on occasion contributed unwittingly to conflict. As a consequence, it takes seriously the "do no harm" approach and seeks ways to prevent and resolve conflicts. Most of this work entails introducing peacebuilding components into relief and development projects. Nevertheless, WV staff is cautiously moving into peace education, conflict prevention, resolution and transformation.

WV attempts to address the emergence of conflict, the escalation of conflict and the re-emergence of conflict. It does so primarily at the community level rather than at the regional or national levels through both conflict prevention in high risk situations of violence and peacebuilding in post-conflict contexts. In pre-conflict settings, WV's development strategies contribute to the reduction of violence in three ways: (1) poverty reduction and reduction of economic disparities between rich and poor; (2) civil society development, including appropriate participatory processes for community decision-making and conflict resolution; and (3) enhancing respect for human rights.

WV's research reveals that participatory processes to identify community needs and promote community development can help prevent violent conflict. According to Michelle Garred, these planning processes contribute to peace by bringing community leaders together across ethnic/religious divisions and intermixing groups that oppose each other (U.S. Institute for Peace 2001, 4). When a larger geographic area is involved in the planning process, the impact on peace is usually greater, since larger areas usually encompass more diverse populations. WV's experience is that intensive community development programmes are likely to decrease ethnic and religious prejudice; increase respect for the dignity and rights of other groups; encourage wider social identities; and enhance a community's ability to resolve local disputes peacefully. Conflict prevention is thus indirect but intentional. The primary purpose is community planning and development, but the indirect benefit is conflict prevention. In some cases, however, as in its church-based peace training in Rwanda, WV's approach to peacebuilding is more explicit and direct because its explicit purpose is to contribute to peace (U.S. Institute for Peace 2001).

Underlying values at WV

The underlying values of WV provide a strong social justice foundation for the building of a strategic vision for future peace education programmes. The powerful Christian values at WV serve as a guide. Some of the most relevant of these values are:

- to serve the neediest people of the earth
- to relieve suffering and promote the transformation
- to promote justice, peace, reconciliation and healing
- to give priority to people before money, systems and institutional machinery
- to respect the dignity, uniqueness and intrinsic worth of every person
- to celebrate diversity in human personality, culture and contribution
- to work using a participative, open, enabling style
- to recognise that values cannot be legislated – they must be lived

Clearly, many of these values relate directly to inner and interpersonal peace. They are also the reason for the many different, independent WV activities that have been initiated around the world in recent years.

WV PEACE EDUCATION ACTIVITIES

A conceptual map of WV peace education programmes worldwide

The development of a conceptual map of WV's peace education programmes seeks to summarise the variety of programme responses to peace made by the various WV country offices. A number of topics were identified representing the common terminology used for peace education programmes. Below are the principal categories of WV programme responses to peace education with brief descriptions or examples:

1. A school-based curriculum and teacher training: these types of interventions typically consist of the systematic development of activities related to peace for use in schools by teachers. School based curriculum may be implemented with or without teacher training. Sometimes teachers are trained in peace-related issues without a formal curriculum being developed.
2. Life skills: the World Health Organization has developed a life skills educational curriculum which teaches a wide range of skills to schoolchildren to improve their psychosocial skills. The skills include problem solving, critical thinking, communication, interpersonal skills, empathy and methods to cope with emotions. These skills enable children and adolescents to develop sound and positive mental health.
3. Peace camps: peace camps usually consist of one- to four-week summer camps that have special peace-related activities. Typically, children from conflicting groups are brought together to learn about each other and to break down stereotypes.
4. Tolerance and diversity: these activities often address stereotypes, prejudices and discrimination through multicultural activities. They seek to make children more accepting of differences and more understanding of the benefits of diversity.
5. Conflict resolution: conflict resolution often has a focus on skills development for resolving interpersonal conflict by addressing such topics as communication, problem solving, negotiation, mediation and conflict

analysis. In some cases this is done by isolated activities; in others, through comprehensive curriculum.

6. Arts and kids' publications: these activities usually include skits, plays, puppets, music, dances, shows, painting, storytelling and other cultural activities that address conflict and peace activities. Some are one-time activities, like Peace Days at schools or in the community, while others may include Peace Wagons that perform such activities throughout the region to many different audiences over a long period of time. Often a kids' publication is mass produced every two or three months addressing a different, important theme of peace education each time, and then sent to thousands of kids or schools.

7. Civic education: this involves activities that promote participation, democracy, responsibility, justice and similar issues to build awareness and skills for meeting the duties of citizenship. The target group is usually youth.

It is extremely important to note that different WV offices have formulated very different responses to similar problems. For example, school-based activities in Burundi and Bosnia are quite different, as we see in detail later. These differences require tolerance for different terminology and frameworks, yet provide excellent examples of how diverse interventions provide unique opportunities for replicating effective peace education interventions. The data collected comes from proposals and reports collected in 2002 for programmes which generally had been implemented between 1998 and 2002.

The following conceptual map provides a summary of different peace education–related programmes correlated by country, based on information obtained in this study.[4]

Summaries of WV country projects

The following summaries of WV's peace education projects are taken somewhat verbatim from WV proposals and evaluation reports.[5] Among other things, this allows the reader to identify similarities and differences in language used in the various WV country offices. Also, it is worthwhile to note that some documents were very short, limiting the ability to generalise across programmes, while others were comprehensive and tremendously informative as to context, goals, strategies, methods, evaluation and resources. Also, note that programme dates are not always identifiable. Due to limited space, only peace education–related objectives or methodological documentation is included.

Figure 1–1. WV peace education projects

Country	Project key word						
	School-based curriculum and teacher training	Life skills curriculum	Peace camps	Tolerance and diversity activities	Conflict-resolution activities	Arts and kids' publications	Civic education
Burundi	✓			✓		✓	
Kenya				✓	✓	✓	
Liberia	✓				✓		
Rwanda							
Sierra Leone	✓	✓		✓	✓	✓	✓
Uganda	✓	✓			✓	✓	
Indonesia					✓	✓	
Philippines	✓		✓	✓	✓		
Sri Lanka	✓						
Bosnia-Herzegovina	✓		✓	✓	✓	✓	✓
Montenegro	✓			✓	✓	✓	
Kosovo	✓			✓	✓	✓	✓
Colombia			✓			✓	✓
Central America and the Dominican Republic	✓			✓	✓		

At the end of each country programme summary I have provided a few comments on the given project. These comments discuss the probability that more peaceful values, attitudes and behaviours will be generated given the intervention used by the local ADP programme. The evaluation is based principally on the intensity of the peace education activities, the variety of activities directly related to peace, and the amount of hands-on practice given with skill building and personal reflection. For example, a six-week curriculum is considered more likely to teach peace than a one-day culture fair at a school. In general, I attempt to evaluate whether the proposals intentionally seek to promote peace through education or whether that is a secondary goal or byproduct. This is not intended to demean the value of any project but simply to classify projects by their ability to promote inner and interpersonal peace.

Burundi

WV Burundi initiated a two-pronged reconciliation, peacemaking and Christian witness project in Burundi to work directly with interfaith church leaders and to include peace and reconciliation activities in all of WV Bosnia's projects. The project goal was to affect a radical heartfelt change in the lives of Burundi's citizens at the national church level and at the grassroots level to begin to move the country towards peace. Planning included clear activities and indicators for each of the three objectives:

- to decrease the fear and distrust among 40 respected leaders in Karusi province based on biblical teaching and the gospel message of grace and forgiveness.
- to bring together ten interfaith leaders to design a strategy to promote a unified involvement in peace and reconciliation activities in Burundi.
- to affect change in the hearts and lives of 1,000 primary and secondary school-aged children in Karusi province through teaching biblical principles and sharing the gospel message of forgiveness and grace.

The adults chosen to participate in the seminars met in groups of 10 every three months for an intensive two-day seminar dealing with issues surrounding the past, the present and how to move into the future. The beneficiaries were chosen from a tightly targeted geographical area in Karusi that has both ethnic groups living in close proximity. Smaller group size was chosen to facilitate close support and monitoring. Collaboration and social integration were encouraged. The school component was initiated in the Karusi area so that the children and adults in the same area receive similar messages and, it is to be hoped, be able to encourage each other. Adults and child beneficiaries were chosen is such a way that in-school and community activities support each other.

Peace education was not clearly defined in the available documentation. Reconciliation activities for schoolchildren and community leaders are intensive and should lead to significant attitudinal and behavioural changes. While the participative approach to reconciliation activities should increase support and local-level implementation, it is uncertain whether the intensity of the interventions (curriculum and other activities) in the church-leader facilitations will be adequate to instill inner and interpersonal peace. Two indicators point towards ideal peace education design: 80 per cent of students pass tests with 70 per cent accuracy based on curricula; and 50 per cent of students voice and demonstrate changes in attitude and behaviour as a result of in-school teaching and Vacation Bible School activities.

Kenya/Uganda

The POKATUSA Peacebuilding Project drew its name from the four ethnic groups involved: Pokot, Karamojong, Turkana and Sabiny. The primary goals of the POKATUSA Peacebuilding Project were to reduce the frequency of violent conflict and to establish lasting peace and reconciliation among the four warring ethnic groups in Kenya and Uganda. The project pursued the following objectives over three years:

- increased understanding of the causes of conflict and effective skills in conflict resolution
- increased levels of contact, interaction and communication within and among families, religious groups, ethnic groups and tribes
- improved co-operation, unity and interdependency among warring ethnic groups
- reduced frequency of conflicts and tension among the pastoral communities in Kenya and Uganda
- increased willingness by community members to engage in joint activities
- reconciliation among long-standing enemies
- increased intercommunity trading activities

The following activities were completed:

- trained 40 peace and reconciliation facilitators
- conducted 40 peace and reconciliation awareness rallies
- broadcast 12 national radio programmes, in four ethnic languages, promoting peace and reconciliation awareness
- trained 30 church leaders to conduct 15 church-related forgiveness and reconciliation seminars
- trained 20 reconciliation trainers
- organised 40 inter-ethnic cultural exchanges
- conducted 6 district peace and reconciliation committee meetings
- organised drama, dance, art and poetry competitions at 40 schools

Liberia

In 1999 in the Madina area WV began a trauma-healing project called the Psycho-Educational Trauma Healing (PETH) Programme. The programme was developed for teachers because of their important role in the healing of their students. Once the teachers learned how to deal with their own trauma and how to help students in their classes, they encouraged their students to bring the images and painful memories of the war into the open by drawing pictures of their life now and in the future. By the end of the trauma-healing activities many of the students were drawing pictures of themselves contributing to the life of their communities.

The first phase of the PETH programme ran from February to July 1999, working with 42 teachers from 6 schools in Grand Cape Mount County with over 700 schoolchildren. WV Liberia then sought funding to continue the programme to cover 31 primary schools and 6,200 schoolchildren. A new initiative of the programme was to train students in managing conflicts, enabling them to help and counsel their peers. The overall goal of PETH was to promote psychological and emotional aspects of mental health of teachers and schoolchildren. This approach strengthens and promotes basic education and training of students in language and social studies through conflict resolution, stress management, peace education and the use of popular local traditional songs and dances that give value to interpersonal relationships.

The documentation available does not define peace education or clarify how the objectives would be met. While the quality of teacher training and curriculum is uncertain, the range of topics in the school activities and intense focus on those issues should promote peaceful behaviours and attitudes. This project is close to the ideal type of peace education programme due to its range of interventions and its intensity.

Rwanda

Peace education activities in Rwanda were unique due to the 1994 genocide and unprecedented levels of exposure to traumatic events among children and adolescents:

- virtually all children witnessed some form of violence during the 1994 conflict
- more than two-thirds of the children saw someone being injured or killed
- around 80 per cent experienced death in their immediate family
- almost all children saw bodies or parts of dead bodies
- the majority believed they would die during the massacres
- 16 per cent reported they had to hide under corpses in order to survive

WV believed that reconstruction and rehabilitation of the Rwandan society would only take place if healing, forgiveness, repentance, reparation, reconciliation and restorative justice occurred. The main mechanism was the traditional *Gacaca* trials for responding to the genocide and providing restorative justice. *Gacaca* is a mixture of conflict resolution, community solidarity and reconciliation. Since the trials are public, however, feelings of revenge and trauma may surface that require managing in order to limit future violence.

To respond to this situation, various interventions were developed. Personal development workshops addressed trust, grieving, expression of emotions and forgiveness. The community-health mental recovery programme addressed trauma identification and therapy and included a drop-in counselling centre for victims of sexual assault and rape. Children Heading Household healing and reconciliation workshops addressed reconciliation among church and governmental leaders. A community capacity peacebuilding tool called DELTA promoted peace education by building dialogue, trust and community solidarity. There was also the Way of Peace radio programme.

The programme goal was to contribute to the development of Rwandan society through healing and reconciliation initiatives in the community. The documentation provided specific indicators for healing, peacebuilding and reconciliation, including definitions of *attitudes of change, steps of change* and *action of change* (meaning both attitudes and behaviours) for individual, family, church and community levels. The proposal also contains a framework for evaluating peacebuilding and reconciliation activities.

While no definition of peace education was found, some indicators point to interventions oriented towards comprehensive peace education activities. The indicators and evaluation framework are especially insightful. However, the programme seems to lean more towards responding to trauma and general peacebuilding than peace education. This is determined in part by the uncertain nature of the participative DELTA project work. It may or may not develop specific, concrete peace education interventions, depending on the facilitation and orientation of participants.

Sierra Leone

The Youth Reintegration Training and Education for Peace Program (YRTEP) was established by the USAID Office of Transition Initiatives (OTI) to provide immediate and appropriate activities to support the enfranchisement and empowerment of youth and thus help break the potential cycle of violence in Sierra Leone. To reach these goals, OTI devised four interlinking objectives:

- assist the reintegration of ex-combatants and war-torn communities
- provide remedial education for youth bypassed by schooling during 10 years of war
- strengthen civil society's peacebuilding initiatives
- build public support for efforts in demobilisation of ex-combatants, reconciliation between war-affected youth and ex-combatants, and reintegration of ex-combatants into society.

The YRTEP curriculum was developed jointly with partners and included five modules:

Module 1. Who Am I? This self-awareness course was designed to facilitate movement of youth from a world of warfare to an environment promoting values related to peace.
Module 2. Learning Mind, Body and Spirit. This life-skills course enabled youth to improve their ability to manage their daily lives, make sound judgements, communicate effectively, manage emotions and solve daily problems.
Module 3. Our Environment. This course addressed what the environment is, how to preserve it and how to use it effectively.
Module 4. Health and Well-Being. This course dealt with local diseases, medicine, clean drinking water, sexually transmitted diseases and maternal and child health.

Module 5. Democracy, Good Governance and Conflict Management. This course focused on democracy, corruption, conflict management and how citizens could contribute to rebuilding Sierra Leone.

The YRTEP curriculum was based on the Regenerated Freirean Literacy through Empowering Community Techniques (REFLECT) methodology, although OTI's analysis showed that it borrowed more from peace education models. The REFLECT model is based on Paolo Freire's work in Brazil and is a structured participatory-learning process which facilitates people's critical analysis of their environment, placing empowerment at the heart of sustainable and equitable development. REFLECT is supposed to be a participatory, bottom-up approach that emphasises literacy, but the analysis of the YRTEP curriculum found it to be directive, with few opportunities for participatory interaction between instructors and students.

Many participants and community members reported significant improvements in youth behaviour. Youth became less violent and rude after completing the programme. YRTEP also got youth off the streets and into productive and educational activities. Participants reported that they were better able to function within their communities because of better understanding of cultural norms and anger control. Frequently ex-combatants reported positive behaviour change as well, no longer committing violent acts such as rape and murder, partly due to an internalisation of the moral consequences of their actions. This underscored the lack of knowledge that ex-combatants had of social norms and traditional community values prior to the training, due in part, for some, to the young age at which they were conscripted. Significant impacts were made emotionally, spiritually and socially.

OTI evaluators compared the goals and curricula of the three approaches: REFLECT, Education for Peace and YRTEP. The YRTEP training materials combine themes and methods from the other two sources.

The Education for Peace models were influential in the development of the YRTEP model, since behavioural and attitudinal transformation of participants and ex-combatants was seen as the main goal. Peace education as a field of endeavour is closely related to conflict-resolution initiatives; both address the themes of peace, co-operation and reconciliation, and also training people in problem-solving skills. The significant difference lies in how these issues are approached. Conflict-resolution training generally addresses specific, context-based conflicts that already exist, while peace education trains participants in how to prevent conflicts before they take place. In most peace education programmes, individuals are the primary focus and training is directed toward changing the behaviour and attitudes of individuals. The principles taught are assumed to be universal and, therefore, transcend the values inherent in the specific cultures.

Peace education programmes have taken many different forms, from emergency workshops in refugee camps to curricula to be interwoven within the existing subjects of national formal instruction. The range of programmes is great; what they have in common is instruction, discussion and activities around the role of the individual in bringing about peace. No systematic evaluation has been carried out to evaluate the relevance and impact of peace education experiences and approaches.

> The YRTEP programme specifically addresses peace education through curriculum. While no peace education definition was found, considerable thought was given to the attitudes and behaviours needed for inner and interpersonal peace, as evidenced by the five modules. Self-reflection was combined with communication, conflict resolution and civic issues to form a comprehensive programme. However, some criticism was raised of the REFLECT methodology based on a perceived lack of hands-on practice of necessary peace skills.

Uganda

The Gulu-Pader Psycho-Social Project Proposal for 2003–5 was a first draft document submitted to the Canadian International Development Agency. WV had worked in this area since 1995, resettling many children. Over 5,000 former child soldiers (5,102 male and 782 female) were rehabilitated from the centre and reintegrated into the community. The effects of this decade-long war have included ill health, trauma, loss of family members and the disruption of social order. Many people still have problems coping. The children who were born 15 years ago have never seen peace and love.

This project enhanced community capacity in resilience, psychosocial and peacebuilding skills. Specific outputs of the project included:

- counselling and resettling of war-affected children
- training community leaders in conflict resolution and peacebuilding skills
- training social groups and children's clubs to carry out participatory community dialogue and psychosocial support
- training youths in vocational and business skills

- establishment of a community-based health-care system by training community health workers, and preventive health awareness and immunisation
  campaigns

This project adopted two approaches, the centre and the community approach.
The centre approach focused on receiving, counselling and resettling the formerly abducted children and former child soldiers. The community approach
focused on addressing the community psychosocial issues and the inherent
effects of war through established community structures like local churches,
social groups and religious institutions.

Deliberate efforts were made to work with relevant government structures
during training. Care givers and counsellors were trained in peacebuilding and
conflict resolution. Counselling of returning child soldiers was done at reception centres. Several different outputs specifically identify peacebuilding and
conflict-resolution needs assessments, then training for WV staff, community
leaders and trainers, to be followed by implementation of activities with children.

This project seems to focus more on psychosocial development and
trauma therapy than peace education. However, the psychosocial interventions may contribute to inner peace, depending on their design.
If the conflict resolution and peace activities are extensive and intensive, including hands-on practice of peace skills, this project could
provide an excellent peace education programme while addressing
critical psychosocial issues.

Indonesia

The principal programme in North Maluku – Peacebuilding through Children's
Education in North Maluku – was a response to violence between Christians
and Muslims in 1999–2000 and aimed to "increase capacity of civil society to
engage in activities that will foster sustainable peace and encourage reconciliation among the people in the conflict zone of the Maluku Islands." Twenty
war-affected communities were chosen to provide services to 6,000 school-
aged children through the services of 300 teachers and 45 community trauma-
support workers. It responded to the violence and needs of the 200,000 internally displaced persons by having parents and community leaders focus on the
educational and psychosocial needs of children. This project was started in

early 2002, with extensive partnering work done with the Indonesian government, religious organisations, universities, NGOs and UN agencies.

Using the local capacities for peace (LCP) model, initially developed by
Mary Anderson in *Do No Harm*, World Vision Indonesia (WVII) identified
dividers (existing and potential tensions or capacities for violence) and connectors (capacities and resources for peace that already exist despite the conflict) and developed a plan to respond to local needs using appropriate yet
flexible planning and implementation strategies. Each of the 20 project sites
included about 300 children from grades 1 to 9, 15 teachers, 3 or 4 trauma
support workers, 1 improvised teaching centre (a rehabilitated school building), an inclusive educational committee and special peacebuilding activities. Of the 20 project locations, 10 had a "Happy House" for trauma-response activities with war-affected and internally displaced children. Teachers
and trauma support workers were trained by WVII and other experts on peace
education and trauma-response activities. A supporting peace and tolerance
curriculum magazine was distributed to over 13,000 kids in 160 schools in
North Maluku, with 750 teachers receiving a teacher's guide for leading peace
and tolerance activities in the classroom. Contents addressed such topics as
appreciation of diversity, co-operation, communication, being a peaceful child
and creative problem solving.

At the national level, WVII developed and promoted a comprehensive peace
education curriculum model based on Eleanor Snyder's *Kids and Conflict:
Resolving Problems the Jesus Way,* which was translated and adapted to the
Indonesian context by the Children and Peace Education Working Group com-
posed of Christian agencies, church organisations and other individuals. The
material was field tested, revised, and then 5,000 copies were printed. Training
on its use was provided to key educational leaders through a training of trainers
workshop: 50 teachers in Central Java, 50 in the Jakarta area, 50 in North Sumatra
and 25 in Central Sulawesi.

Programme intervention based on the LCP framework included the LCP
Integration Project, which placed three LCP disseminators in ADP areas of
high risk for violent conflict. Many WVII staff members have received mediation training through the Empowering for Reconciliation training courses. By
June 2001, 10 staff members were also trained in peacebuilding fundamentals
at the Mindao Peacebuilding Institute. They now lead the development of a
WVII peacebuilding core team which responds to short-term requests for specific assignments. WVII worked on peacebuilding at three levels – grassroots
community, middle and national – through collaborative endeavours with religious, educational, interfaith and nongovernmental organisations.

This programme views peace education as a significant component of its peacebuilding programme with a variety of intensive and specific peace education interventions. The concept of peace is very well thought out. Also, strategies were developed to circumvent and minimise interreligious hostilities by focusing on the needs of children while seeking repatriation or settlement for internally displaced persons and long-term, sustainable development for all Indonesians.

Philippines

Within the broader Philippine peace movement, humanitarian NGOs were very active in the peacebuilding process. Their efforts to introduce development at the grassroots level in far-flung areas facilitated the empowerment of rural communities, opened doors to long-term sociopolitical change and promoted social values such as intergroup or interreligious solidarity, which in turn have enhanced the quest for a society of peace. In 2000 and 2001 WV carried out Local Capacities for Peace/Do No Harm workshops in Mindanao. The LCP tool provides communities and youth with a forum to examine and understand the dividers and connectors in their communities. It also assesses the impact of project activities on these dividers and connectors, so that where negative impacts are identified, other options can be explored and used.

In Zamboanga, three sponsored teenagers led the local youth organisation and activities, such as sports competitions, which promoted interfaith fellowship among young people. Children were active in peace rallies and advocacy, like the Week of Peace celebrations in Mindanao, in which they pledged to work for peace by signing the United Nations Manifesto of Peace 2000. Subsequently, they held a gathering on the theme of reconciliation among people of different faiths that was attended by young people from all over the province.

Since 1998 WV has facilitated regional children and youth assemblies that gradually fostered a better understanding of and respect for the diversity in ethnicity and religion among the peoples in Mindanao. As a key implementer of the Expanding Children's Participation in Social Reform initiative, WV encouraged children to take the lead in conducting activities that promote interaction, especially between children and youth. Training and seminars, sports, fellowships and theatre groups were favourite activities for fostering a deeper sense of camaraderie and solidarity.

Some observations from the peace education work in the Philippines include:

- The impact of events such as ethnically mixed children's and youth assemblies should never be underestimated, as young people have proven to be enthusiastic peacebuilders capable of influencing others positively.
- While linguistic differences can cause divisions, joint education and other activities can connect youth of all faiths. And, through these young people, intercommunity relations, peace and understanding have been strengthened.
- If these children are educated about their rights and the laws of their country, then their communities will not lose their lands due to ignorance of these laws. If they can then use legal means to protect their resources, conflict and tensions will be reduced. Therefore, in the long term, educating children of all ethnic groups will help reduce tensions over land-ownership issues.
- There are strong links between conflict and poverty. Alleviating poverty can both reduce intra-community and intercommunity tensions and help build a stable environment that supports peacebuilding at a broader level. The causes of poverty must also be addressed.

Children's peacebuilding was a key potential of community development in areas affected by conflict. Children's simplicity, humility and peace-loving nature best exemplify the character that all individuals need in order to coexist with others. Rather than having fixed views, most children are flexible and open to new ideas and initiatives. They see simple answers to problems which adults often fail to see, yet they are often blind to religious or ethnic differences that pose obstacles for adults. Perhaps looking at adult problems and carrying out peace initiatives from a child's well-meaning, pure-intentioned perspective may lead us to a genuine answer in the long quest for peace and solidarity in the Philippines. Both Muslim and Christian children have said that peace will be possible when people "learn to understand and accept differences," "exercise liberty to practice their own beliefs and traditions without trepidation," and are "afforded equal opportunities for development." They also believe that peace must "begin within oneself."

LCP analysis in Mindanao reveals that children and youth are key stakeholders who unite communities and can act to bridge divides. At the same time, WV has found that LCP workshops have helped adults to overcome long-entrenched obstacles by seeing their situation with new eyes. Indeed, in the LCP workshops adults sometimes express their wish to begin again – to become like children who are able to accept and forgive and to develop non-violent ways of dealing with conflicts.

The WV peace education efforts in Philippines include a variety of strategies that seek to build tolerance and inter-ethnic relations. While no document was found detailing peace education programming and definitions, the extensiveness of certain activities, like the peace camps and conferences, is evident. Also, the peace education work in this country seems to exemplify how difficult it is to work in isolated, poor, conflict-ridden and violence-prone areas. Successes in this context are difficult to make happen. However, WV Philippines has made improvements in the lives of many children, youth and families.

Sri Lanka

WV Sri Lanka initiated a major peacebuilding programme with several peace education projects, including a Peace for Children programme, a Children as a Zone of Peace component and a peace education/conflict-resolution curriculum. There also were some intergroup sharing experiences between Sinhala Buddhists and Tamil Hindus, attempting to break down stereotypes and to learn how the other really lives.

Meetings were held to determine what kind of school curriculum to develop and what topics to include in that curriculum. This work was facilitated by the local Quaker group Peace and Community Action. If the peacebuilding outcomes are any reflection of the future peace education outcomes, the quality of the peace education training will be very high, as shown by the following list of peacebuilding outcomes that were identified:

Participants List of Topics and Skills for the Applied Peace Building Training Course:
- understanding our duties and responsibilities towards achieving peace: self-awareness; changes in our attitudes and behaviours; our responsibilities and roles; dedication; mutual respect through mutual understanding; social animation skills; team-building skills; stress management; understanding of different histories; political knowledge
- methods and skills for theory and practice: communication skills; mutual trust-building skills; critical-analysis skills; networking skills; non-violent conflict-resolution skills; confidence building and positive mental exercises; understanding values; a balanced study on religions and cultures; facilitation roles and skills; resource management
- skills needed for deeper understanding of non-violent peacebuilding processes: knowledge about our personal capacities for peacebuilding;

knowledge of the costs of conflict; advocacy of non-violence; giving equal status to all languages; leadership qualities; relationship building; new knowledge and methods of awareness on facing challenges, for example, dialogue with armed groups; approaching problems in a sensitive manner; human rights awareness.

The WV Sri Lanka peace education programme was just starting at the time data was collected. While goals and strategies are still being planned, information points to a programme that addresses the fundamental concepts of inner and interpersonal peace through both attitudes and behaviours.

Bosnia-Herzegovina

WV Bosnia had three separate peace education–related projects recently.

Creative Activities for Reconciliation and Trauma (first project): The project goals and objectives were:

- to increase the coping skills of vulnerable children in Republika Srpska, Tuzla canton and Brcko district through participation in Creative Activities workshops
- to increase the participation of parents in the education of their children in order to complement what children learn at school with what they learn at home
- to raise awareness about tolerance and conflict resolution among children, parents and teachers living in an environment of ethnic tension
- to increase participation of parents and teachers in community affairs

The above goals and objectives were tackled through a fully integrated programme designed to provide assistance to children, their parents and their teachers. The process of improving children's coping skills was initiated through their participation in Creative Activity workshops. There were festivals, a multiethnic peacebuilding camp, and Creative Activity workshops addressing prejudices and peaceful conflict resolution. Positive results were shown on pretest and post-test measures on self-esteem, relationships, tolerance and understanding of other groups. A 15–workshop curriculum was undertaken to improve parent-teacher relationships and to improve the curriculum in order to reduce intolerance. Themes explored included:

- strategy of co-operation in conflict resolution
- tolerance and discrimination
- conflict resolution, prejudice and discrimination
- teaching peace
- human rights, the *Convention on the Rights of the Child*

Brcko Town and Parent Teacher Associations (second project): WV worked with the town of Brcko through parent-teacher Associations to develop a unified curriculum to reduce the intolerance taught in schools and ethnic tensions. Also, WV and UN partners initiated promotion of civic education through informal parent-teacher associations and encouragement of citizen participation and confidence-building by facilitating a community-police dialogue. After a considerable number of meetings, the parent-teacher group accepted the idea of a unified curriculum. It emphasised that a unified curriculum should be employed in a one-ethnic environment, at least at the beginning, because it was concerned about the possible consequences of placing children of all three ethnic groups together. WV recognised this change of attitude as significant progress, taking into account that the parent-teacher group had been the toughest to work with. The parent-teacher group of the Fourth Primary School included additional recommendations: history, language and religious education should be separated from the other two ethnic groups; science should not be changed; and English language should be introduced as a first step toward unification.

Reconciliation Summer Camp in Bosnia (third project): Encouraging reconciliation and non-violent conflict resolution among children will have a profound and long-lasting effect on the Bosnia-Herzegovina of the future. Summer camps promoting these values will be one of the most effective tools to help children learn to trust one another, to overcome prejudices they encounter in their daily lives and to start a process of reconciliation.

WV identified short-term and long-term goals and expected results and indicators for the project. The wider objective (purpose) of this project was to promote reconciliation and non-violent conflict resolution with children to whom ethnic confrontation and conflict are a daily reality. The immediate objectives were:

- to give 200 children an understanding of prejudices/reconciliation and of conflict/conflict resolution which they can apply to their daily lives
- to help children challenge accepted patterns of behaviour relating to ethnic hatred and conflict generation and to reduce their fears

- to encourage children to form friendships across ethnic divides
- to give children from disadvantaged families an opportunity to enjoy themselves in a stress-free environment and to recover from their psychological wounds

The summer camp worked to build on the ongoing Creative Activities program. Target groups included 200 children from areas in Bosnia-Herzegovina close to the inter-ethnic border line or where minority repatriation leads to ethnic conflict. The identified geographical areas were Brcko, Tuzla and Gorazde. The IES (impact and events scale) survey, a standard questionnaire to assess depression and post-traumatic symptoms, was used to identify at-risk children for the programme.

Activities included a summer camp for 200 children (two 10–day sessions, for 100 children each) near Split, Croatia. The theme was developing friendships. The sessions addressed topics of confidence-building, communication, building trust, non-violent conflict resolution and reconciliation. Workshops used several means of expression: art, music, dance, drama and sport. The Developing Friendships curriculum's topics included introduction and establishing the group; who we are; same versus different; tolerance versus discrimination; non-violent conflict resolution; my new friends; and a message for peace.

WV Bosnia has developed a variety of intensive interventions addressing many different aspects of peace education, from trauma and inner peace issues to communication, conflict resolution and tolerance for interpersonal peace development. The existing curriculum was modified participatively with teachers and parents to reduce causes of intolerance and prejudice. Programmes address peace issues directly with reflection on the long-term need for education to build more peaceful social relationships. The programme in general takes specific steps towards the ideal peace education type of programme development.

Montenegro

In 2001 WV jointly implemented with UNICEF a peace and tolerance curriculum in every school in Montenegro. The themes included peace, tolerance, creative problem solving, peaceful resolution of conflict and leadership development. Some methods incorporated traditional stories, songs and dance. In 1999–2000, 25 teachers from nine elementary schools were trained, reaching about 5,000 children. In 2000–2001, another 25 teachers from partner schools were trained. The curriculum for this training addressed five issues: building co-operation, co-operative communication, giving affirmations, appreciating diversity in the classroom and creative problem solving in the classroom (similar to the Quaker Children's Creative Response to Conflict model). The project ended in August 2001, although additional activities may have been implemented through March 2002.

This project seems to be both intensive, with many activities for children addressing critical peace issues, as well as extensive, with a large number of beneficiaries.

Kosovo

The main Kosovo programme is called Community Council for Peace and Tolerance (CCPT) and is based in Mitrovica. Following the October 2001 conflict-resolution and strategic-planning workshop in Caux, Switzerland, CCPT entered a new phase of development. The first year focused on internal group formation and the second phase emphasised public outreach through increased member activity and small-group meetings.

The Gift Exchange Committee did an inter-ethnic gift exchange between elementary schoolchildren in North and South Mitrovica to mobilise children and educators for peace by creating a tangible, personal link between Albanian and Serbian schools. Children from other minority groups (Bosniac, Ashkali, Turkish, and others) were included to ensure equitable relationships with all ethnic communities. Multiethnic committee work highlighted the need for training in participatory decision-making.

A Kids for Peace programme proposal was developed by WV Kosovo in June 2002 to support the Children's Peace Movement in Kosovo. Over a one-year period it included work with schoolteachers and directors through activities on co-operation, communication, affirmation, tolerance, diversity and problem solving. The materials used were adapted from UNESCO's Inter-Agency Network for Education in Emergencies Peace Education model.

The programme goal for the Kids for Peace programme will impact the children of Kosovo positively by promoting peace and understanding among elementary schoolchildren throughout the province. The four distinct objectives are:

- outreach to local schools in the targeted municipalities by eliciting support and encouraging active participation of schoolteachers and directors in this Kids for Peace programme

- children learn strategies to enhance co-operation and collaboration, and to promote good communication and listening skills, through activities on positive affirmation, appreciation of diversity and creative problem-solving techniques
- children are encouraged to express themselves and their interest in promoting peace through music, poetry and drama
- children are encouraged to perform their artistic programme at various schools across the province to promote public outreach

---

The proposal includes an excellent list of bibliographic, organisational and training resources. The use of the UNESCO curriculum and variety of activities with teachers points towards a well-developed peace education programme.

Colombia

The Peace Builder Girls, Boys and Youngsters Movement was born to respond to the evident need for children and youth to participate in the construction of a culture of peace. Their participation allows them to live out their potential and their experiences with the hope of a present and future. The movement includes kids between from 6 to 18 who belong to different ethnic groups and live in various regions of the country. During 2001 this movement held six regional meetings, with over 2,800 participants, intended to strengthen the basic concepts of peace, culture and culture of peace.

Currently there are 8,300 girls and boys taking part in the movement from nine municipalities (Santander de Quilichao, Silvia, Cali, Armenia, Ibagué, Bucaramanga, Barranquilla, Montería and Bogotá). The second national meeting of the group in 2002 was led by 70 national youth representatives and had 750 youth participants at the main conference. The topics selected by the peacebuilders for this event were:

- infant maltreatment
- children and youth in armed conflict and the urban violence (child soldiers, forced displacement, gangs, urban delinquency)
- children and poverty
- child participation in civil society and construction of peace
- child labour
- better opportunities for young people (education and employment)

- land mines
- child exploitation (sex and work)
- identity of the movement (hymn, creed, social movement)

Each participant is expected to share his or her knowledge and experience with at least five other children, especially through didactic games and artistic processes.

> The multiplication strategy in this peace education project has tremendous potential for reaching a large number of children. While children and youth participate in some didactic activities, such as the peace magazine, it is uncertain if there are enough activities to change behaviour and attitudes significantly. Also, while the inclusion of a large number of related issues may promote a holistic environment for the generation of peace, it may reduce time focused specifically on peace education activities. This project is an example of making children a zone of peace in the midst of an ongoing war characterised by considerable terror and human rights violations.

Central America, Dominican Republic and Mexico

A recent peace education project called the Education with Tenderness Campaign was started in the region. It brings together government agencies and NGOs with the goals of promoting more peaceful relationships between children and adults and halting child abuse and neglect. It utilises alternative forms of conflict resolution and positive forms of discipline and education. Educational materials were developed. An annual media campaign promoted its message to the general public. This year's campaign focused on schools and child abuse by teachers. The campaign runs in Central America, Mexico and the Dominican Republic, with WV actively involved in most countries. WV Mexico is currently the point agency.

The model focused on developing coherence between what adults say and do with children, as well as providing appropriate guidance, training and education. This was combined with adult responsibility for providing a safe environment. In sum, it means balancing education and discipline, with a strong emphasis on positive methods for socialising children, not negative or violent means. The model included the four key concepts developed by Cloy Ramirez in *Discipline in the Classroom: A Guide for the Educator*:

- mutual respect: respect must be earned and comes from respecting others; eliminate negative criticism; talk with the kids when situations are tense; create an agreeable environment at home and school
- time: devote quality time to the kids; share time during your working day; and accompany them at least once a week on an extracurricular activity, such as going to the park or an artistic or sporting event
- stimulation: play down importance of kids' mistakes; acknowledge their virtues and potential; affirm their efforts
- expressions of love: show kids that we love them by hugging them, holding their hands, and other actions; maintain friendship with the kids

---

The model used to guide this programme is widely respected and touches on critical issues for peace education development.

CONCLUSIONS
AND RECOMMENDATIONS

The range of peace education responses by the different WV country offices to problems of violence and conflict is indeed tremendous. While realising that peacebuilding and peace education are necessary for long-term sustainable social development, each WV office's path to arriving at that conclusion and then moving forward through programme development and implementation is often unique. This makes generalising about programme similarities and differences especially problematic, since each WV office faces contextually specific issues and local implementation constraints. However, some noteworthy conclusions can be drawn.

First, the initial 13 categories used to select data for this study included some types that fit more appropriately under the peacebuilding theme than the peace education theme. The categories of community outreach, intergroup relations and religious activities often had limited educational components in their work. Instead, they sought to improve relationships between two groups in conflict. If they had (or would have in the future) more extensive educational components, they could be considered within the peace education umbrella.

Second, it is worthwhile to ask which among the final seven peace education programme interventions best promote sustainable peace. For example, do intensive school-based activities or conflict-resolution curricula promote more significant positive change in values, attitudes and behaviour than other programme interventions? Some agreement, even if only intuitive, on which types of peace education intervention are more likely to promote inner and interpersonal personal peace in children and adults may be worthwhile for programme development. This discussion also highlights the need to clarify the goals of peace education – Is there just one, or are there multiple goals? What exactly are they? How does one evaluate them? If there are multiple goals, there may be more effective peace education interventions for each one. When clear goals and indicators become available, qualitative and quantitative research should be done to assess the levels of interpersonal value and behavioural change as well as community levels of conflict, violence, empathy and co-operation. The comments made at the end of each country programme summary discussed *ideal* peace education programme development. The questions posed in this section help to clarify what an ideal peace education programme would look like.

Another interesting dynamic is the surprising range of models used to guide these peace education programmes. One often used model is the Quaker model, as evidenced by the Children's Creative Response to Conflict programme, which addresses affirmation, communication, conflict resolution and co-operation. Other models include those from UNHCR, UNICEF and UNESCO that may have been designed for use in intense conflict situations such as refugee camps. Unfortunately, the peace education programmes usually were not sufficiently documented in the available reports to enable identifying the underlying models. Clarifying which models and philosophies are being used can improve discussion about the values and paradigms influencing and guiding the peace education programme.

With this range of models we also find a range of sophistication in theory and programme development. Some programmes are well researched (the theoretical and resource development of some WV proposals truly impressed this author) while others have very limited foundations. However, the variety of background understanding of peace education may reflect the difficulty of finding good peace education literature in some parts of the world and the limited WV staff experience and training related to peace education.

Also, it is interesting to note the intervention levels of the peace education programmes found in this study. While some interventions are local (a few schools or a town), others address regional issues and populations (like counties, departments or states) and some work nationally (Ministry of Education teacher training or curriculum work). While this probably reflects WV resource constraints in some countries, it also highlights the extensiveness of some projects, with a corresponding larger number of beneficiaries. It would be interesting to explore creatively how to replicate the more effective interventions to much larger populations while limiting additional costs. For example, if a

Figure 1–2. Considerations for designing a peace education initiative

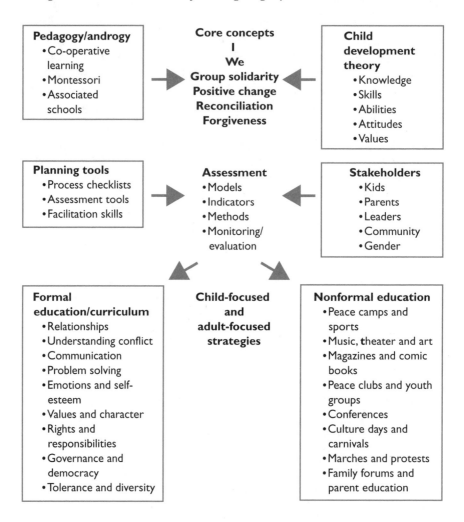

peace education curriculum is developed for a town or region, could it be expanded to the national level for a small additional expense?

Similarly, some programmatic responses are focused specifically on children and others on families and communities – similar to the idea of nested levels of intervention. While each type of intervention may have strengths and weaknesses, it is worthwhile to consider how the focus on one group may affect the other group or the overall success of the programme. In a few cases this was consciously considered by WV staff; in others it did not seem to be reflected upon as much. It would seem that increased integration of child-focused and family/community-focused interventions would more likely lead to relationships built on peace, justice, tolerance and creative conflict resolution. Figure 1–2 illustrates an integrated design process which begins with core concepts and theoretical underpinnings and moves to assessment strategies which determine stakeholders, beneficiaries and curriculum content.

In this context the overall goal of WV's peace education programme could be to provide flexible programmatic responses to assist in the development of culturally sensitive peace education programmes, so as to provide children, adolescents and adults with the skills, attitudes and values needed for living harmoniously and in peace with everyone in their communities.

NOTES

[1] WV local development programmes are called area development programmes (ADPs). For a description of ADPs, refer to Chapter 2.

[2] Initially there were 13 types of peace education programmes identified, but several were more related to peacebuilding than peace education, so they were dropped from the final report.

[3] "Prosocial" values and skills include what are commonly referred to as social skills (communication, problem solving, building relationships, etc.) but take the concept a step further with additional promotion of beliefs and behaviours that encourage co-operation and interpersonal peace. These include tolerance for differences, empathy and concern about other people, and a desire to empower those who are less fortunate.

[4] It is important to note that other WV peace education country projects may also exist, but they were not identified during the data-collection phase of this study.

[5] Due to space limitations and continual changes in each of the countries cited here, no background information is given on these countries. To see the latest information about these conflicts, see the Carter Center website (www.cartercenter.org), the Crisis Report website (www.crisisreport.org) or other continuously updated sites.

RESOURCES AND BIBLIOGRAPHY

World Vision documents

Bosnia. Reconciliation Summer Camps in Bosnia. August 2001.
Bosnia. Brcko Community Building Project. Second Interim Report February–June 2002.
Bosnia. Creative Activities for Reconciliation and Trauma Treatment of War Affected Children in Bosnia. Third Quarter Report. May–July 2002.
Bosnia. Building Confidence in the Zone of Separation and Brcko Town through the Formation of Parent-Teacher Associations and Police-Community Initiatives. February 2001.

Burundi. Concept paper. Reconciliation, Peacemaking and Christian Witness. October 2002.

Colombia. Concept paper. Second National Meeting of Children Peace Builders. June 7, 2001.

Colombia. Peace Builder Girls, Boys and Youngsters Movement of World Vision Colombia. No date.

Costa Rica and Central America. Campaign for Educating with Tenderness: A Shared Responsibility between Parents, Teachers and Adults. Jorge Delgado Salazar, Costa Rica Ministry of Justice and Crime Prevention. No date.

Indonesia. Peacebuilding Initiatives Fund: A Proposal for Funding. September 2001.

Indonesia. Opportunity Project Description, Indonesia Peacebuilding Initiative Fund. FY 2003.

Indonesia. Kids and Conflict: Curriculum Development for Children and Peace Education Project Proposal. Children and Peace Education Working Group. No date.

Indonesia. Maluku Peace and Reconciliation Program: Peacebuilding through Children's Education in North Maluku. June 2001.

Indonesia. Annex C LFA WV Indonesia Magazine Project for North Maluku. No date.

Kenya. Pokatusa Peace and Reconciliation Project. Quarterly Reports. January–March 2002 and October–December 2001.

Kosovo. Kids for Peace: A Proposal. June 13, 2002.

Kosovo. Improving Ethnic Relations in Kosovo: Community Council for Peace and Tolerance. Mitrovica. July 2002.

Kosovo. Proposal: Community Council for Peace and Tolerance: A Sustainable Voice for Peace in Mitrovica. June 2002.

Rwanda. Project Proposal. Peacebuilding and Reconciliation Program. October 2002.

Rwanda. Training Outcomes Local Capacities for Peace Workshops 1 and 2. May and June 2002.

Serbia and Montenegro. Final Program Report. March 2002.

Serbia and Montenegro. Activity Report. June–July 2001.

Serbia and Montenegro. Progress Report for Adult Evening Classes Berane Community Center. June 7, 2001.

Sierra Leone. Final Evaluation of the Office of Transition Initiatives' Program in Sierra Leone" (Draft, April 2002). Basic Education and Policy Support Activity.

Sri Lanka. Opportunity Project Description, Peace-building in Sri Lanka. FY 2003.

Sri Lanka. Peace Building Initiative Start Up Proposal. No date.

Uganda. Gula-Pader Psycho-Social Project: Project Proposal 2003–2005. No date.

Uganda. Children of War Rehabilitation Project. Third Quarter Report. April–June 2002.

Uganda. Congolese Children Transit Center Project. March 2001.

Additional works cited

Anderson, Mary B. *Do No Harm: How Aid Can Support Peace – Or War.* London: Lynn Rienner Publishers, 1999.

Lederach, John Paul. *Building Peace: Sustainable Reconciliation in Divided Societies.* Washington, DC: USIP, 1997.

Sandy, Leo, and Ray Perkins, Jr. "The Nature of Peace and Its Implications for Peace Education." *The Online Journal of Peace and Conflict Resolution* 4, no. 2 (2002): 1–8. www.trinstitute.org/ojpcr

Synder, Eleanor. *Kids and Conflict: Resolving Problems the Jesus Way.* A VBS curriculum for age 4–grade 8. Living Stones Series of Children's Resources. Newton, KS: Faith and Life Press, 1997.

U.S. Institute for Peace. *Faith Based NGOS and International Peace Building.* Washington, DC. June 2001. www.usip.org/pubs/reports

2

Potential for peace education in international development programmes

Concepts and strategies from World Vision's area development programmes

Robert Krech

INTRODUCTION

In the years following the end of the Cold War, dramatic changes in patterns of conflict and their destructive impact on the most vulnerable precipitated among international agencies a new interest both in conflict resolution and peacebuilding and in the rights and protection of children, who are among the most vulnerable in conflicts. Among the resources available to communities and agencies working to build peace in contexts of armed conflict, peace education continues to present a vision of and call for transformation. Peace education is a relatively old concept, dating back to before the First World War (Stomfay-Stitz 1993), and yet, despite its history, it is unclear what peace education is. Ian Harris suggests this is in part because "the problems of violence are so enormous and complex that peace education is practically amorphous, trying like an amoeba to address all the different forms of violence that occur on this planet" (Harris 2002, 16). Indeed, peace education seems to take all forms of conflict within its scope of concern, from the inner to the planetary. As once noted by Betty Reardon, "There are no clear and precise limits to, nor standards for, what should be included in peace education" (Reardon 1988, 14).

The amorphous nature of peace education becomes an acute problem within the context of aid agency programmes. Uncertainty exists regarding how peace education can meaningfully contribute to development and humanitarian programmes implemented in such violent contexts. Important to how peace education functions as a programme are questions of what peace education is and how it builds peace. In an attempt to explore these questions, this chapter examines some of the conceptual and practical issues associated with international NGOs implementing peace education programmes. It does so by exploring the potential of select World Vision (WV) area development programmes (ADP)[1] that are operating in settings of armed conflict to support peace education programming for children. This chapter began as a report commissioned at the initiative of WV's Asia Pacific Regional Office/Paxnet to provide input for a WV peace education consultation in September 2003, but it could apply to other NGOs with similar programmes. Taking WV ADPs as the unit of analysis, this chapter begins by describing the main areas of policy and practice within which ADPs function. This is followed by discussion of the kinds of conflict WV's ADPs experience, and then a presentation of the findings of a survey of the strengths, weaknesses, opportunities and threats facing ADPs wishing to incorporate peace education in their programmes. The chapter concludes with a number of recommendations, including a model to guide conflict analysis and to integrate peace education into relief and development programmes.

There are four areas of policy and practice important to understanding how peace education can assume a programmatic form for WV. The first is the current context of armed conflict worldwide, the second is the protection of war-affected children, the third is conflict resolution and peacebuilding, and the fourth is the policy environment of an aid agency. The first three areas exist in the wider discursive practices of the aid agency–donor world (of which WV is a part), linking understandings of violent conflict with their impact on children and with the urgent need to resolve conflict and build peace. The fourth is WV's unique policy context as an institutional orientation that frames all programming, including future peace education programmes. Every agency has its own policy environment that similarly shapes how programmes are conceptualised and developed by that agency. All four are important to understand for a number of reasons. Understanding these contexts will help ground subsequent discussion in this chapter on peace education. But more expansively, a large number of aid agency programmes – including WV's ADPs – function within each of these contexts. Clear links among the reality of violent conflict, protection of children, peacebuilding, an agency's institutional ethos, and peace education will help decision-making bodies at all levels of an aid agency support new peace education programmes. Moreover, clear links among these areas will assist with programme planning at the local level, equipping aid agencies to be attentive to critical implementation issues, and thus will contribute to existing research and practice in peace education.

The current context of conflict

Violent conflict in its various forms can encompass interstate war at the international level, civil wars, insurgencies, ethnic and community-based conflict at the state and sub-state levels, and domestic violence and abuse at the level of the family. It is widely acknowledged that the majority of armed conflicts since the end of the Cold War have been within states rather than between states. Approximately 90 per cent of the casualties in these conflicts have been women and children (Gantzel 1997; UNDP 1994). The majority of ADPs that participated in the survey experience conflict at the state and community levels, often with state-level violent conflict (whether political, economic, or social in manifestation) affecting children at the community level. Given this reality of experienced conflict, this chapter focuses on the problem of armed conflict as civil wars, insurgencies, and ethnic and community-based conflict.

Recent literature on contemporary violent conflict and war rejects notions of conflict as a regressive collapse into chaos driven by mechanistic forces. Instead, while violent conflict and war have definite discoverable causes, they are viewed as organic processes involving a range of players who constitute new and competing arrangements of power, legitimacy and livelihood. These players include governments, rebel groups, local warlords and strongmen, ethnic groups, and criminal organisations (including gangs), as well as NGOs, donors, private companies and private security forces. Market deregulation, structural adjustment programmes, and foreign aid through NGOs have created a context in which governments, rebel or militia groups and ethnic groups can forge global-local links with state donors, private companies, NGOs, and criminal and terrorist networks to control aid, populations, territories, resources and illicit commodity trade for profitable ends. Violent conflict often involves attrition, terror and human rights abuses against civilians. Violence is frequently carried out by the youngest members of a population, facilitated at times by the media and an abundant and accessible supply of small arms. In this context of conflict, power and legitimacy is based on violent control rather than popular consent (Macrae 2002; Duffield 2001; Kaldor 1999; Holsti 1996). In what is seemingly intractable violence, children are among the most affected.

The imperative to protect children affected by armed Conflict

As observed in the UN study *The Impact of Armed Conflict on Children:*

> More and more of the world is being sucked into a desolate moral
> vacuum. This is a space devoid of the most basic human values; a
> space in which children are slaughtered, raped, and maimed; a space
> in which children are exploited as soldiers; a space in which chil-
> dren are starved and exposed to extreme brutality. Such unregu-
> lated terror and violence speak of deliberate victimization. There
> are few further depths to which humanity can sink. (United Nations
> 1996, para. 3)

These strong words express a grief at the experience of children in situations of
violent conflict, suggesting that children's victimisation is the "last straw" and
it must stop. Violence kills and maims children disproportionately and often
violates their right to be at home with their families, to healthy development
into their full potential, to education, and to protection from exploitive labour
(Sommers 2002; UNICEF 2002).

The Convention on the Rights of the Child (CRC), ratified by every country
except Somalia and the United States, embodies the principles of the best interests of the child and the child's right to survival and development. Led by
UNICEF, the CRC has been the basis for a child rights regime that has concerned itself in particular with war-affected children. This concern is recognised
in documents such as *The State of the World's Children 1996* (UNICEF 1996),
conferences or summits like the Winnipeg Conference on War-Affected Children in 2000, and civil society movements and information networks like the
Global Movement for Children and the Children's Rights Information Network (CRIN). While the notion of rights for children has spread since the introduction of the CRC in 1989, much still remains to be done to ensure children's
rights are upheld. Children can be victims of violence; tragically, children are
also perpetrators at times. Still, children remain one of the most important resources for peace. Their participation in conflict resolution and peacebuilding
is imperative to a transformed world that respects children's rights.

Conflict resolution and peacebuilding

Conflict resolution and peacebuilding, though obviously related, are conceptually and operationally distinct. Conflict resolution in its classical form developed during the Cold War era and is largely actor oriented, viewing conflict as

a function of the negative attitudes, violent behaviours, and clashing interests of conflicting parties. Conflict resolution as applied to violent conflict among states, ethnic groups or other groups primarily relies on third-party intervention in negotiation, mediation or problem solving. *Peacebuilding* as a term emerged following the end of the Cold War in various U.N. documents. In these and other similar documents, peacebuilding was envisioned to occur in post-conflict countries following peace settlements with the purpose of supporting political, economic and social structures that consolidate newly achieved peace into the long term (Boutros-Ghali 1995; Carnegie Commission on Preventing Deadly Conflict 1997). Peacebuilding differs from traditional notions of conflict resolution because it focuses less on third-party interventions and more on conditions of human security such as economic opportunities for sustainable livelihoods, political participation at all levels that allows everyone to have a voice in decision-making, and social inclusion in cultural institutions or in public services like education or health care. The conditions of failed human security are what J. Galtung calls "structural violence" (Galtung 1976) and are often the structural causes of grievance and conflict that have turned violent in many situations.

Contemporary thinking fuses conflict-resolution principles and those of peacebuilding, with *peacebuilding* being the chosen term for a more robust notion of possible interventions for peace. Peacebuilding should be better understood as a

> comprehensive concept that encompasses, generates, and sustains the full array of processes, approaches, and stages needed to transform conflict toward more sustainable, peaceful relationships. The term thus involves a wide range of activities and functions that both precede and follow formal peace accords. Metaphorically, peace is seen not merely as a stage in time or a condition. It is a dynamic social construct. (Lederach 1997, 20)

In this view, peacebuilding is for more than civil wars and includes chronic political and community violence, is both actor oriented and structure oriented, and serves to prevent conflict as well as end conflict and build positive peace. Peacebuilding so conceived takes new recognition of bottom-up efforts normally seen as "track III" (grassroots) interventions, valuing local culture and capacities for peace as necessary for long-term transformation of relationships and structures implicated in the causes of conflict (Miall, Ramsbothan and Woodhouse 1999).

WV's Policy Environment

WV is organised internationally in a federal system, with a partnership office, regional offices, and national offices. National offices are full partners, and the partnership office is structured primarily as a service centre for the whole partnership. Policy development involves a participatory process that leads to adoption at the partnership level. WV's policy environment is informed primarily by its vision, mission statement, core values and transformational development (TD) framework. WV's commitment to the norms of child protection and peacebuilding, shared among most agencies in the wider development and humanitarian aid community, is integrated into it TD framework. TD is one of WV's ministry objectives (along with emergency relief, promotion of justice, strategic initiatives, public awareness and witness to Jesus Christ) informed by WV's mission statement and core values (World Vision 2001b).[2] TD is defined as "a process and actions through which children, families, and communities move toward wholeness of life with dignity, justice, peace, and hope, as the Bible describes the Kingdom of God." WV's approach to TD is "child-focused, community-based, value-based, sustainable, and holistic" (World Vision 2003). The TD framework identifies TD programming elements, such as TD indicators to guide programming outputs, and impact areas or domains of change where TD programming is expected to make a difference (World Vision 2003). Their relationships can be represented in a basic flow chart (see Figure 2–1).

WV's child protection and peacebuilding policies can both be located within its TD framework. WV has historically championed the rights of children suffering from family abuse and violence, exploitive labour, sex and gender-based violence, poverty, HIV/AIDS and violent conflict. Through its advocacy work WV urges governments to honour their commitments to the CRC, supporting the creation of national policies and actions that are in line with their commitments. WV has also been active in the Global Movement for Children and the international campaign against the use of children as combatants, and in general attempts to protect children affected by armed conflict. Through its ADPs and other programmes WV provides for children's survival, education and healing, and facilitates opportunities for children to participate in their own development through leadership projects and community education campaigns (World Vision 2001a; World Vision 2001b). As indicated in Figure 2–1, child protection and a child-focused orientation to relief and development are not standalone components to its policy but are integrated into its overall approach to its work.

Figure 2–1. A transformational development flow chart

Transformational development frame

Five domains of change:
- well-being of children, families and communities
- empowered children as agents of change

- transformed relationships
- interdependent and empowered communities
- transformed systems and structures

Transformational development programming cycle

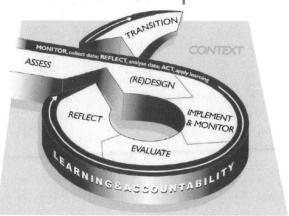

Transformational development cross-cutting themes:
- gender
- disability
- peacebuilding
- Christian commitments
- the environment
- protection

Transformational development indicators:
- child immunisation
- child nutrition
- primary education
- safe water
- diarrhoea management
- household resilience
- % poorest households
- community participation
- social sustainability
- caring for others
- emergence of hope
- Christian commitment

Graphic taken from "LEAP for Quality: Learning through Evaluation with Accountability and Planning," WVI (February 2005).

As with child protection, WV is committed to peacebuilding in its ADPs (O'Reilly 1998), but unlike child protection, which has a longer history within WV, the concept and language of peacebuilding was formally introduced into its TD approach relatively recently, even though peacebuilding was practised using different language. As part of this integration WV has invested important resources in participating in the inter-agency local capacities for peace (LCP) project by Mary Anderson, and has developed an LCP initiative and peacebuilding network within the WV organisation. Conflict, conflict resolution and peacebuilding as policy areas are defined within WV documents and linked to its TD framework. WV defines conflict as "disagreement between two or more parties that is rooted in incompatible goals, positions, views, needs, or behaviours." Conflict resolution is defined as "the process of addressing root causes and core issues that have generated conflict and finding reasonable solutions that allow parties to the conflict to agree on ways to live and work together in a constructive manner." Peacebuilding is defined as "programs and activities that address the causes of conflict and the grievances of the past to promote long-term stability and justice, and that have peace-enhancing outcomes" (World Vision 2001d). Peacebuilding strategic processes are linked to the TD impact areas or domains of change (World Vision 2003; World Vision 2001c), as demonstrated in Figure 2–2.

Figure 2–2. The relationship between peacebuilding strategic processes and TD domains of change

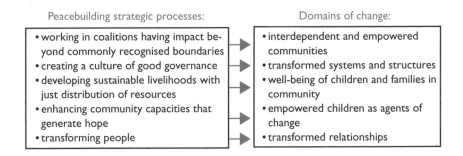

As will become apparent in the sections that follow, one of the central issues facing future peace education programming is determining where peace education fits in to an organisation's policy environment, and for WV's policy environment in particular, how peace education fits with its TD paradigm.

Peace education and drawing the contexts together

Reflecting its fundamental purpose – to construct the defences of peace in the minds of men – a culture of peace requires that education be the principal means of accomplishing this task. This includes not only formal education in schools, but also informal and non-formal education in the full range of social institutions, including the family and the media (UNESCO 1998).

In keeping with its amorphous quality, peace education does not exist as a separate discipline, theory or approach. Although many universities may offer peace and conflict study programmes, there is no programme of study in peace education itself. Rather, peace education draws from numerous disciplines such as psychology, sociology, anthropology, education, political science, international relations, environmental studies and others. Academically, it often appears as anti-racism education, multicultural education, conflict-resolution education, curriculum and pedagogical reform, democratic citizenship or civics education, environmental education, peace studies or development education.

In general, peace education programmes assume as their domain of change people's attitudes, behaviours, knowledge and skills. People benefit from peace education by obtaining new ways of seeing the "other," learning to reject racist, sexist and other stereotyped prejudices to become more empathetic, tolerant and accepting of others and their differences. People also learn to relate to others differently, practising behaviours through (for example) decision-making that is respectful, inclusive, participatory and democratic. People also acquire new knowledge about conflict, peace and how to resolve conflict peacefully, which is accompanied by new skills of conflict resolution (Bickmore 2002; Rosandic 2000). Owing to its largely Western origin (other cultures may practice peace education even if it is called something else), peace education as it is conceived takes children as its primary target group and the classroom as the primary site for teaching peace education (Sommers 2001; Harris 1999). Although a number of peace education programmes in conflict or crisis areas do not rely on classrooms or schools (for example, UNHCR's peace education programme in Kenya), the preferred model for delivering peace education still seems to be a classroom setting with corresponding curriculum and pedagogy.

Peace education has been criticised for at least four serious shortcomings. As noted already, peace education is conceptually vague, and this has resulted in unclear programming and uncertainty regarding how it prevents violent conflict. Peace education seems to be valued on the basis of thinking that peace is desirable, and it places a high premium on the utility of education to inculcate peace. It is assumed that educating children about peace will lead to a peaceable future, but how this will happen is unclear. In the absence of a clear theory of change, sentiment and visceral appeal cannot substitute for results.

A second criticism is that peace education is poorly evaluated as a programme, partly because of its poor conceptual clarity. This only reinforces the already existing vagueness of peace education, increasing the impression that peace education is too soft or indefinite for serious programming. Despite this criticism, peace education programmes are supported by both UNHCR and UNICEF (Nevo and Brem 2002; Aguilar and Retamal 1998).

A third criticism is that peace education is weak on addressing structural and systemic causes of conflict because of its emphasis on the individual in understanding conflict and peace. In keeping with the insight suggested above, peace education assumes that structural change will occur indirectly as individuals change through exposure to peace education. The theory is one of a "trickle up" effect, where changed individuals change structures and systems. But again, it is not clear how this happens. Moreover, this theory of change underestimates the way political, economic and social structures create and constrain choices and contribute either to empowerment or to oppression, the latter of which may contribute to ethnic and civil violence. It also poses the danger that without deliberate attention to structures and systems causing conflict they will be ignored in favour of interpersonal conflict resolution approaches.

Lastly, peace education has been criticised for placing too much emphasis on children as its target group instead of involving more adults from the wider community. This could be said to cause a disjunction between what children are taught and the conflict behaviour of adults in the wider community. This discontinuity can undermine the impact of peace education lessons (Sommers 2001).

THE FINDINGS OF THE SURVEY OF WV ADPS

The scope of this study includes 18 selected ADPs from WV's four main operational regions – Asia Pacific, Latin America, East Africa and the Balkans/ Middle East. With the assistance of WV staff in the partnership, Indonesian, and Canadian offices, ADPs were contacted by telephone and/or email with an explanation of the purpose of the survey and an invitation to participate. The ADPs were chosen based on whether they are operating in a conflict setting and geographic location (to ensure representation from a variety of WV operational regions). The 18 included in this chapter were those that responded to the invitation. After consent to participate was obtained from each ADP, an easy-to-use survey tool (see the Appendix to this chapter) was sent by email. Included with this tool was an explanation of the purpose of the survey, basic information on peace education and instructions on how to implement the survey. The time frame for the survey design, implementation and return was August 2002 to February 2003.

The purpose of the original report was to understand the context of conflict in which each participating ADP operates and then to assess the opportunities and challenges of integrating peace education goals and strategies at the ADP level through a SWOT (strengths, weaknesses, opportunities, threats) analysis. Recommendations on possible approaches to peace education programming would follow. A SWOT analysis is an environmental scan that serves the purpose of strategic planning for organisations. This form of analysis seeks to assist organisations (or projects and programmes) to respond effectively to opportunities and threats within its environment based on an understanding of internal strengths and weaknesses. In the course of programme planning, internal organisational weaknesses and external threats to programme success can be addressed, and existing strengths and external opportunities can be exploited for further programme development (Bryson 1988). As a tool, a SWOT analysis provides a means to explore future programming by raising salient issues and questions.

In order to be cost effective and as participatory as possible, the survey was designed to be implemented in approximately one day by one to two focus groups from each ADP. Ideally, each focus group would reflect a balance of gender, ages, beneficiaries and staff. The survey instructions encouraged the use of group facilitators with prior experience in leading participatory small groups. We strove to make questions open ended and yet sufficiently structured that the survey would be clear and usable. The questions also invited participants to identify what conflict they saw in their experience of the ADP and to define what peace education means or would mean for them. Within the limitations of ADP financial resources, overworked ADP staff, the potential inexperience of small-group facilitators and possible language barriers, this methodology was chosen to be practical and to provide opportunity for focus-group participants to speak from their own experiences. It should be noted that this survey is not a rigorous quantitative survey owing to the limitations in methodology. Rather, it is qualitative, providing valuable insights into the strengths, weaknesses, opportunities and threats of the participating ADPs for future peace education programme planning.

Forms of conflict in participating ADPs

Given the range of conflict experienced by ADPs, it is difficult to make generalisations. At the same time, some ordering of conflict must be attempted to make sense of the complex manifestations of conflict. The forms of conflict experienced by surveyed ADPs are represented in Figure 2–3. The levels of conflict in the matrix are somewhat self-explanatory but are better illuminated with accompanying examples taken from the ADPs surveyed. An example of conflict on the level of the *individual or family* is domestic violence linked to substance abuse such as experienced in ADP Vila Nova Contagem, Brazil, and ADP Casitas, Nicaragua. An example of conflict on the *community* level is the blood feuds experienced by ADP Lezhë, Albania or the ethnic violence in ADP Pontianak, Indonesia. Conflict on the *state-social* level might include discriminating laws against women as in Pokot ADP in Kenya or conflict between religious denominations in ADP Nyamagabe, Rwanda. Examples of *state-economic* level conflict are the cattle-rustling in TOT ADP in Kenya and violence between drug gangs and police in ADP Amigos para sempre, Brazil. An example of *state-political* level conflict is anti-government violence from insurgent militia groups in ADP Agusan del Sur, Philippines, and an example of *regional* conflict is influxes of refugees who compete for already scarce resources with local populations such as reported in an ADP in southern Lebanon (this ADP asked to remain anonymous).

As Figure 2–3 reveals, the majority of conflicts in the participating ADPs for this report occur at the community level or at the social, economic, or political levels of the state, with only one ADP experiencing conflict at the regional level due to refugee inflows. It is interesting to note that some of the conflict includes violence, but other forms of conflict are structural and linked to violence. This fits in with the description of conflict given in the section above. It also suggests that successful peace interventions in these ADPs will have to target conflict at the community and state levels cognizant of structural causes of conflict and violence.

The strengths, weaknesses, opportunities, and threats Facing ADPs

Some brief comments about how the results presented here were obtained are warranted. As already mentioned, this survey is qualitative, drawing from participants' perceptions to form the basis of interpretations. The analytical approach used here was to begin with respondents' answers and read them carefully searching for emerging themes, issues, comments or categories. These emergent categories were coded and then tested against the survey form emailed to ADP staff. Only what was said was coded. If, for example, an ADP mentioned

Figure 2–3. Levels of conflict experienced by surveyed ADPs

Region	ADP	Individual/family	Community	social	State economic	State political	Region	Global
Asia Pacific	Pontianak, Indonesia	✓	✓		✓			
	Southern Philippines		✓	✓	✓	✓		
	Agusan del Sur, Philippines		✓		✓	✓		
East Africa	Tot, Kenya		✓	✓	✓	✓		
	Pokot, Kenya		✓	✓	✓	✓		
	Marigat, Kenya		✓		✓	✓		
	Kolowa, Kenya		✓		✓	✓		
	Mudasomwaed, Rwanda	✓	✓	✓	✓	✓		
	Nyaruguru, Rwanda	✓	✓	✓	✓	✓		
	Nyamagabe, Rwanda	✓	✓	✓	✓	✓		
Latin America	Vila Nova Contagem, Brazil	✓	✓		✓			
	Vila União, Brazil	✓	✓					
	Amigos para sempre, Brazil	✓	✓		✓			
	Educação Popular, Brazil		✓		✓			
	Casitas, Nicaragua	✓	✓	✓		✓		
	Colombia National Office	✓	✓	✓	✓	✓		
Balkans/ Middle East	Lezhë, Albania	✓	✓		✓	✓		
	Southern ADP Lebanon	✓	✓	✓	✓	✓		

Source: This matrix is taken from H. Miall, O. Ramsbotham and T. Woodhouse, *Contemporary Conflict Resolution: The Prevention, Management and Transformation of Deadly Conflicts* (Cambridge, UK: Polity Press, 1999), 77. Southern Philippines and Southern ADP Lebanon are so titled because this is how participants chose to title them. In the case of Lebanon, the ADP's identity was hidden for security purposes.

community support four or five times, it was still only scored once for that ADP under its appropriate code. A number of categories ended up reflecting the questions provided in the survey form to guide discussion. However, a number of categories or issues not reflecting the questions on the form were evident. In addition, a number of themes usually associated with external opportunities or threats (such as community participation or attributes) appeared as strengths or weaknesses according to participants' responses. While this is normal (as some opportunities or threats can be understood as strengths or weaknesses and vice versa), in this case it may suggest a deeper affinity between ADP staff and members of the communities or programme beneficiaries with whom they work.[3] This in itself represents an opportunity as such an identification of community members with an ADP means there is potentially a resource in terms of commitment and solidarity that could be channelled into programme success (in fact, 12 out of 18 of the participating ADPs reported there was community support for the ADPs, and, in some cases, support for peace education).

The reported strengths of the ADPs

Peace education does/would fit with or strengthen other ADP programmes: 14/ 18 or 77.8 per cent
   Key words: integration, easily fit, fit well, meets needs, strengthens, peacebuilding programmes already in place[4]
Interest/ willingness of ADP/WV staff: 13/18 or 72.2 per cent
   Key words: interest, willingness
Capacity of ADP/WV staff: 12/18 or 66.7 per cent
   Key words: trained, possess knowledge (of LCP), have capacity, enhanced skills, good managers, staff education level
Success of existing ADP programmes: 8/18 or 44.4 per cent
   Key words: significant changes, worked, outputs achieved, community appreciated, in line with objectives and implementation plan, achieved goals
Positive relationship between ADP staff/ WV and community: 5/18 or 27.8 per cent
   Key words: mutual discussion, trust, mutual understanding, cooperation
Participatory approach to programmes *: 4/18 or 22.2 per cent
   Key words: active involvement, interventions based on community thought, programme design based on community needs
Support of ADP/WV staff *: 3/18 or 16.7 per cent
   Key words: supports, motivated, sacrificed
Peace education programmes already exist *: 3/18 or 16.7 per cent

Key words: Peacebuilders Program, existing programmes that focus on peace education named

The reported weaknesses of the ADPs

Lack of funding: 13/18 or 72.2 per cent
   Key words: project budget limited, scarce financial resources, lack of financial resources, no direct funding
Low capacity of staff: 9/18 or 50 per cent
   Key words: need more training, needs consult on peace education/conflict resolution, not prepared, lack of skills, do not have full technical competence, limited capacity, no qualification
Lack of ADP/WV staff to take on new programmes: 6/18 or 33.3 per cent
   Key words: not cover the needs, no sufficient staff, not enough human resources, lack of staff
Inequalities and conflict between staff and community: 3/18 or 16.7 per cent
   Key words: inequalities, unequal distribution of work, gender prejudice
Lack of integration of LCP *: 2/18 or 11.1 per cent
   Key words: lack of integration of LCP, programme contributes to conflict
Difficulties in relationship between ADP and WV partnership *: 1/18 or 5.6 per cent
   Key words: difficulties in relationship
Weakness of existing ADP education programmes *: 1/18 or 5.6 per cent
   *Key words:*N/A

The reported opportunities in the ADPs

Legal or traditional structures opposing violence or supporting peace: 16/18 or 88.9 per cent
   Key words: law on children, laws contribute to peace, *Gacaca, Kasfala, Barangay* peace councils, reconciliation councils, policing, judiciary, laws that prohibit threats or contribute to peace
Community participation **: 15/18 or 83.3 per cent
   Key words: active participation, inputs from communities of resources, labour, finances, proposals, peace education curriculum
Strong relationship between ADP/WV and churches, government, schools, CBOs: 12/18 or 66.7 per cent
   Key words: good relationship with local leaders, good relationship with government leadership, partnership with schools, support of local churches, working relationship with local government units

Support of community: 12/18 or 66.7 per cent
  Key words: commitment, support, very supportive, available
Community interest in peace education **: 12/18 or 66.7 per cent
  Key words: interested, keen, readiness of stakeholders to participate, everyone wants peace,[5] willingness to solve problems, peace education raised at community meetings
Perceived donor support: 11/18 or 61.1 per cent
  Key words: possibilities of negotiating resources, high likelihood for donor support, willing donors, donor support, support of other WV offices
Positive attributes of the community **: 10/18 or 55.6 per cent
  Key words: hope, resilience, solidarity, goodwill, positive attitudes towards peace, people care for one another, respect and tolerance
CBOs, other NGOs, churches, other organisations or institutions doing peacebuilding or peace education: 10/18 or 55.6 per cent
  Key words: Roman Catholic centre for development and dialogue, churches advocating for reconciliation, partner NGOs, police "peace blitz," child protection councils
Community capacity **: 7/18 or 38.9 per cent
  Key words: dynamic, creative, strong leadership, good community leaders, qualified, teenagers trained and able to train
Shared community traditions, holidays, beliefs, places, practices, ethnicity, language:
6/18 or 33.3 per cent
  Key words: common meeting places, same language and culture, intermarriage, fiestas, cultural fair
Regular open communication within community: 6/18 or 33.3 per cent
  Key words: peace messages shared in various forums, community attends meetings, free and frequent discussion, routine or regular meetings
Low levels of insecurity *: 6/18 or 33.3 per cent
  Key words: insecurity hasn't gotten out of hand, accessible
Government doing peacebuilding: 6/18 or 33.3 per cent
  Key words: presence of government to promote peace, existing government efforts on peace, governmental disarmament campaign, government efforts in solving problems
Presence of youth groups in churches or civil society *: 4/18 or 22.2 per cent
  Key words: youth groups, children's movement, children's theatre group, teenagers willing to get involved
Acceptance from factional groups: 2/18 or 11.1 per cent
  Key words: recognition of work, confidence of leaders of main groups
Past experience as victims of war *: 2/18 or 11.1 per cent

Key words: experience negative impact of the war and conflicts, victims of war

The reported threats to the ADPs

Community attitudes: 10/18 or 55.6 per cent
Key words: prejudice, self-glorification, suspicion, community relief attitudes, dependence, fear, personal interests, hypocrisy, negligent leaders
Militia, ethnic, or gang violence *: 9/18 or 50 per cent
Key words: hostile environment, armed forces, cattle rustling, persistent conflict in area, unstable order in area, insurgents, drug gang disputes
Government corruption or inefficiency *: 9/18 or 50 per cent
Key words: bias, decisions of government contribute to conflict, fiscal laws contribute to conflict, lack of prompt action, nepotism, corruption, lack of political will, false promises
Poverty or unemployment *: 9/18 or 50 per cent
Key words: poverty, decay, not able to find job, underdevelopment, low employment (often referring to youth)
Lack of community participation ***: 8/18 or 44.4 per cent
Key words: community participation low, weak community participation, involved passively, lack of participation, little mobilisation and involvement
Lack of unity among stakeholders: 8/18 or 44.4 per cent
Key words: conflict of interests, no synchronisation with government, lack of collaborative approach towards peacebuilding, resistance from opinion leaders
Unjust access to resources or opportunities *: 7/18 or 38.9 per cent
Key words: resource competition, physical and material barriers to access school, lack of adequately trained teachers, low level of resources, resource distribution not equal, insufficient resources
Lack of regular open communication: 7/18 or 38.9 per cent
Key words: no routine meetings among community leaders, irregular meetings, talking about violence taboo
Local practices or traditions: 6/18 or 33.3 per cent
Key words: high bride price, leaders pushing culture on newcomers to area, *kanun* (blood feud), gender discrimination, child abuse
Poor understanding of peace education or community development ***: 4/18 or 22.2 per cent
Key words: low level of awareness, misunderstanding of leaders, lack of knowledge of rights

Exclusion or under use of youth *: 4/18 or 22.2 per cent
  Key words: social stigmatisation, not activating youth, not enough
  programmes
Low capacity of community ***: 3/18 or 16.7 per cent
  Key words: illiteracy
Laws unfilled or not enforced: 3/18 or 16.7 per cent
  Key words: deteriorating observance, law not respected
Drug use *: 3/18 or 16.7 per cent
  Key words: drug addiction, influence of drugs
Lack of community support ***: 2/18 or 11.1 per cent
  Key words: low commitment
Health risks *: 2/18 or 11.1 per cent
  Key words: HIV/AIDS, STIs (sexually transmitted infections), malaria
Lack of involvement by church, government: 1/18 or 5.6 per cent
  Key words: limited involvement with local religious leaders
International events *: 1/18 or 5.6 per cent
  Key words: September 11

Discussion of Results

The most significant strengths to adding new peace education programming to
ADPs seems to be that peace education would fit well with or strengthen ADP
programmes, adequate interest on the part of ADP staff and the assessment that
ADP staff have adequate capacity. The three largest weaknesses confronting
ADPs are lack of funding, low staff capacity and insufficient staff. The fit of
peace education with existing ADP activities and the interest of staff are positive features that could be said to reflect the same basic openness of ADP staff
and beneficiaries to peace education programming.

Regarding weaknesses, lack of funding and insufficient staff to take on new
programmes are obvious. It is interesting that some overlap exists in the reported statements on staff capacity (12 out of 18 ADPs said staff capacity was
a strength, but 9 out of 18 said staff capacity was a weakness). One of the
guiding questions on the SWOT survey form was, "Does the staff and leadership have the capacity to start up peace education programming?"

The most likely possible explanation for these contradictory answers seems
to be that participants felt that staff members possessed a general capacity that
makes them competent, but regarding new peace education programmes they
did not feel secure in their knowledge or abilities to run such a programme.
This is expressed by the ADP in Southern Philippines that stated as a strength
"strong capacity built" but under the weakness heading said, "starting a purely

peace education programme in the ADP would pose difficulty to the project since it may not have full staffing and technical complementation as of yet." Similar sentiments were expressed by Amigos para sempre ADP in Rio de Janeiro, Brazil, which said, "The ADP staff is well prepared and qualified for the current activities. As for a new peace education activity, they do not know if they are qualified." This was also echoed by Pokot ADP in Kenya, which said, "There is capacity but needs more enhancements through further training on peace and conflict resolution."

Two additional comments on two of the reported strengths are worth mentioning. The first is that 8 out of 18 ADPs responded by saying past programme success is a strength of the ADPs. This could be construed as a reason for adding new peace education activities, but this reporting should be treated carefully as there are numerous reasons why programme success could be claimed. At best, it is only supportive evidence of the general competency of staff and should only slightly suggest that ongoing success at the ADP level is a reason peace education programmes would fit well. A second comment is the reporting on staff interest versus staff support. Interest may be perceived as a form of support and so could count towards this category. However, interest is different from support in that interest has a more passive connotation than support, which connotes more active involvement. In the scoring under the categories "Interest of ADP/WV Staff" and "Support of ADP/WV Staff," the words *interest* and *support* were taken separately as their meanings were not explained by respondents.

The most significant opportunities present for ADPs are legal or traditional structures opposing violence or supporting peace, community participation, strong relationships between ADP staff and other institutions and organisations, community support, interest in peace education, perceived donor support, positive attributes of the community, and other local peacebuilding or peace education efforts. Shared community features and regular open communication within the community were not very strong opportunities (both were counted as opportunities by only 6 out of 18 ADPs) but worth mentioning. The largest threats facing ADPs are community attitudes, militia, ethnic or gang violence, government corruption or inefficiency, poverty or unemployment, lack of community participation and lack of unity among stakeholders. A noteworthy threat is local practices that cause conflict.

As with discussion on staff capacity as a strength or weakness, there is overlap in the responses from some ADPs regarding whether the level of community participation is an opportunity or a threat (O = 15/18; T = 8/18) and whether quality of relationships with other organisations and unity among stakeholders is an opportunity or threat (O = 12/18; T = 8/18). The most likely explanation regarding community participation is that focus-group members said participation was both an opportunity and a threat (as did ADP Vila Nova Contagem, Brazil, ADP Casitas, Nicaragua, and the ADP in Lebanon), reflecting the diversity of opinion within focus groups. It could also reflect the sensitivities of different participants as to who is participating and who is not. Regarding relationships and stakeholders, it is possible that positive relationships with other organisations and unity among stakeholders meant two different things to participants. To clarify these overlaps further, follow-up questions probing the specifics of participation and who is a stakeholder and what constitutes disunity should be addressed to ADPs.

A number of opportunities within the ADPs appear to fit together and make for interesting contrasts with some of the threats challenging ADPs. Having strong relationships between ADP staff and other institutions and organisations, community support, interest in peace education, perceived donor support, positive attributes of the community (like hope, resilience, tolerance or respect) and having other local groups engaged in peacebuilding or peace education efforts all indicate in general a supportive environment for future peace education programmes. It also indicates definite LCPs that should be brought together synergistically as resources to strengthen any new initiatives. The threats to peace, however, are grave. Alongside positive community attributes are negative attitudes (like selfishness, fear or suspicion), ongoing violence, government ineptitude, poverty, low participation, low unity among stakeholders and, in a few cases, local practices that contribute to conflict.

Though this will vary in specifics from programme to programme, the aggregate picture of the potential for peace education programming emerging from this exploration of WV ADPs is complex. In most cases where aid programmes are being implemented, important questions to ask will be which of the opportunities listed above exist in a given ADP and which of the threats are present? Can strong relationships with other bodies also doing peacebuilding or peace education and a generally supportive and interested community with positive intra-group dynamics be drawn out and connected profitably? Do ADP staff members possess the skills necessary to facilitate these local capacities and connections to leverage greater peace dividends? Would these connections be enough to counter government corruption, poverty, negative attitudes, low community participation and disunity among stakeholders, as well as certain practices that cause conflict in a context of violence?

Based on the specifics of each ADP, the challenge is to explore creative combinations of people and relationships that can be directed at the transformation of negative attitudes and broken relationships. The more significant challenge, though, is how to do this in the midst of crisis or violence that has become the texture of daily life, and how to address the structural causes or contributors of conflict and violence such as poverty and government corruption.

Definitions of peace education from the ADPs: Voices from ADPs

This section contains selected definitions of peace education from ADP participants. Its purpose is to let participants' own thoughts come forward,[6] to hear something of how they define peace education, perhaps in ways beyond what the SWOT categories permitted. While every expression of what peace education is from every ADP could not be included here for reasons of space, these definitions represent common statements. They are organised under headings to draw attention to how they reflect the traditional notions of the intended impact areas of peace education. As well, some interesting references to the need for more than changed attitudes or behaviours is contained under the heading "Structural supports." Each ADP is different in its definition of peace education, depending on how people living in those circumstances perceive the type and nature of conflict. Despite how negotiated the term *peace education* is likely to be within each ADP, these definitions indicate that resident definitions are more or less similar to those given in the wider literature.

Peace Education is . . .

Attitudes
"Peace education is an activity that promotes understanding of each other's culture and beliefs." – *ADP in the Philippines*

"To not have any kind of prejudice." – *Montes Carlos, Brazil*

"Developing the idea of respect towards all people (male/female/child) regardless of the nationality, religious background, social status or political view of the person." – *ADP in Lebanon*

Knowledge
"It is to study and train people about how to live together. It has to do with knowing our rights and obligations as citizens, to be taught about how to relate to each other and solve conflicts." – *Casitas, Nicaragua*

"Educating for peace is teaching how to love. It is to teach first of all, how to love yourself, and after, how to love and respect others, even [those who are] different from me." – *São Paulo, Brazil*

Behaviour
"For us the Peace education can be defined as actions which contribute to the welfare of the community including human rights, respect, prevention of quarrels (social inequality, conflict of interest . . .) in society for sustainable and holistic development." – *Nyamagabe, Rwanda*

"Involvement of the population in decisions through local institutions, which, in some way, avoid the outbreak of violence. Peace Education depends on each one of us. It cannot be imposed." – *Recife, Brazil*

Skills
"It is a process of empowering individuals, families, institutions and the community as a whole to be able to identify and resolve both internal and external conflicts." – *Pokot, Kenya*

"Use of nonviolence in problem solving." – *Lehzë, Albania*

Organised Programmes or Activities
"Peace education is a process in which communities are mobilised to participate in activities that foster peaceful coexistence among people based on shared values, common resource base and heritage." – *Tot, Kenya*

"[Peace education] focuses on community level culture of peace workshops, conflict resolution workshops, starting with the children in communities." – *ADP in the Philippines*

"[Peace education] is done through transformational development and community empowerment, the promotion of tolerance, dignity and mutual respect, healing and reconciliation." – *Mudasomwaed, Rwanda*

Structural supports
"Peace education is more realistic if the stomach is full." – *Agusan del Sur, Philippines*

"Those relations (established by peace education) should be based on conditions such as food sufficiency, potable water and sanitation, education for all (formal, informal and non-formal), good housing, and for everybody to have access to the power of country. When a society fails to the above elements, good relationships between people are broken and there is disagreement, violence, lack of unity and lack of communication among each other without forgetting the conflicts." – *Nyaruguru, Rwanda*

"It is about opportunities like access to better education for all." – *Lehzë, Albania*

"When we do not have disadvantaged groups who feel they are weak and they are a minority, we work on solving the conflict. People should have acceptable conditions and then they will be able to work on peace." – *ADP in Lebanon*

RECOMMENDATIONS AND A MODEL OF CONFLICT ANALYSIS AND PEACE EDUCATION PROGRAMME PLANNING

The recommendations put forward in this section are directed primarily at WV's ADPs, as they were the subject of analysis in previous sections. However, the recommendations and model of conflict analysis and peace education programme planning could legitimately be applied to other similar NGO programmes, and certainly the analysis of institutional policy and ADP programmes in this chapter could be reproduced for the programmes of other agencies. Regarding WV's ADPs, it appears that the potential for peace education in WV's ADPs is high. The recommendations brought forward in this chapter are divided into policy recommendations and programme recommendations.

Policy recommendations

Peace education as an approach to peace is a concrete application of the cross-cutting theme of peacebuilding in WV's TD framework. As articulated above, it is obvious that the empirical experiences of violent conflict and peacebuilding are deeply connected at the conceptual level. Likewise, established peacebuilding literature and practices firmly posit the protection of children at risk of suffering harm in conflict. WV links these concepts to its institutional policy through its TD framework, which gives priority to child protection and peacebuilding. But while these observations suggest receptivity on the policy level to new initiatives that might fall within these existing commitments, the relevance of peace education highlights important issues.

Generally speaking, the wide scope of peace education can be easily accommodated within WV's Christian values and view of peace as *shalom,* as the concept of *shalom* is itself quite broad.[7] Additionally, the tie between child rights and peace education is established in children's right to an education that prepares them "for responsible life in a free society, in the spirit of understanding, peace, tolerance, equality of sexes, and friendship among all peoples, ethnic, national and religious groups and persons of indigenous origin" (CRC 1989, art. 29). This overt statement of the child's right to an education that includes education for peace not only links peace education with the child's right to education but also is easily associated with WV's TD framework, both in its commitment to child protection and in WV's Taskforce for Education's affirmation that "education has, arguably, the highest potential for Transformational Development, as it can address the way we see and interact with our world" (World Vision 2002, 3).

This affirmation contains within it some of the main ingredients of peace education in the conviction that education can alter the perceptions, attitudes and behaviour of the individual in a transformational manner. In combination, the child's right to education is paired with the notion that education is a vital tool for peace and for transformation. Theoretically, the child's right to education can be fulfilled in a manner that enhances peace. This signifies important points of connection with WV's policy. In addition to the fit with WV's child protection mandate, peace education, with its emphasis on the attitudes, knowledge, behaviour and skills of the individual, fits well within WV's policy statement on peacebuilding, as peacebuilding policy statements emphasise a view of conflict and intervention for peace that is personal and relational. But this important fit presents its own challenge to how peace education programmes could be conceptualised in the context of WV's peacebuilding work in its ADPs.

While WV includes both systems and people in its approach to peacebuilding, a less holistic approach would create a serious limitation that could undermine the coherent inclusion of peace education programming in integrated development and successful engagement with violent conflict. As suggested in the criticisms of peace education above, how peace education contributes to peace is not well known. As well, peace education is weak in addressing political, economic and social structures that are underlying causes of state and community violence. NGOs need to include within their definitions of conflict and peacebuilding a clear distinction between peace interventions that target people and interventions that target systems and structures. Within conflict-resolution and peacebuilding literature notions of peacebuilding seek to encompass actor-oriented understandings of conflict and its resolution as well as changing underlying structures that cause or exacerbate conflict. As well, most ADPs experience structural forms of violence contributing to if not functioning as significant causes of conflict. As S. O'Reilly states, "The complexities of modern conflict predicate the need for a multifarious approach" (1998, 18). Within WV there is an institutional assumption that building peace must rest on wider human security, and conflict analysis and peacebuilding programmes within WV take account of the structural causes of conflict and the structural resources for peace. One result of the WV Peace Education Consultation was a redrafting of the peacebuilding definition so that systemic and structural issues were explicitly included.[8]

Peace education was defined as "the learning and teaching that nurtures the knowledge, attitudes, values, skills, habits, and behaviors that enable people to proactively engage with conflict and violence and build a peaceful world for children and adults." Among the assumptions undergirding peace education are that peace education seeks to facilitate engaging the world, takes violent behaviour as the central problem and peaceful behaviour as the central desired outcome, assumes that everyone has the capacity for both participation in violence and destructive conflict and participation in peace and peaceful conflict transformation, and that knowledge, attitudes, values, skills and habits are important to why people either participate in violent conflict or participate in peace. The theory of change that accompanies this definition of peace education is that when individuals are nurtured in appropriate knowledge, attitudes, values, skills, habits and behaviours, they are equipped for peaceful relationships and empowered to engage critically with violence and people in conflict. Peace education so defined can be understood as an actor-oriented approach within the larger sphere of peacebuilding, addressing the knowledge, attitudes, values, skills, habits, behaviours and in general the capacities of individuals or groups for more peaceful behaviour and relationships.

Programme recommendations

Because policy guides programmes, the necessity of making the dimensions of peacebuilding distinct in this regard has implications for defining peace education both conceptually and operationally. Conceptually, among the chief criticisms of peace education, as stated above, is the amorphous scope of meaning around what peace education is and its poor response to structural causes of conflict in the promotion of peace. Operationally, this is also important to solid programme design, implementation, and especially monitoring and evaluation, given that peace education programmes are frequently criticised for being poorly evaluated. Conceptual clarity would help in establishing goals and results-oriented objectives as well as specific, measurable, achievable, realistic and time bound indicators that would help close the evaluation gap and provide insight into the impact of peace education in its peacebuilding role. Defining peace education conceptually and operationally would aid policy integration and assist with gaining support for peace education from relevant decision-making bodies within WV – or any aid agency. With these thoughts in mind, I advance the following specific recommendations[9] regarding future peace education programmes:

- What peace education includes should be established both conceptually and in programmatic terms so that programmes can be designed and so that the *limitations of peace education can likewise be discerned.* Peace education must not come to be regarded as some kind of panacea because of a lack of conceptual clarity and a poor sense of what kind of impact it can have for peace.

- Peace education is not well suited to create direct changes to the structural conditions underlying conflict. Thus, peace education should be complemented by other structure-oriented interventions and other actor-oriented interventions. This addresses the complex causes of conflict and violence to build peace. For example, while peace education could affect the attitudes, perspectives, and behaviour of two groups in conflict, peace education alone would not change the underlying issues, whether economic or political or other, that are contributing to the conflict.

- At a pedagogical level, peace education incorporates many of the best practices found in quality education. Quality education promotes relationships of care, respect and collaboration. Yet peace education involves more than the formation of peaceful learning environments. Peace education works for change at multiple levels, enabling learners to build peace within self, family, peer group, community and the world (for example, culture or structures).

- The monitoring and evaluation aspect of the design, implementation, monitoring and evaluation process for each pilot programme should receive considerable attention for reasons discussed in this chapter. Technical considerations in this process include the following:

  - Goal statements present an excellent opportunity to harness a community's dreams for peace and draw on the creativity that may exist among people, especially children.

  - The monitoring and evaluation aspect of peace education programmes is of particular importance because peace is difficult to measure, and determining how to attribute change in conditions of peace to a programme intervention is likewise difficult. Of particular interest are indicators for peace education. Given the conceptually fuzzy nature of peace education, indicators that are specific, measurable, achievable, realistic and time bound would strengthen any programme. Because peace education results or outcomes are difficult to quantify with direct indicators, programme staff should invest time in choosing helpful proxy indicators to strengthen their evaluations.

  - Peace education outputs are more concrete and perhaps easier to plan. Output indicators to measure programme delivery could focus on programme delivery (number of people receiving training, number of community-based peace education activities held, number of peace education curricula materials delivered to peace education training sites and so forth). Outcome indicators to measure change could focus on aspects of negative and positive peace and whether participants show a difference in attitudes, behaviours, knowledge, or skills related to peace education principles. Measurement of negative and positive peace could look at whether violence is reduced and whether there is better or more successful conflict management. Measurements of positive peace could include whether those features associated with transformation, human security and *shalom* are present and what difference this is making. Measurements focusing on new learning as a programme outcome could be obtained based on a baseline measurement prior to the peace education programme compared to post-programme surveys.

- The major challenge of conducting a rigorous evaluation of the impact of peace education is obtaining control and intervention groups that are stable. Conflict settings often disrupt communities, heightening the possibility of eroding the difference between the control group and the intervention groups. Additionally, it is unethical to keep a control community from benefitting from something that could reduce violence and provide relief and protection. The UNHCR peace education programme in Kenya was more amenable to an evaluation because programme beneficiaries were in a refugee camp and less likely to leave the programme. However, the challenge of new arrivals to the camp who also wanted peace education training remained. One possibility is that new arrivals could be scheduled for the next peace education session and in the interim act as the control group to the intervention group currently targeted with a peace education programme. Programme staff should plan the evaluation scheme when planning the peace education intervention.

- Peace education programmes should be piloted, with more in-depth case studies analysing the causes of the conflict and the actors involved to clarify the complex phenomena of conflict and the strengths, weaknesses, opportunities, and threats unique to each programme. The design phase of pilot peace education programmes could then be accompanied by a more rigorous LCP analysis.

- Peace education programming should not be pursued simply because a high level of demand exists among programme staff (as reported by ADPs, staff expressed a high level of interest in peace education and a desire for training). Programme staff should demonstrate a commitment to gaining a deeper understanding of how peace education programmes can be effective and whether or not peace education is in the best interests of children. Programme staff and community receptivity along with unique environmental opportunities in the programme areas that support peace education should guide implementation.

- Future peace education programming would seem to build best on the strength of a fit with current programme activities, staff interest, and general staff capacity. But sufficient funding and staff to run new programmes are necessary, and staff needs to be trained in peace education principles and methodologies as a basic foundation. Curriculum materials could be provided as examples, but ideally staff members would adapt these materials or create their own based on their setting. The greater challenge would be to extend peace education into the community, building on the kind of opportunities and mitigating the kind of threats mentioned in the analysis of WV's ADPs.

- As peace education by nature is meant to be democratic and inclusive, the participatory nature of programme planning, implementation, monitoring and evaluation should be strengthened among programmes taking on new peace education projects. Only 4 out of 18 ADPs said a participatory approach to current programmes is a strength.

- Slightly below half of responding ADPs (7 out of 18) said capacity of the community was an opportunity, and 3 out of 18 said it was a threat. In such a situation it would seem that community members and their leaders, CBOs, and other relevant stakeholders in the community should be considered for "train the trainer" activities to build the capacity of the community in peace education practices. As well, peace education (like many other programmes) would benefit from literacy skills that encompass inclusive and consensus-based decision-making practices and conflict-resolution skills.

- Shared community features and regular open communication within the community were not considered very strong opportunities among the ADPs surveyed. This is not necessarily a threat, but it certainly suggests that in such situations the shared opportunities for communication that do exist should be enhanced, if possible, and more work should be done to improve communication within the community, especially around difficult topics like community-level violence or abuse within homes.

A model for conflict analysis and peace education programme planning

A model of conflict analysis and peace education programme planning based on the types of conflict that the participating ADPs experience (as do many other aid agency programmes) – and one that anticipates the criticisms levelled against peace education – is shown in Figure 2–4. Recalling the concern that peace education is weak in addressing structural causes of conflict, the model in this section is a child-focused, community-based peace education model. This model of peace education retains the traditional impact areas of peace education, namely, the attitudes, knowledge, behaviour and skills of individuals associated with peace. But how effective can peace education be if it emphasises conflict in interpersonal relationships and assumes children and the classroom and school are the target group and site of learning when conflict is far more encompassing?

As noted earlier, conflict is mostly between groups and in the context of communities. Causes of conflict are found in the structural and underlying as

Figure 2–4. A child-focused framework
of conflict mapping and peace education

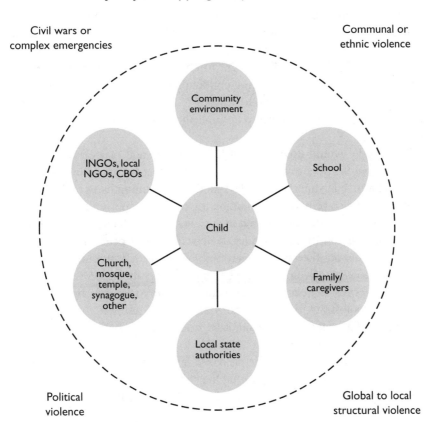

well as at the immediate actor level. Unless peace education includes or is accompanied by measures to structure justice into a community or society, it will lack meaning. In addition, school- or classroom-bound peace education may not be able to contend with drug-related gang violence, land disputes or civil conflict affecting the neighbourhood, village or region. Aid agencies must account for the call for peace education programmes that keep hold of peace education's impact areas in combination with other peacebuilding interventions that address underlying systemic causes of conflict often linked to human insecurity. This child-focused model of community-based peace education suggests that peace education programming ideally should be diffused throughout a community as part of other programmes and not necessarily as a separate programme.

Because the socioeconomic and political contexts determine what kind of peace needs to be built, better links among institutions within communities need to be made. Peace education and political action are deeply intertwined, and adoption of peace education programmes strongly implies activism in tandem with other programmes to change hearts, minds, relationships and structures—important TD ingredients. Peace education must include the adults and community institutions that surround children in order to mitigate the negative messages of conflict taught to children through the attitudes and behaviours of the adults occupying children's lives. This type of hidden curriculum creates a gap between the lessons of peace education taught to children and the violent response to conflict modelled by adults outside those lessons.

This model would dovetail with LCP analysis and peacebuilding work, searching out the opportunities within communities and matching them with the comparative advantage of ADPs found in their strengths. A child-focused model would also provide a foundation for creating opportunities to enhance the participation rights of children in peer-peer outreach and as peace educators in the community. As Bush and Saltarelli state of peacebuilding education, the model put forward in this report "would be a bottom-up rather than top-down process driven by war-torn communities themselves, founded on their experiences and capacities. It would be firmly rooted in immediate realities, not in abstract ideas or theories. It would be applied, immediate, and relevant, which means that it cannot be restricted to the classroom" (2000, 23).

The model of peace education proposed in this chapter identifies the main institutions that affect children within the child's broader community. Focusing on these institutions takes into account local and more distant sites of conflict and provides a context for the threats and opportunities facing aid programmes that would implement peace education interventions. Put another way, this model provides a concrete way of mapping conflict that includes both actors and structures that cause or conflate conflict, along with recognising the capacities for peace also found in the broader community, placing the child at the focus of the analysis.

Conflict and violence can occur in or between each of the six shaded areas representing six key institutions immediately affecting children. Peace education programmes would involve these six institutional areas, including members from each of these institutions who are either part of the conflict or act as a resource for peace. Outside of the sphere are forms of violent conflict that also directly affect on children, as suggested by the permeable sphere. These forms of conflict involve individuals, groups, institutions and structures that peace education traditionally does not address, except where opportunity arises through interpersonal contact.

Each of the shaded areas and the forms of conflict outside the permeable sphere can be explained as follows. Regarding the shaded areas, *family* includes the child's immediate and extended family or whoever cares for the child, and *school* is whatever form of learning institution the child attends (or should attend). The religious institutions are those in which the child participates, and local state authorities include local political offices and ministries, the police and the military. *INGOs, local NGOs and CBOs* are those institutions engaged in aid work. The *community environment* is the village or neighbourhood or even refugee camp in which the child lives, including the people who live there, local or traditional leaders, the market areas, places of labour, public spaces and play areas. While not an institution, like the other areas, it bears similar features because it has social, political and economic arrangements with leadership and rules governing interactions. This is also the place in which traditional conflict mechanisms could be located. Most of the other circles could be contained within the community environment circle, but they are given separate circles because community is a porous reality. People participate in numerous overlapping communities, sharing institutions of learning, religion, state authority (where it exists), or participating in the programmes of one or more development agency. Analysis should not stop at the community level, assuming it is a unified entity, but should recognise each of the institutions within the wider community because they are all integral to building peace. It is partly for this reason that this child-focused model of conflict draws attention to institutions immediately affecting children and the individuals who participate in these institutions, especially as leaders.

Regarding the forms of violence given outside the sphere, civil wars and complex emergencies are self-explanatory. Political violence could be state repression, the violence of militia groups or even election-time violence from rival parties. Communal or ethnic violence occurs between groups of different religions, ethnicity or races. Global to state structural violence is political, economic or social policies, or practices from the global to the state levels. It can be unjust trade practices; the exclusion of an ethnic or religious group from access to political participation, economic opportunity or social benefit by another group; unjust laws; or restriction from local resources. Though all of these forms of violence are positioned outside of the circle in the diagram, their impact is felt within the circle, often manifesting among these overlapping communities. The forms of conflict outside of the sphere are representative and could be articulated at length with greater sophistication than the discussion here. Our main concern is the sphere of influence for peace education.

As a way of illustrating this model for analysing conflict and peace education programme planning, the conflict of Amigos para sempre ADP in Rio de Janeiro, Brazil, is analysed using the model, its strengths, weaknesses, opportunities and threats are described, and possible peace education programming is outlined using the components of the model in Figure 2–4. The Amigos para sempre ADP is used as an example because its survey response provided a sufficient amount of detail for such an illustration.

Community environment: Violent conflict within the ADP community consists of violence between drug gangs and the police along with the predation of the gangs on the community. Violence and conflict also feed into the permeable circle in the form of *structural violence* as poverty, hunger, social inequality and unemployment. Related to the conflict, *threats* within the community consist of the parallel power structure of drug gangs and "outlaws" who control the community, fear of talking about violence, community resistance to police efforts if the community is not involved in decisions and a lack of recreational opportunities for children and youth. *Opportunities* within the community are the availability, solidarity and support (including that of volunteers) for ADP programmes.

Child: In addition to the above, violence and conflict exist among adolescents and children. ADP activities that directly target children and youth are spiritual training, child health activities, day care and nurseries, sports and recreation (*capoeira* dancing) and pregnant adolescent support.

Schools: ADP programmes at the school level are school-based evangelisation.

Family/caregivers: A *threat* in this area is the lack of responsibility of parents. ADP activities targeting families are religious and civic action, food aid, and family visitations. An *opportunity* among families is their availability for involvement in peace programmes.

Local state authorities: Threats in this area include lack of financial support for communities. In addition, the police increase conflict within the community. *Opportunities* consist of government attempts to disarm the community, pro-peace laws passed by the government, and scholarships and family educational support from the government.

Church, mosque, temple, synagogue and other: There is limited involvement by religious leaders; ADP staff described this as a *threat.*

INGOs, local NGOs, CBOs: Cited as *opportunities* was the ongoing work of such groups as Nova Canaã, Local Samba Group and Youth for Peace.

The direction
of peace education programmes

While ventures into the specifics of peace education cannot be undertaken without the lead of ADP staff and community members, some preliminary thoughts are possible. Clearly, the conditions of unemployment, social inequality, hunger and lack of recreation that create and perpetuate human insecurity are not incidental to the appeal of drug use, drug trafficking and violence as means of generating income, social status or self-esteem. The pressure drug gangs exert on local communities as "parallel power" arrangements in turn exacerbate these conditions. It is a vicious cycle. Future peace education programmes could seek to expand existing activities that directly target children and families, including school-based programmes beyond evangelism, to include peace education learning opportunities; they could integrate peace education "learning moments" into the activities of Nova Canaã or the Youth for Peace clubs. Greater involvement by religious leaders – attending pro-peace events and activities, making public calls for greater government efforts and criticising drug gangs (admittedly extremely dangerous) – could help publicly stigmatise violence and erode the culture of silence surrounding violence and drug gangs. Closer collaboration among community members, the police and local CBOs and NGOs could support increased knowledge, attitudes and skills that create a culture and a practice of peace, thus providing a necessary context for children's peace education learning. Having said all this, such efforts would be greatly compromised without addressing poverty, hunger and unemployment as incentives to violence and the drug trade.

CONCLUSION

The ongoing work to build sustainable peace and create the freedom of opportunity that helps people realise greater dignity and wholeness could be assisted
by peace education. But drawing on peace education is fraught with conceptual
and operational challenges. The conceptual fit of peace education with any aid
agency will depend on how peace education is defined and how peace education, so defined, fits with the agency's institutional ethos and policy. The potential of peace education lies perhaps in what aid agencies like WV already know
about successful programmes and effective education. Sound programme design that includes rigorous monitoring and evaluation will benefit not only those
participating in these programmes but also contribute to a better understanding
of how peace education actually builds peace. Implemented by a variety of
agencies in programmes across regions, the knowledge generated would help
agencies successfully engage in peace education work and increase support
and acceptance among donors.

NOTES

[1] ADPs are "baskets" of programmes that are geographically bounded, often approxi-
mating the size of an administrative district within a country. The programmes depend on
the needs of the communities within the geographic area, but they might consist of micro-
credit, education, health, agriculture, or infrastructure projects. ADPs rely on local resi-
dents of the communities included in an ADP, as well as local churches, if any exist within
the ADP. The time frame for ADP operations is 10–15 years (O'Rielly 1998, 34). At the
time of writing, there were approximately 1,100 ADPs worldwide.

[2] WV's vision, core values and TD framework can be accessed on its website. This
chapter quotes published WV documents or documents available from its Internet data-
bases, especially with regard to Figures 2–1 and 2–2.

[3] I have indicated with an asterisk (*) which emergent categories or themes were
generated by participants themselves. Themes marked with a double asterisk (**) under
the opportunities list appeared as a strength in the responses. Themes marked with a triple
asterisk (***) under the threats list appeared as a weakness in the responses. I have rear-
ranged them in the presentation to preserve the basic logic of the SWOT analysis without
obscuring how participants responded.

[4] *Key words* are examples of words or phrases recorded by participants that guided the
formation of the categories.

[5] The apparent contradiction of "everyone wants peace" in a setting where there is conflict can be explained by violence against a community perpetrated by groups outside of the
community or lack of agreement between groups who want peace on the terms of peace.

[6] Quotations are taken from returned survey forms.

[7] *Shalom,* a word found in the Hebrew scriptures, means not just lack of violence but the positive relationship of individuals with the people around them, the integration and healthy relationship of individuals with their community, and a healthy relationship among communities and between communities and the earth.

[8] Refer to this book's Appendix 1, titled "Unpacking Peace Education," for a full discussion of the ramifications of this definition.

[9] I am indebted to Vachel Miller, with whom I collaborated to consolidate a definition and formulate the assumptions about peace education emerging from the WV consultation in September 2003.

REFERENCES

Aguilar, P., and G. Retamal. 1998. *Rapid Educational Response in Complex Emergencies: A Discussion Document.* Geneva: IBE. Available online.

Bickmore, K. 2002. "Education for Peacebuilding Citizenship: A Proposal for Teaching and Learning in the Context of Fragile Peace." *Canadian Issues/ Thèmes Canadiens.* September 2002.

Boutros-Ghali, B. 1995. "An Agenda for Peace." In *United Nations, Divided World: the UN's Roles in International Relations,* ed. A. Roberts and B. Kingsbury. Oxford: Clarendon Press. AUTHOR – Though *An Agenda for Peace* came out in 1992, I refer to the copy cited in this report.

Bush, K., and D. Saltarelli. 2000. *The Two Faces of Education in Ethnic Conflict: Towards a Peacebuilding Education for Children.* Florence: Innocenti Research Centre/ UNICEF.

Bryson, J. 1988. *Strategic Planning for Public and Non-profit Organizations: A Guide to Strengthening and Sustaining Organizational Achievement.* San Francisco: Jossey-Bass.

Carnegie Commission on Preventing Deadly Conflict. 1997. *Preventing Deadly Conflict: Final Report.* Washington, DC: Carnegie Commission on Preventing Deadly Conflict.

CRC (Convention on the Rights of the Child). 1989. Geneva and New York: Centre for Human Rights, United Nations Office, and UNICEF.

Duffield, M. 2001. *Global Governance and the New Wars: The Merging of Development and Security.* London: Zed Books.

Galtung, J. 1976. "Three Approaches to Peace: Peacekeeping, Peacemaking, and Peacebuilding." In *Peace, War, and Defence – Essays in Peace Research,* ed. J. Galtung. Copenhagen: Christian Ejlers.

Gantzel, K. 1997. "War in the Post-World War II World: Some Empirical Trends and a Theoretical Approach." In *War and Ethnicity: Global Connections and Local Violence,* ed. David Turton. Rochester, NY: Univ. of Rochester Press.

Harris, I. 1999. "Types of Peace Education." In *How Children Understand War and Peace: A Call for International Peace Education,* ed. A. Raviv et al., 299–317. San Francisco: Jossey-Bass.

———. 2002. "Conceptual Underpinnings of Peace Education." In *Peace Education: The Concept, Principles, and Practices around the World,* ed. G. Salomon and B. Nevo, 15–25. London: Lawrence Erlbaum Associates.

Holsti, K. 1996. *The State, War and the State of War.* Cambridge: Cambridge Univ. Press.

Kaldor, M. 1999. *New and Old Wars:Organized Violence in a Global Era.* Cambridge: Polity Press.

Lederach, J. 1997. *Building Peace: Sustainable Reconciliation in Divided Societies.* Washington, DC: United States Institute of Peace Press.

Macrae, J., ed. 2002. *The New Humanitarianisms: A Review of Trends in Global Humanitarian Action.* Humanitarian Policy Group Report 11.

Miall, H., Ramsbotham, O., Woodhouse, T. 1999. *Contemporary Conflict Resolution: The Prevention, Management and Transformation of Deadly Conflicts.* Cambridge, UK: Polity Press.

Nevo, B., and I. Brem. 2002. "Peace Education Programs and the Evaluation of Their Effectiveness." In *Peace Education: The Concept, Principles, and Practices around the World,* ed. G. Salomon and B. Nevo, 271–82. London: Lawrence Erlbaum Associates.

O'Reilly, S. 1998. *The Contribution of Community Development to Peacebuilding: World Vision's Area Development Programs: Final Report.* Milton Keynes, UK: World Vision International.

Reardon, B. 1988. *Comprehensive Peace Education: Educating for Global Responsibility.* New York: Teachers College Press.

Rosandic, R. 2000. *Grappling with Peace Education in Serbia.* Peaceworks No. 33. Washington, DC: United States Institute of Peace Press.

Sommers, M. 2001. "Peace Education and Refugee Youth." In *Learning for a Future: Refugee Education in Developing Countries,* ed. Jeff Crisp, Christopher Talbot and Daiana Cipollone. Geneva: UNHCR.

Sommers, M. 2002. *Children, Education and War: Reaching Education for All (EFA) Objectives in Countries Affected by Armed Conflict.* Conflict Prevention and Reconstruction Unit Working Paper No.1. Washington, DC: World Bank.

Stomfay-Stitz, A. 1993. *Peace Education in America, 1828–1990: Sourcebook for Education and Research.* Metuchen, NJ; London: Scarecrow Press.

UNESCO. 1998. *Preliminary Consolidated Report to the United Nations on a Culture of Peace.* Item 8.5, 1545EX/42. Paris: UNESCO.

United Nations. 1996. *The Impact of Armed Conflict on Children.* Report of the Expert of the Secretary-General, Ms. Graça Machel, submitted pursuant to General Assembly Resolution 48/157, A/51/306, 26 August 1996.

UNDP. 1994. *Human Development Report.* New York: Oxford Univ. Press.

UNICEF. 1996. *The State of the World's Children, 1996.* New York: Oxford Univ. Press.

UNICEF. 2002. *Children Affected by Armed Conflict: UNICEF Actions.* New York: UNICEF.

World Vision. 2001a. *Here We Stand: World Vision and Child Rights.* Monrovia, CA, and Milton Keynes, UK: World Vision International.

World Vision. 2001b. *Protecting Children: 2001 International Annual Review.* Monrovia, CA, and Milton Keynes, UK: World Vision International.

World Vision. 2001c. *Strategic Processes and Success Indicators.* Internal World Vision document.

World Vision. 2001d. *Track III: Operational Definitions, Concepts, and Definitions: Peacebuilding.* Revised draft. 30 October 2001. Internal World Vision document.

World Vision. 2002. *Taskforce on Education for Transformational Development.* Powerpoint presentation for Mnet. October 2002. Internal World Vision document.

World Vision. 2003. *Transformational Developments: Core Documents.* Internal World Vision document.

Appendix

Peace Education Survey

INFORMATION SHEET

Purpose of Survey

The purpose of this survey is to assess the potential of World Vision's ADP and other programs to incorporate peace education. This survey is being sent to select ADPs in the LACRO, MEERO, EARO, and APRO [Latin America, Balkans/Middle East, East Africa and Asia Pacific, respectively] operational regions of the World Vision partnership. With full recognition of how busy and 'over-surveyed' so many ADPs are, this survey is meant to be simple, inexpensive, and able to be conducted within one day. The survey method is a SWOT analysis, which is explained in the next section. The Survey Worksheet and Guide that follows this page gives direction on how to conduct a SWOT analysis.

What is a SWOT Analysis?

SWOT stands for Strengths, Weaknesses, Opportunities, and Threats. This is an easy to use tool that can help staff articulate what internal strengths and weaknesses an ADP has, and what external opportunities and threats an ADP faces. The idea is to aid staff in assessing whether an ADP's strengths can build on opportunities to minimize its weaknesses and threats. This also allows for ADP staff to plan new programs aware of possibilities and challenges facing them for greater success. The SWOT analysis needs group discussion to be successful and so is done in focus groups.

What is Peace Education?

Peace education is a vague term that has different meanings, different names, and refers to a range of program activities depending on the cultural context in which it is used. Peace education can be defined broadly as a means to facilitate learning:

- Attitudes, ways of thinking, and behaviour conducive to peace, such as understanding, tolerance, and respect for others
- Understanding that the 'others' are as equal in dignity and rights as one's own group
- Conflict resolution skills (i.e. mediation, cross-cultural communication, and negotiation) to help resolve conflict without violence.

The goals of peace education also vary, including reconciliation, eliminating racism, prejudice, and discrimination, increasing empathy and understanding, the reform of unjust political, economic, and social structures, and the upholding of human rights. As with its definition and goals, peace education in practice draws from different sources, such as antiracism education, multi-cultural education, conflict-resolution practices, curriculum and pedagogical reform, democratic citizenship education, and religious ecumenism.

Peace education is neither a separate subject nor a project but an educational orientation that helps existing programs identify and mitigate potential areas of conflict, while also promoting areas of common interest. Peace education ideally builds on local strengths and opportunities and includes the whole community in achieving its goals.

SURVEY WORKSHEET AND GUIDELINES

This Worksheet and Guide is meant to assist in the implementing of the peace education survey. It provides questions to help establish the context for each ADP, an outline of a possible process of how to conduct the survey, as well as suggested questions to guide discussion around the ADP's strengths, weaknesses, opportunities, and threats when considering introducing peace education. The worksheet leaves sufficient space for participants to write answers. If it is possible, please e-mail these completed worksheets back to me, or fax the completed worksheets to the World Vision Canada office for analysis. My e-mail address and the World Vision Canada fax number are provided below. Your own insights or analysis can be included in the comments section if you desire.

How to Conduct the SWOT Analysis in Your ADP Area

The SWOT Process

The SWOT analysis will work well with 1–2 focus group discussions and a few interviews involving knowledgeable staff and program beneficiaries at each

ADP over 1–2 days maximum, depending on who is available, difficulty of travel, how busy staff are, availability and willingness of staff. Each focus group should have between 5–9 people. A balance of gender, ages, and staff in each focus group is desirable. Each focus group should have a facilitator to lead the discussion, someone to record responses on the worksheets, and someone to make observation notes of the focus group discussion. Ideally, the facilitator will be someone with experience with SWOT analyses or with experience leading or participating in small group discussions. Please keep all notes and answers in case further information is needed. When providing answers, please be specific about who, what, where, when, or any other detail that makes your answers concrete. Please also complete this survey by September 28, 2002.

Thank-you.

Context

Conflict and peace (like peace education) have a variety of meanings depending on context. The questions below set the context for your ADP's work, identifying what is the conflict there and what kind of peace ADP staff and beneficiaries want. Conflict can exist within and between families, communities (i.e. schools, local leadership), regions, ethnic groups and castes, and where great inequalities exist between political, economic, religious, and ethnic groups. Please answer the following questions in the boxes provided below:

- What is peace education to you? Please give your own definition according to peace education work in your ADP.
- Please describe the major form of conflict(s) currently experienced by those living in your ADP. Who is the conflict between? What are the issues in the conflict?
- Please describe the sectors of work which are currently underway in the area. What kind of work is being done? In what setting is this work being done? Who are the beneficiaries or participants in the education work (age, gender, ethnicity, religion, etc.)?
- In what ways is your current work contributing to conflict or peace? Would you say peace education is currently being done in your ADP? Please describe this.

Suggested Questions to Guide Discussion of Strengths, Weaknesses, Opportunities, or Threats

The following suggested questions are a guide and participants are encouraged to answer the basic questions **"What are our strengths and weaknesses, and what opportunities and threats do we face when considering adding peace education to our existing programs"** as freely as possible. Some strengths may also be weaknesses, and some opportunities may also be threats. Please feel free to include the same answer under different headings, but please provide an explanation in the comments section why something fits into more than one category.

Strengths and Weaknesses

- What financial resources are available for a new or expanded peace education project?
- Is there currently sufficient staff to develop peace education programming?
- Is there sufficient interest among staff for peace education programming?
- Does the staff and leadership have the capacity to start up peace education programming?
- What is the level of staff involvement in programming decisions?
- How well would peace education fit with current program activities?
- What conflicts currently exist between ADP staff and how are they being managed?
- How well have outputs fulfilled program objectives in recent and/or current ADP activities? Why or why not? This information will reveal a lot about the capacity of an ADP to take on peace.

Opportunities and Threats

- What kind of relationship does the ADP program have with the local, regional, and/or national government or leadership?
- Are there any laws, policies, or practices from a government body that either contributes to peace or to conflict?
- What is the likely level of support and interest from donors for peace education?
- Who currently provides the greatest support or resistance to ADP program activities within the ADP or local communities?

- How accessible are local communities who participate in ADP activities?
- What resources do they or can they contribute?
- How much do local communities actively discuss, plan, and implement program ideas?
- How supportive of a peace education project are local community members?
- How much is the conflict experienced in the ADP openly discussed by those affected?
- Are there already other peace education activities being done by local community members, or other agencies?

SWOT ANALYSIS RECORD WORKSHEET

Strengths	Weaknesses

Opportunities	Threats

Comments, Suggestions, Explanations, Insights

Thank-you for your time and effort to complete this survey. Your assistance is much appreciated.

PART II

ENCOUNTERING THE CORE

*Growing a peace education curriculum
and teacher/learner concept*

3

Where's the peace?
What's the education?

Part I: A closer look at existing curricula

Vachel W. Miller

The primary task of education for peace is, therefore, to reveal and tap all those energies and impulses that make possible the full human capacity for a meaningful and life-enhancing existence.

– IAN HARRIS, PEACE EDUCATION

AN EVOLVING FIELD

Ultimately, peace education has to do with the creation of peaceful, just societies that nurture human potential and cultural pluralism. Given such grand ambitions, what do contemporary peace education programmes actually look like? What concepts and skills do they offer children? What aspects of peace education curricula are unique to specific places, and what aspects are shared globally? What lessons do peace education curricula neglect? What conflicts do they avoid?

Despite growing interest regarding the potential offered by peace education, there is no internationally accepted standard model of peace education. Nor are there universal guidelines for what peace education curricula should include. It is an evolving field with open boundaries. Over the past three decades peace education has taken on many different forms in different cultures in response to pressing social and political concerns. For instance, peace education has focused on "A-bomb" education in Japan; in Northern Ireland and Israel peace education focuses on intergroup relations and dialogue (Harris 2002).

In a review of peace education programmes in the United States conducted in the early 1970s, S. L. Carpenter (1975) identified five major approaches: war prevention, conflict resolution, world order, social justice and non-violent action. Some of these approaches to peace education focused on analysis of global systems; others focused on effective management of interpersonal conflict. In the years since Carpenter's study, profound differences in approaches to peace education remain.

Yet a certain consensus seems to be emerging on key curricular dimensions of school-based peace education programmes for children. This chapter analyses a small group of peace education programmes, exploring what they have in common and the significance of their differences. This set of peace education curricula, in use by educators in different sites globally, was evaluated to compare different approaches to peace education and potentially to assist in constructing new approaches grounded in a solid conceptual base.

Peace education is a rich field – rich with curricular models, concepts and possibilities for innovative approaches. The analysis presented here does not attempt to capture that richness fully. It is not intended as a representative review of all current peace education programmes or curricula. During the last two decades many varieties of peace education programmes have emerged, both in non-formal settings and in schools. Rather than provide a comprehensive overview, World Vision commissioned an in-depth review of a sample of models and materials of particular interest to its September 2003 Peace Education Consultation. Some of these programmes have become models for peace education programmes internationally, particularly within the development community. In this respect the questions raised here will be useful for practitioners interested in creating or enhancing their own peace education programmes. Furthermore, some of the materials analysed here emphasise a religious or spiritual dimension that is particularly relevant for World Vision's commitment to transformational development. Specifically, transformational development includes concern for the emotional nurturance of children, protection from abuse, the creation of inclusive and equitable relationships in households and communities, and the prevention of conflict – all related to a vision of a more just and dignified future for children.

The following descriptions provide an overview of the goals and characteristics of each programme. The most comprehensive programmes are described first and in greatest detail. The descriptions are followed by a comparison of learning objectives, as well as a quantitative analysis of the relative emphasis placed on the acquisition of knowledge, skills and values in the programme guidebooks. I then continue to compare the programmes with respect to their inclusion of elements focused on improving intergroup relations. In the chapter that follows I explore a series of critical questions about the content of peace education, questions which extend those introduced in this chapter.

The analysis in this chapter attempts to identify strengths and gaps and to point towards broader parameters for project design. Overall, my intention is to make visible the ways in which peace education curricula have been constructed and suggest alternative possibilities. In conjunction with the following chapter's foundational questions, an overarching purpose of this review is to provide insight for practitioners to use in the construction of their own vision and strategies for peace education.

PROGRAMME DESCRIPTIONS

UNHCR Peace Education Programme

Designed to prevent conflict in refugee camps, the UNHCR Peace Education Programme (PEP) emerged from discussions with refugee communities in Kenya in 1997. A consultant facilitated discussions within the refugee community about the refugees' interests in peace education and the desired content of the programme. Based on those discussions, the programme features both an in-school component and a community-workshop component; taken together, they affirm the importance of peaceful behaviour in the camps (Baxter 2001).

The school-based component of the PEP features a spiral curriculum; that is, students cycle through a set of primary themes in each grade level, with topics addressed through new activities in increasing depth as students mature. This format enables students to grow increasingly familiar with core concepts and have repeated opportunities to practise new skills over several years in peace education courses. Like other peace education curricula, the lessons are activity oriented and could be used in any setting.

The PEP curriculum, developed under the guidance of Pamela Baxter, is the most comprehensive example of a peace education programme among the materials reviewed here. Programme materials have been carefully designed for use in resource-poor environments with multiple groups. The entire package contains guidebooks for teachers and teacher trainers, as well as for community workshop facilitators and their trainers. The curricular materials for the school-based programme are designed to guide novice teachers with a well-designed lesson framework and detailed instructions for activities. Activity instructions are complemented by a set of teaching tips, discussion questions and concluding thoughts. The overall programme materials also include a teacher training manual and teacher resource guide, each of which provides practical advice for teachers new to peace education and generally unfamiliar with activity-based pedagogy.

More than any other programme reviewed here, the PEP emphasises the importance of congruence between the teachers' behaviour and the learning objectives for students. Programme materials stress that participants must learn the skills they teach and act as models of peacebuilding.

Evidence indicates that the programme has been effective. According to a comprehensive evaluation, programme participants have internalised a sense of individual responsibility for building peace in the refugee camps and demonstrated active conflict reduction behaviour (Obura 2002). Participants repeatedly assert that the programme workshops help bring people closer together. Crime rates in the camps have decreased significantly since the inception of the programme.

Education for Conflict Resolution

Designed for the training of peace education facilitators/teachers, this manual was developed by Susan Fountain for UNICEF. The *Education for Conflict Resolution* (Fountain 1997) manual has a rich collection of activities covering key peace education topics. As a resource for programme designers, it also has distinctive strengths. The introductory discussion of the cultural dimensions of curriculum and pedagogy is especially useful for adapting the curriculum to different contexts.

Based on a framework for interpreting cultural differences, the introduction suggests how issues of authority, power, emotional control and individualism may affect teaching and learning in different cultural settings.[1] In cultures that emphasise emotional control, for example, activities that ask participants to share feelings about experiences of prejudice may yield little response. The guidebook encourages facilitators to be sensitive to cultural norms and make appropriate adjustments.

The second strength of the manual is its concluding section on programme design. In introductory sessions participants are asked to brainstorm about the knowledge, skills and attitudes that should be included in peace education. At the end of the training, participants are guided to identify their priorities and select peace education lessons for their own settings.

The *Education for Conflict Resolution* guidebook is also unique in including a section on decision-making. This is a topic that other guidebooks either ignore or touch upon tangentially. One of the activities invites participants to use various decision-making strategies and then evaluate their positive/negative aspects and rank them according to their potential contribution to peacebuilding. Because decision-making processes in groups often contribute to conflict, the guidebook's emphasis on alternative decision-making strategies and their relation to peacebuilding is important, especially for trainers and group leaders. The activity on building consensus, for example, guides participants through a structured process for generating agreement on group-level goals. Although it is intended for adults, practice in consensus building could also be beneficial in activities to help children develop their own rules for classroom behaviour.

Panagtagbo sa Kalinaw
(Culture of Peace)

This peace education manual, published in 1998, is designed for the training of community workers on the island of Mindinao, Philippines, an area suffering from inter-ethnic and interreligious tensions. In contrast to the other material reviewed here, this manual directly addresses the origins, issues and identities associated with a particular conflict setting. Although it could also be adapted for use by teachers, it is geared towards adult participants interested in improving relations and building lasting peace in their local communities. While other curricula emphasise a general set of skills and values, the Culture of Peace programme starts with existing conflicts and embeds skill development within that context. In this sense the programme has a more overt liberatory/empowerment agenda than the other materials reviewed here.

The training programme is divided into three modules for use over a four-day training seminar. The first module focuses on the historical dimensions of the conflict in Mindinao. The second module – the one most similar to other peace education curricula – focuses on approaches to peacemaking. The third module invites participants to elaborate their vision of a culture of peace for their home communities.

Among this set of peace education materials, only the Culture of Peace training treats religious identity as an explicit dimension of the peacebuilding agenda. Activities suggested in the guidebook reflect this religious dimension. The programme was developed by Catholic Relief Services, in collaboration with governmental and local organisations in the Philippines.

Living Values

The Living Values programme is unique in several ways. The programme grew out of a guidebook on values prepared by the Brahma Kumari World Spiritual University in 1995 on the occasion of the fiftieth anniversary of the United Nations. The school-based component of the guidebook inspired the development of the Living Values programme by an international network of educators. Some 1,800 educators in more than 64 countries now use the Living Values programme, adding their own cultural elements to the core programme developed by educational psychologist Diane Tillman.

Unlike other programmes reviewed here, Living Values is not designed as a peace education programme per se. It is considered a values education programme in which children explore and deepen their understanding of 12 "universal" values: cooperation, freedom, happiness, honesty, humility, love, peace,[2] respect, responsibility, simplicity, tolerance and unity.[3] The curriculum offers activities designed to help children explore the meaning and importance of each of the 12 values in their personal lives and in society. The values units contain reflections, group activities, visualisation exercises, artistic expression and analysis of social issues. A special set of materials for use with war-affected children has also been developed.

Creating an environment of safety, respect, understanding and love is emphasised because such environments enable students to thrive academically, socially, and spiritually. Skills of conflict resolution, trust building and problem solving are viewed as integral to the creation and maintenance of values-based environments. In addition to the curriculum guidebooks, the Living Values programme has developed an extensive set of complementary materials to assist parents and programme facilitators.

Adventures in Peacemaking

Adventures in Peacemaking, written by William Kreidler and Lisa Furlong (1995), is oriented towards use in non-formal, out-of-school settings such as child-care centres or youth centres. Although the activities are organised into thematic blocks, the guidebook is intended as a compendium of possible activities from which facilitators can select any given activity rather than as a structured, sequenced progression of activities. The programme emphasises that conflict can be used constructively for growth and should not be treated as problems to eliminate. In fact, the guidebook makes the important point that, because conflict is a ubiquitous part of children's lives, they are highly motivated to learn constructive ways of dealing with it.

Overall, the activities in this guidebook are the most creative of the set reviewed here. They are intended be adventurous, that is, to invoke children's imagination and embed learning in games and other imaginative exercises. There is an emphasis on play and less explicit attention to skill and knowledge acquisition in a didactic sense. As with most other programmes, activities are complemented with reflection and discussion periods. With more than 150 activities, the guidebook offers enough possibilities for facilitators to create unique and varied lessons.

From an international perspective, one of the limitations of this guidebook is that it is written for a North American cultural context.[4] Activities to stimulate creative thinking and help children synthesise their learning might need to be thoughtfully redesigned for non-U.S. contexts.

Creative Problem Solving in the Classroom

This curriculum was developed for schools in Montenegro in 1999-2000 by Ljiljana Krekrjlic and Judy Slobig. At that time Montenegro faced social instability, with inter-ethnic violence on its borders. A host of international NGOs initiated relief and development programmes to improve living conditions for refugees from Kosovo and support civil society development within local communities. The Creative Problem Solving in the Classroom curriculum was developed in this context by World Vision and UNICEF. It was intended to support the needs of all children, with special attention to mitigating the impact of traumatic events in children's lives.

Like other peace education curricula, the Montenegro programme highlights skills and values related to co-operation, creative problem solving and conflict resolution. One of the strengths of the programme is its emphasis on issues of conflict escalation and understanding of others' perspectives.

Compared with others, however, the overall set of activities is relatively weak. The curriculum offers little structured practice in conflict resolution skills. For example, the lesson on understanding differences for children in the lower primary grades involves children guessing one anothers' birthdays.[5] The unit on creating a collaborative classroom only asks students to generate rules for the classroom.

Despite these curricular weaknesses, there is anecdotal evidence that the programme is having a constructive impact. A pilot programme involved nearly 200 teachers working with some 4,800 students in Montenegran primary schools. A preliminary report by the implementing agency indicated that teachers found the programme helpful in reducing classroom conflict (Slobig 2001).

Creating Peaceful Individuals

This curriculum was developed by World Vision and the Mennonite Central Committee for use in Cambodia. As the title declares, the programme focuses on formation of peaceful children who "know their own worth and can solve their problems in creative, constructive ways" (iii).

The programme is designed to supplement existing curricula, rather than as a stand-alone programme. Although it can be used in schools, the activities in this guidebook are intended primarily for use outside of schools in various non-formal settings or in children's clubs to provide a positive environment for children's growth.

The guidebook includes a variety of creative activities, with strong emphasis on co-operation, self-esteem and understanding emotions. However, the conflict-resolution section is relatively small. In this sense the programme is more oriented towards the psychological well-being of children and to the formation of peace-oriented attitudes/values than to the development of techniques and concepts related to conflict resolution.

Conflict Manager Training Manual

This manual is the most skill specific of the curricula reviewed here. Prepared by the Community Board, an organisation in San Francisco, California, USA, as one of a series of resources for conflict resolution in schools, this manual includes a short set of lessons to prepare students to serve as peer mediators in schools. While including standard topics such as "I messages" and active listening, the training focuses on practical issues related to peer mediation. The training is brief but provides opportunities for students to rehearse and deepen their skills in ways that may increase the likelihood of the skills being used.

Let's Talk

Intended for use by adults in Christian churches, this guidebook provides a strong set of lessons related to conflict resolution and interpersonal communication (Bartel 1999). Bartel's approach was influenced by the work of the Mennonite Conciliation Service and places strong emphasis on the values and virtues of constructive conflict management for deepening relationships, taking inspiration from Christian Scriptures. Reflection questions in the guidebook encourage learners to consider the theological foundations and implications of various approaches to conflict. However, the *Let's Talk* manual restricts itself to issues of interpersonal conflict over everyday problems, with special emphasis on church-related dynamics. It does not extend further into religious approaches to group-level conflict or issues of social justice.

Guidebook summary

As a prelude to further commentary, Figure 3–1 provides an overview of the key elements of the various guidebooks reviewed here. The matrix itself may serve as a tool for assessing additional peace education materials, alongside analysis of learning objectives and discussion of critical issues (introduced here and elaborated in the following chapter).

ANALYSIS OF LEARNING OBJECTIVES

This analysis finds that peace education curricula have converged around central themes. Almost all of the guidebooks reviewed here include the topics of co-operation, problem solving, understanding emotions, appreciation of self and others, and conflict resolution. Within these broad topics, however, there are many differences with regard to choices of specific learning objectives as well as the relative emphasis placed on knowledge, skills and attitudes/values. Consequently, it is important to look more closely at the specific nature of the activities in each programme, as well as the strengths and limitations of the core curriculum that tends to be shared across programmes.

To illuminate programme differences and shared concerns, I first summarise the learning objectives embedded in each guidebook. Second, I compare in a quantitative manner the distribution of knowledge, skills and values across programmes. A framework for prejudice reduction is used to compare strengths of the different programme guidebooks.

For purposes of this analysis, most programme guidebooks have been reviewed in their entirety.[6] However, sampling choices have been made in some cases. For the Living Values programme I selected 7 of the 12 units, those that most closely related to the standard themes of other peace education programmes – "Peace," "Tolerance," "Love," "Respect," "Co-operation," "Freedom" and "Unity" – using the curriculum for 8-14 year olds. For the PEP, which repeats key topics at each grade level, I analysed lessons for grade 5 as representative of the larger curriculum.[7]

Figure 3–1. Overview of key elements

	Living Values	**Peace Educa-tion Program (PEP)**	*Education for Conflict Resolution*	**Culture of Peace**
Intended contexts	School or non-formal settings; international	Schools and com-munity settings in African refugee camps	International; to be adapted to lo-cal culture/con-text	Community de-velopment in Phil-ippines
Orientation and goals	Cultivate under-standing and commitment to universal human values	Build skills for constructive en-gagement with conflict; help min-imise conflict	Help trainers de-velop skills for conflict resolu-tion and design own curriculum for children	Understand his-torical conflict; build skills and commitment to peace locally
Curriculum structure	Overall, 12 val-ues; each value (e.g., peace) con-tains ordered set of activities	Spiral; repeating set of topics for each grade, 1-8; 28 lessons to be offered once per week	Activities for key themes; planning exercises; sample children's activi-ties	3 modules to be offered over a 3-4 day-long seminar
Strengths	Cultivation of imagination; non-didactic develop-ment of moral values; compre-hensive materials	Comprehensive, well written ma-terials; rich sup-plemental resour-ces; school and community-level program	Focus on appro-priate adaptation and cultural norms; planning activities; social justice	Inclusion of reli-gious and cultural identity; analysis of local conflict, inspiration for change
Gaps and limitations	Weak in skill de-velopment	Limited gender focus; limited analysis of conflict in community	Lack of self-re-flection	Inadequate prac-tice in conflict resolution skills
Culture specific?	No; generic; de-signed for use in-ternationally	Somewhat (pri-marily through supplemental ma-terials)	No; generic; de-signed for use in-ternationally	Yes; only for use in local context
Source and origin	Brahma Kumaris; ideas from net-work; written by consultant	Requested by ref-ugees; written by consultant after input from com-munities	Written by UNI-CEF consultant; input and testing globally	Collaboration of grassroots NGOs and CRS
Target conflict	Interpersonal conflict among children; violence in world	Interpersonal conflict within refugee commun-ity	Interpersonal conflict and, to lesser extent, structural conflict	Individual and group-level con-flict locally
Explicit theoretical foundation	Inspiration from Brahma Kumari philosophy; psy-chological influ-ence of value-based environ-ments for learn-ing	Maslow (Hierar-chy of Needs); Kohlberg (stages of moral develop-ment); Bloom (Taxonomy of ed-ucational objec-tives)	Hofstede (ele-ments of cul-ture);Activities based on com-mon conflict res-olution topics	None; inspiration from religious teachings on peace/justice

Adventures in Peacemaking	Creating Peaceful Individuals	Conflict Manager Training	Creative Problem Solving in the Classroom	Let's Talk
After-school; child-care; non-formal settings in the United States	Schools and non-formal settings in Cambodia	School settings	Schools in Montenegro	Adult education in American Christian churches
Provide fun activities to reduce conflict and improve children's ability to interact peacefully	Help children interact more peacefully and use non-violent conflict resolution strategies	Preparation of peer mediators for mediation of school-based conflicts	Help children interact more peacefully and use non-violent conflict resolution strategies	Building communication and conflict resolution skills from Christian perspective
Large set of activities; no necessary sequence; coded for age level, activity type, time needed, etc.	Single set of activities for key themes	Sequence of activities for 6 lessons in a 2 day workshop	2 sets of 12 lessons; adapted for lower and upper primary	10 chapters with conceptual lessons and exercises
Wealth of imaginative activities; learning embedded in games	Focus on appreciation of self and others; support for active teaching	Focus on peer mediation; practical preparation for actual mediation	Emphasis on democratic, active pedagogy	Grounding in Christian tradition, focus on value of conflict, practical examples
Weak structure for capacity development; creativity at the expense of content	Weak in skill development; no attention to community context	Narrow focus excludes larger peace-oriented lessons	Few activities; lack of reinforcement; no attention to context	No attention to gender or power in conflict; predominantly conceptual focus
Somewhat; some activities based on American culture	No; no reference to local culture	No; no reference to local culture	No; instructions oriented toward local teachers	Yes; designed for American cultural context
Authors	Mennonite Central Committee, World Vision	Community Board	Response to refugee influx; written by consultant for UNICEF, WVI	Based on work of Mennonite Conciliation group and workshops
Interpersonal conflict among children	Interpersonal conflict among children	Interpersonal conflict among children	Interpersonal conflict among children	Interpersonal among adults, especially in church context
None; Emphasis on creative framing of messages for active learning	None; Activities based on common conflict resolution topics	None; Activities based on common conflict resolution topics	None; Activities based on common conflict resolution topics	None; based on common conflict resolution topics and inspiration from Christian tradition

Learning objectives

As noted above, the central themes of peace education curricula appear to be shared universally in the materials reviewed here. However, the different programme guidebooks do vary in terms of their specific learning objectives. To highlight these differences, I have "boiled down" each programme guidebook in terms of learning objectives; I have examined each guidebook, page by page, to determine the main learning objective(s) of each activity or lesson.

In some cases the objective is clear and easily identified; in other cases an activity may contain a mix of objectives or a complex, multidimensional objective that is difficult to capture in a few words. Further, some lessons focus on one objective in the main activity, but connect it to related concepts in follow-up discussion. There is a degree of uncertainty and subjective judgement inherent in this analysis, and another review might yield a slightly different "snapshot" of the curricula. I have attempted to err on the side of inclusivity, giving programmes credit for those objectives they touch upon in a significant manner.

For the sake of making the matrix (see Figure 3-2) manageable, not all objectives have been included. As a rule of thumb, I have included only those objectives that are shared by two or more curricula. Given its focus on many different values, of which peace is only one, the Living Values curriculum includes several learning objectives that are not common to other curricula and are not included here. The *Panagtagbo sa Kalinaw* manual also includes several objectives specific to understanding the social/historical situation in Mindinao, objectives unique to that programme.

I would like to suggest several initial observations about this summary comparison. For one, it indicates the extent to which many objectives are held in common across the programmes. Understanding of co-operation, active listening, recognising emotions, appreciating others, steps in conflict-resolution processes and group membership are found in almost every case.[8] In this sense these topics can be seen as core elements of the kind of peace education currently being practised internationally. Of course, the precise boundaries of this core are not fixed. Depending on their orientation and scope, programmes may focus more explicitly on certain skills or feature a broader range of concepts.

At another level the summary indicates that several key elements are not included in all cases. With regard to conflict resolution, for example, the concept of conflict escalation is found in only two of the curricula. Presumably, it would be helpful for students to understand how conflict escalates in order to better diffuse it. Although several guidebooks do include activities related to decision-making,

Figure 3–2. Programmes and learning objectives

	Living Values	PEP	Education for Conflict Resolution	Culture of Peace	Adventures in Peacemaking	Creating Peaceful Individuals	Conflict Manager Training Manual	Creative Problem Solving in the Classroom	Let's Talk
Vision of peaceful society	✓		✓	✓					
Communication problems	✓	✓	✓	✓	✓	✓			✓
One-way/two-way communication		✓			✓	✓			
Active listening	✓	✓	✓		✓	✓	✓		✓
Paraphrasing		✓	✓		✓				✓
Observing	✓	✓	✓		✓				✓
Open questions		✓	✓						✓
Recognising emotions	✓	✓			✓	✓	✓	✓	✓
Empathy	✓	✓	✓	✓	✓			✓	
I-messages	✓	✓	✓			✓	✓	✓	✓
Dealing with anger	✓	✓	✓		✓				
Assertiveness	✓	✓	✓			✓			
Relaxation	✓	✓	✓						

	Living Values	PEP	Education for Conflict Resolution	Culture of Peace	Adventures in Peacemaking	Creating Peaceful Individuals	Conflict Manager Training Manual	Creative Problem Solving in the Classroom	Let's Talk
Appreciating others	✓	✓	✓	✓	✓	✓		✓	
Building self-esteem/self-respect	✓	✓	✓	✓	✓	✓		✓	✓
Sharing talents	✓	✓			✓	✓			
Put downs	✓	✓			✓	✓			
Cooperation	✓	✓	✓		✓	✓		✓	
Trust building	✓	✓		✓	✓	✓			
Problem-solving strategies		✓			✓				
Decision-making strategies			✓	✓		✓		✓	
Consensus building			✓					✓	
Meaning of conflict	✓	✓	✓	✓	✓		✓		✓
Types/sources of conflict	✓		✓	✓		✓			
Personal conflict styles			✓		✓			✓	✓
Win/win outcomes		✓	✓		✓	✓			✓

Topic	1	2	3	4	5	6	7	8
Escalation of conflict	✓				✓		✓	
Collaborative problem solving	✓	✓			✓		✓	
Creative problem solving		✓			✓		✓	
Steps in problem solving/conflict resolution	✓	✓			✓	✓		✓
Conflict mapping	✓	✓	✓					
Negotiation (positions/interests)		✓	✓				✓	✓
Mediation	✓	✓	✓			✓		✓
Dialogue			✓					
Group membership		✓	✓		✓		✓	
Stereotypes		✓	✓		✓			
Inclusion/exclusion	✓	✓	✓		✓			
Discrimination	✓	✓	✓		✓			
Inequality			✓					
Perspective taking	✓	✓	✓		✓		✓	
Understanding perceptions	✓	✓			✓	✓		
Challenging prejudice	✓		✓		✓			
Public peace advocacy	✓		✓		✓			
Creating a co-operative classroom	✓	✓					✓	

they fail to promote processes for more inclusive decision-making. The process of consensus building, for instance, is found in only one of the curricula.

The programme guidebooks reviewed here seem inadequate in other areas as well. For instance, most programmes neglect the cultivation of students' personal visions and aspirations for peace. Only three of the guidebooks include lessons that invite students to envision a peaceful society and develop their own vision of peace. Developing such a vision enables students to transcend a foreclosed vision of the future, that is, a vision of the future that extrapolates future possibilities from current realities and accepts violent narratives as inevitable (Hutchinson 1996). Just as most curricula neglect to nurture alternative visions of the future, only three of the curricula include relaxation and visualisation exercises to develop the resources for inner peace.

Generally, the programme guidebooks reviewed here do not equip learners with tools to better understand the dynamics of group-level conflict or more systemic forms of violence. Engaging students in analysis of social issues is a rare activity. The curricula favor skills in interpersonal conflict resolution, neglecting issues in group-level conflict such as scapegoating or discrimination. In this respect the curricula tend to reinforce a passive acceptance of the economic, cultural and social forces underlying many types of interpersonal conflict in local communities.

One of the missing pieces in these programmes is an affirmation of students' capacity – and even responsibility – for critical thinking about social issues, especially issues related to the use of violent force. The programmes lack activities that help students develop what Shapiro calls the critical facility to question dominant discourse about the necessity of military interventions, the superiority of one group over another and structures of violence embedded within their social systems.

A related weakness is that the curricula tend not to be action oriented. It is noteworthy that only two of the guidebooks include objectives related to advocacy of peace and conflict resolution outside the children's immediate learning environment. Most programmes lack mechanisms for helping students become public actors. In this respect they fail to engage students in a larger agenda of peacebuilding. The programmes tend not to connect students' lives outside the classroom with their classroom learning in an explicit manner. Overall, the curricula lack frameworks for understanding and addressing different levels of conflict and their interrelationships. For example, students are not encouraged to explore the connections between patterns of exclusion on the playground and issues of social or economic exclusion in the lives of families within their community.

Relative emphases of knowledge, skills and values

Another step in this analysis involves an examination of the types of learning objectives included in each programme guidebook. Does the curriculum emphasise skills, knowledge, attitudes and values in a balanced way, or does it focus more on one area than another? To answer this question, I coded each of the activities provided in the guidebooks and made a judgement about the primary purpose of the activity and what the learner would gain from it. I have given each activity only one coding, even if it contains multiple objectives.[9]

The coding was based on the following schema:

Type of Learning	Characteristics
Knowledge (1)	Understanding frameworks, concepts or issues; usually related to discussion activities
Knowledge (2)	Understanding of self; reflection on past events or personal history, especially with regard to conflict and group membership
Skill (1)	Fundamental, general capacities such as creativity, problem solving and collaboration; usually developed through activities which are not in themselves found in daily life (such as solving the "9 dots" problem)
Skill (2)	Specific, applied skills, such as active listening and mediation; usually developed through practice of that skill in role plays or other simulations
Attitudes and values (1)	Appreciating and respecting others and one's self; increasing awareness of the specific individuals within the learning community, their talents and cultural backgrounds
Attitudes and values (2)	Heightened awareness and commitment toward peace-oriented values; usually developed through stories or experiences which highlight social problems (for example, exclusion games)
Attitudes and values (3)	Cultivation of one's vision of peace and a peaceful society; developing the imaginative vocabulary associated with peace
Emotional intelligence[10]	Recognising and understanding one's own emotions and those of others; managing difficult emotions (such as anger)

I developed this schema as an elaborated version of the traditional "knowledge, skills and attitudes" framework in order to better capture subtle differences among the learning objectives. It seemed to me that it is important to distinguish, for example, skills to be used directly in a conflict situation, such as mediation procedures, from more fundamental problem-solving skills which might be employed in a variety of contexts.

Of course, the borders of these designations are fluid and my coding of the activities might be idiosyncratic. My understanding of *skill* or *knowledge* may be different than others' understanding. To complicate matters, many activities could be said to fall into more than one category or to straddle the boundaries between categories. I found it difficult to categorise several activities that could be said to involve attitudes, skills and knowledge. The guidebooks often include reflection questions to be asked at the conclusion of an activity, and such questions sometimes develop the conceptual and attitudinal dimensions of otherwise skill-oriented activities. Without describing the coding challenges in more detail, the point here is that there is a certain degree of ambiguity in the analysis. It is intended as a starting point for further dialogue and analysis, not as a definitive judgement about the nature of the curricula in question. A summary table indicating the distribution of learning objectives found in each guidebook is given in Figure 3-3.[11]

A quick overview of the results indicates that different curricula have very different emphases in terms of knowledge, skills and values. Unlike other guidebooks, the *Panagtagbo sa Kalinaw* and *Let's Talk* manuals give some emphasis to personal reflection – a feature appropriate for adult training programmes. For children, the Living Values curriculum is deeply sensitive to reflection and the cultivation of imagination, whereas other programmes tend to neglect this dimension. Although children are often encouraged to reflect on personal qualities or talents in order to build self-esteem, they are rarely invited to reflect on their own habits of interaction or attitudes towards other groups.

In terms of skills most programmes focus more clearly on applied skills than on fundamental skills. Such emphasis would be expected to lead to stronger outcomes in terms of students' abilities to work constructively with conflict. Both the PEP and *Education for Conflict Resolution* focus more on building specific conflict-resolution skills than general problem solving or co-operative skills. The *Conflict Manager Training Manual* puts maximum emphasis on the development of applied skills related to conflict mediation. Such skills are also emphasised in *Let's Talk*. In contrast, *Adventures in Peacemaking* is heavily oriented towards building fundamental skills (largely involving co-operative games). The Creative Problem Solving in the Classroom curriculum, despite its title, is comparatively weak in skill development.

Figure 3–3. Distribution of learning objectives (numbers in per cents)

	Living Values	PEP	Education for Conflict Resolution	Culture of Peace	Adventures in Peacemaking	Creating Peaceful Individuals	Conflict Manager Training Manual	Creative Problem Solving in the Classroom	Let's Talk
Knowledge 1	24	29	22	38	13	9	31	23	47
Knowledge 2	8	0	4	15	1	6	0	0	16
Skills 1	11	18	9	4	40	26	0	8	0
Skills 2	8	29	27	12	10	6	62	15	21
Attitudes and values (1)	9	7	4	15	14	11	0	31	5
Attitudes and values (2)	22	7	24	8	6	23	0	15	5
Attitudes and values (3)	17	0	2	8	1	0	0	0	0
Emotional Intelligence	2	11	7	0	14	20	8	8	5

In the category of attitudes and values, there is mixed emphasis. Some programmes give greater attention to awareness-oriented activities, while others place emphasis on appreciation of self and others. The Creative Problem Solving in the Classroom curriculum is especially focused on building students' self-esteem and appreciation for diversity within their classrooms. In contrast, the Living Values programme, *Education for Conflict Resolution* and the Creating Peaceful Individuals guidebook place more emphasis on encouraging understanding and commitment to peace-related values. Notably, the Living Values programme is unique in cultivating students' personal vision of peace and imagination about peaceful futures. Related to attitudes and values, some degree of overt emphasis on understanding and managing emotions is found in all curricula, with the exception of the Culture of Peace programme.[12]

Figure 3–4 collapses the distinctions between types and shows the overall distribution of learning objectives in the major categories.

I would point here to the overall percentages as an indication of the relative weight given to the various dimensions. In general, the guidebooks demonstrate a balance among the different kinds of learning objectives. The peace education programmes reviewed here tend to devote about one-fourth of their activities to knowledge development and more than that amount, slightly more than one-third of total activities, to skill development. Slightly less than one-third of activities are devoted to attitudes and values oriented towards peace. Development of emotional understanding and management comprises less than one-tenth of peace education activities. If that category were considered another form of self-knowledge, then the three primary categories – knowledge, skills, attitudes/values – would be roughly equivalent in proportion across curricula.

These overall percentages provide a kind of rough benchmark against which specific programmes can be compared. UNICEF's *Education for Conflict Resolution* manual is balanced in a way that most resembles the overall distribution of knowledge, skills and attitudes. The PEP, in contrast, has a relatively greater emphasis on skills than most other programmes, and a slightly lower emphasis on attitudes and values. The Living Values programme contains almost the reciprocal emphasis, as would be expected from the title. Relatively minor attention is given to skill-building, in relation to the focus on attitudes and values. The *Panagtagbo sa Kalinaw* and *Let's Talk* guidebooks, both intended for adults, are knowledge intensive, whereas the Creating Peaceful Individuals programme and *Adventures in Peacemaking* – both designed as non-formal programmes – tend to de-emphasise conceptual understanding as primary objectives. Creating Peaceful Individuals, also true to its title, has the strongest emphasis on emotional understanding and management of any curriculum.

Figure 3–4. Summary distribution of learning objectives (numbers in per cents)

	Living Values	PEP	Education for Conflict	Culture of Peace	Adventures in Peacemaking	Creative Problem Solving in the Classroom	Conflict Manager Training Manual	Creating Peaceful Individuals	Let's Talk	OVERALL
Knowledge	32	29	27	54	14	23	31	14	63	26
Skills	18	46	26	15	50	23	62	31	21	35
Attitudes and values	48	14	31	31	21	46	0	34	11	30
Emotional intelligence	2	11	7	0	14	8	8	20	5	9

Of course, such interpretations about the nature of these programmes must be made with some caution. This coding of objectives says nothing about the depth or superficiality of a given activity, or the quality of the activities with regard to their potential to engage students in a meaningful way. And even then, the curriculum on paper is a far different matter than the curriculum that is actually implemented. With the exception of the PEP, which has been well documented and evaluated, there is little evaluative material available on how the various curricula actually work in practice and what students really gain from their experience. In sum, an analysis of learning objectives can tell us something about the ideas that the curriculum designers had but tells little about how teachers work with the materials in practice or the experience participants have in the actual programme.

Curricular approaches to improving intergroup relations

All the programmes reviewed here help participants become more skilled in working with interpersonal conflict, that is, in working with conflict constructively at the individual level. Yet conflicts between individuals can be rooted in tensions over group identity, as are many conflicts that generate violence in particular regions. Consequently, an important aspect of peace education is the way in which it contributes to building better relations among groups. In this section I examine the theoretical approach – whether implicit or explicit – used by programmes to create better relations among participants at the group level.

In their recent book on improving intergroup relations, Stephan and Stephan (2001) outline several primary approaches. Capsule descriptions of selected approaches are given below:

- *Expose value-behaviour gaps.* The focus in this approach is for facilitators to point out discrepancies between participants' values and behaviours. A participant may hold as a value such as equality of all people and yet practice discriminatory behaviours. When there is conscious dissonance between values and behaviour, people tend to change behaviours to be more consistent with their values.
- *Reduce threat.* This approach focuses on reducing the perceived threat (especially psychological) posed by another group. Through positive interactions with members of another group, participants will feel more secure and are less likely to respond aggressively. For children, such a strategy might underlie co-operative games, co-operative learning or other forms of activities that build trust among members of different identity groups.

- *Increase empathy.* For Stephan and Stephan (2001), there are two types of empathy: cognitive and emotional. Cognitive empathy involves the ability to take the perspective of the other on a particular issue. It is built on knowledge of the other group (language, culture, etc.) and practice in understanding that group's point of view. Cognitive empathy involves understanding the other and thus feeling more secure and less threatened. Emotional empathy involves concern for the members of the other group, a sense of how the situation feels for them. Vehicles for building emotional empathy include simulations, stories, and role plays in which participants experience a situation from the other's standpoint.
- *Increase perceived similarity.* In general, perceived similarity with another individual or group tends to reduce prejudice and increase liking of the other. Thus, helping members of different groups become aware of the many ways in which they are similar (belonging to a large family, enjoying sewing or cricket, etc.) decreases attention to difference and increases positive valuation of the other.
- *Decategorisation by emphasising multiple identities.* In situations in which ethnic or religious identity is highly charged, it can be helpful for people to realise that ethnicity or religion is only one aspect of their identities. Similar to the above approach, here facilitators would encourage participants to explore their membership in multiple social categories (gender, social class, born in a particular month or season, hobbies, talents, etc.) Participants can then appreciate the richness of their own identity and their connection with others on the basis of those categories. As Stephan and Stephan point out, "It is difficult to dislike people with whom one shares important aspects of identity" (2001, 32).
- *Focus on superordinate groups.* By focusing attention on categories of identity held in common among groups, people can begin to soften their focus on categories of difference. For example, children may be encouraged to see themselves as common members of a school, of a community or even of humanity rather than as members of rival ethnic groups.

These last three approaches share an emphasis on re-orienting participants' perspectives on members of the other group. In fact, the very notion of "other group" is challenged as a particular choice in constructing one's understanding of the situation. The "other group" may be "other" in a particular dimension of identity, such as religion but similar in many other aspects, especially in superordinate categories such as belonging to a particular nation, living in a particular region, or having a shared cultural heritage. An emphasis on aspects of shared identity, of similarity, shifts "other" to "same" and thus tends to soften, even dissolve, stereotypes and prejudice.

The peace education programmes reviewed here all contain elements of these prejudice-reduction strategies. Figure 3-5 suggests which strategies are being employed by each programme. Cells with dark shading give stronger or more explicit attention to a particular dimension, while lightly shaded cells give it some attention.

Figure 3-5 suggests the relative strength of the different programmes in terms of their ability to improve relations among participants at the group level. In most cases, with the exception of the programme designed for adults in the Phillipines, group identity is not an explicit element of the curriculum design. Peace education lessons tend to avoid direct engagement with issues of group identity. Nevertheless, a curriculum may include discussion of similarities, as in the case of the PEP, Creative Problem Solving in the Classroom and Creating Peaceful Individuals programmes. By focusing students' attention on what they have in common, peace education programmes can improve students' sense of appreciation for each other and soften stereotypes. While emphasising similarities, several programmes also place strong emphasis on affirming the value of diversity.

Indeed, most of the peace education curricula reviewed here take a gentle approach to intergroup relations, an approach that seeks to improve relations indirectly, through enjoyable activities, affirmation of individual similarities and increased skills and proclivities regarding collaborative modes of interaction. Engaging students in co-operative learning – a process at the heart of peace education pedagogy – is likely to increase their regard for members of other groups. In terms of improving intergroup relations, co-operative learning has become an increasingly well-documented and respected approach to building trust and friendship among students of different groups (Stephan and Stephan 2001). Several programmes are also effective in increasing cognitive empathy through understanding of cultural traditions. In *Adventures in Peacemaking*, for example, one activity asks children to interview each other about their families and cultures, opening a deeper appreciation of the diversity present in the group.

This indirect approach can be a strength. Focusing on the personal characteristics of individuals rather than problematic group issues can be an intelligent political strategy. By not including ethnic/religious/cultural identity as an explicit issue, the programmes can avoid becoming embroiled in controversy among parents or school officials. Further, skills-oriented curricula tend to be politically neutral. They can be introduced without reference to contentious issues, even though, in practice, there is space to explore such issues during

Figure 3–5. Strategies

Strategy \ Programme	Living Values	PEP	Education for Conflict Resolution	Culture of Peace	Adventures in Peacemaking	Creative Problem Solving in the Classroom	Conflict Manager Training Manual	Creating Peaceful Individuals	Let's Talk
Value-behaviour gap	✓			✓					✓
Reduce threat	✓	✓	✓	✓				✓	
Increase empathy	✓	✓	✓	✓	✓				
Emphasise similarity	✓	✓	✓	✓	✓	✓		✓	
Decategorisation	✓	✓	✓		✓			✓	
Superordinate groups	✓	✓		✓					✓

discussion periods following skill-oriented activities. Such an approach can be especially useful in environments in which identity-related politics are highly sensitive.

Nevertheless, avoiding explicit attention to group identity may leave important problems unexamined. It is not clear whether exercises aimed at improving empathy, will transfer to increased empathy for a specific "other" group. Peace education programmes may not help students develop empathy, either cognitive or emotional, for specific identity groups in their home communities if the curricula do not acknowledge that such group differences exist. Because peace education curricula tend to avoid overt reference to group identities and differences, they may be less effective in eroding stereotypes and softening boundaries between groups. In an evaluation of the PEP, it was found that "most teachers go half way and then fail to name ethnic or religious issues, fail to elicit discussion of ethnic or religious issues, and fail to emphasise ethnic or religious tolerance and respect, which are critical concerns in the Dadaab and Kakuma camps" (Obura 2002, 86).

Several examples of a direct approach to matters of identity come from the *Panagtagbo sa Kalinaw* manual. In one activity facilitators invite participants to name the groups with which they associate themselves. Participants then gather in these groups, and the groups share with each other aspects of their history and culture – a process that contributes to emotional and cognitive empathy. As part of the discussion, participants comment on the strength they have gained from the group, what they would like the group to change, and what they no longer wish to hear about their group. In another activity participants are asked to reflect specifically on their own prejudices as well as an incident that changed their attitudes towards another group. This activity is organised as a healing ritual in which participants share their prejudices with one another, offer apologies and even express forgiveness for those who may have caused the "cultural pains" of prejudice.

Several guidebooks include exercises aimed at increasing sensitivity to inclusion and exclusion. The PEP includes several lessons on this topic, beginning in grade 6, and the Living Values programme also has an extended activity related to dynamics of discrimination. Of the materials reviewed here, *Education for Conflict Resolution* has perhaps the most comprehensive set of activities aimed at sharpening participants' understanding of in-group/out-group behaviours. Participants gain a strong sense of empathy through simulations of exclusion and inequality. Another activity enables participants to practise ways in which they can challenge stereotypes in everyday life; in this way the curriculum moves participants towards a more active stance with regard to encountering prejudice in their home communities.

CONCLUSIONS AND FURTHER QUESTIONS ABOUT THE CONSTRUCTION OF PEACE EDUCATION

One of the enduring frustrations many people express about peace education is that it means so many different things. How can it be a legitimate field of education if there is no common approach? In a dissertation written three decades ago, Carpenter noted:

> Despite current popular interest there still remains great confusion about the field of peace education. People question whether it should include examination of the growth of the military-industrial complex, international political systems, imperialism, ethnic conflict, inner peace, resource distribution, community action or human relations training. Questions are also asked about the most appropriate ways to learn about peace. To date there are no adequate answers for these questions. (1975, 4)

There are still no final answers as to what peace education should and should not include. Perhaps there never will be final answers. The convergence of the peace education curricula reviewed here around central learning objectives represents a response to that frustration; finally, international educators are agreeing that this is what peace education means (collaboration, problem solving, etc.) and now development agencies can replicate such an approach more broadly. No doubt greater coherence and conceptual clarity are important goals in the development of peace education.

Given the wealth of peace education materials now in circulation, it has become a relatively simple task to toss together a set of activities and call it a curriculum. As the core themes of peace education have become more clearly visible, curriculum designer may be tempted to follow a formulaic recipe: start with a base of co-operation, add some problem-solving skills, spice it with emotional intelligence, sprinkle in a few prejudice-awareness exercises, and voila! – a ready-to-eat peace education programme!

In some cases curriculum writers seem to have followed this recipe. They have grabbed interesting activities from other curricula indiscriminately, without a solid theoretical understanding of peace education to inform their choices. The result can be a hodgepodge of activities that cover central topics yet lack a deeper theoretical coherence or grounding in the realities of a given context. In other cases materials have undergone an extensive development process and continue to evolve through ongoing feedback and revision.

Salomon and Nevo (2002) point out that peace education generally lacks a strong conceptual basis. Given the global spread of peace education efforts, perhaps curriculum writers assume that theoretical discussions are no longer necessary. It may also be that peace educators, pressed to develop new curriculum quickly, have bypassed reviewing the theoretical foundations of their efforts in order to get the curriculum writing completed in a hurry and move on to implementation.[13] The danger of replicating old material is that it may perpetuate certain easily digested ideas without engagement with deeper issues in peace education.

Exploring these questions in more depth might lead to different sorts of activities, different programmematic structures and different understandings of peace education than are currently in vogue. Designing curriculum for peace education within a larger conversation can be a powerful contribution to the field (this was the context of the World Vision Consultation on Peace Education for which the chapters of this book were prepared).

On the other hand, many organisations or communities interested in introducing peace education may not have resources – in terms of time, funding or expertise – to explore fundamental questions in depth or construct innovative curricular models based on synthesis of theoretical frameworks. Further, why shouldn't programmes incorporate variations of activities and ideas developed elsewhere? If curriculum developers didn't borrow good practices from a variety of sources, they might end up spending countless hours attempting to "reinvent the wheel" with results that are not necessarily better. In other words, borrowing what others have learned is necessary to get new programmes running. The fact that new programmes tend to resemble existing programmes may be inevitable, if peace education is to spread, especially within the programmeming efforts of international development agencies.

But an openness to an examination of patterns and assumptions in the construction of peace education programmes provides a basis for programmematic evolution. In their review of education for peacebuilding K. D. Bush and D. Saltaralli (2000) conclude with four principles. They believe that peacebuilding education:

- is a process rather than a product
- is long-term rather than short-term
- relies on local, rather than external, inputs and resources
- seeks to create opportunities rather than impose solutions. (34)

These are valuable criteria for any agency to consider as it builds a flexible approach to peace education. They are also challenging criteria, in that they shift the emphasis away from the neatly packaged curricular materials produced by international consultants towards the process of co-creation of peace education for a particular time and place. Organisations interested in implementing peace education in the future might consider a process in which communities generate their own learning objectives, building on the good work already manifest in the many lessons and activities in existing peace education materials. In this way peace education can be something the community seeks to teach itself rather than something an outside agency believes a community should learn.

NOTES

[1] The Western cultural orientation of core peace education material is rarely analysed or criticised. This is surprising, because peace education addresses, among other issues, communication – a process that is highly conditioned by cultural norms. The emphasis on "I messages" or "assertiveness" found in almost every peace education curriculum seems strongly affiliated with a Western cultural disposition for individualism and democratic social dynamics. (An exception here is the UNHCR Peace Education Programme which intentionally does not foreground self-esteem for cultural reasons.) In most curricula, culturally rooted norms about authority, the relation of the individual to the group or even the nature of conflict at a cosmological level are never discussed.

[2] Peace is the largest unit within the Living Values curriculum. The programme recommends that teachers begin with the peace unit because children have an immediate attraction to issues of peace.

[3] Questions might be raised about the degree to which this particular set of values is universal. Not all cultures or societies share this list or see these as distinct values. While the Living Values programme encourages educators to adapt the curriculum to their own cultural setting, the set of 12 values itself does not seem to be open for modification.

[4] In an activity about cultural differences, the facilitator is advised to gather a set of objects that represent American culture. Suggested objects include the flag, a baseball, a photo of the White House, jeans and a TV remote control.

[5] Some of these activities appear to be adapted from *Adventures in Peacemaking*.

[6] It is important to note that the *Conflict Manager Training Manual* is only one part of a larger set of peace education-related materials published by the College Board. This analysis does not include that larger set of materials. For both the PEP and Living Values programmes, only the materials oriented towards children are included here in the analysis of learning objectives. These programmes are quite extensive, including materials for other groups as well as for children. A more complete analysis of the entire programmes would include a review of the objectives used in the teacher/facilitator training as well as the parent/community education components.

[7] Although the theme of inclusion/exclusion and group membership is first introduced in grade 6, I have included it in the listing of learning objectives below to acknowledge that it is an important aspect of the overall programme.

[8] The diverse nature of the materials gathered for this review makes it unlikely that a given topic will be truly universal across all programmes. For example, the *Panagtagbo sa Kalinaw* training manual, designed for community workers in the Philippines, does not feature the kinds of activities for children found in other curricula.

[9] Exceptions here are the *Panagtagbo sa Kalinaw* and *Let's Talk* guidebooks. Each lesson in these guidebook is extensive, containing what would be two or three distinct lessons in other guidebooks. Consequently, I have, in several cases, given lessons two different codes to acknowledge the co-existence of two key objectives.

[10] The term *emotional intelligence* is used in reference to the concept made popular by psychologist Daniel Goleman in his book of that name (1995). It is intended to affirm the importance in daily life of understanding, monitoring and regulating one's emotions while being perceptive about the emotional states of others. Goleman believes that emotional intelligence is as important as, or more important than, traditional conceptualisations of intelligence for success in life.

[11] To arrive at the percentage breakdown, I first constructed a table with the actual number of lessons in each category. Because the number of lessons is vastly different across guidebooks (totaling more than 150 in the *Adventures in Peacemaking* guidebook and 12 in Creative Problem Solving in the Classroom), comparison of percentages seems more useful than a comparison of the actual number of lessons in each category.

[12] Ironically, that programme may be the most emotionally evocative, in that it directly addresses issues of injustice and historical conflict as well as participants' personal contribution to others' pain. Although it does not explicitly address emotions as a curricular topic, it has a very strong emotional/affective dimension.

[13] In my review I noticed an apparent disconnection between the peace education work of international NGOs and the dialogue among peace education theorists. There appears to be a much more expansive conversation about peace education outside international NGOs than inside. This may reflect the fact that international NGOs tend to work in resource-poor, politically volatile and highly constrained settings, whereas many scholars are grounded in resource-rich, low-conflict settings.

REFERENCES

Bartel, B. C. 1999. *Let's Talk: Communication Skills and Conflict Transformation.* Newton, KS: Faith and Life Press.

Baxter, P. 2001. The UNHCR Peace Education Prograe: Skills for Life. Available online.

Bush, K. D., and D. Saltarelli. 2000. "The Two Faces of Education in Ethnic Conflict: Towards a Peacebuilding Education for Children." Florence: UNICEF, Innocenti Research Centre.

Carpenter, S. L. 1975. *The Peace Transformation Process: Toward a Framework for Peace Education.* Doctoral dissertation. Amherst: Univ. of Massachusetts.

Catholic Relief Services. 1998. *Panagtagbo sa kalinaw: A Basic Orientation Manual towards a Culture of Peace for Mindanao Communities.* Mindinao: Catholic Relief Services.

Community Board Programme. 1995. *Conflict Managers Training Manual for Grades 3-6.* San Francisco, CA: The Community Board Programme.

Fountain, S. 1997. *Education for Conflict Resolution: A Training for Trainers Manual.* New York: UNICEF.

Goleman, D. 1995. *Emotional Intelligence.* New York: Bantam.

Harris, I. 1988. *Peace Education.* Jefferson, NC: McFarland & Co.

———. 2002. "Conceptual Underpinnings of Peace Education. In Salomon and Nevo 2002, 15-25.

Hutchinson, F. P. 1996. *Educating beyond Violent Futures.* London: Routledge.

Kreidler, W., and L. Furlong. 1995. *Adventures in Peacemaking: A Conflict Resolution Guide for School-age Programs.* Cambridge, MA: Educators for Social Responsibility.

Krekrjlic, L., and J. Slobig. 1999-2000. Creative Problem Solving in the Classroom programme.

Mennonite Central Committee and World Vision Cambodia. N.d. Creating Peaceful Individuals programme.

Obura, A. P. 2002. UNHCR Peace Education Programme: Evaluation. Unpublished.

Salomon, G., and B. Nevo. 2002. *Peace Education: The Concept, Principles, and Practices around the World.* Mahwah, NJ: Erlbaum.

Slobig, J. H. 2001. "Peace Education in Montenegro." In *Children and Peacebuilding: Experiences and Perspectives,* ed. H. Elliott, 9-13. World Vision Discussion Papers. Melbourne, Australia: World Vision Australia.

Stephan, W. G., and C. W. Stephan. 2001. *Improving Intergroup Relations.* Thousand Oaks, CA: Sage.

Tillman, D. 2000. *Living Values, An Educational Program: Living Values Activities for Children Ages 8-14.* Deerfield Beach, FL: Health Communications.

4

Where's the peace?
What's the education?

Part II: Questions asked of peace education curricula

Vachel W. Miller

> *Teaching for peace means eliciting and affirming that part of our worldview that sees life as of inestimable and transcendent value.*
> – Svi Shapiro, "Toward a Critical Pedagogy of Peace Education"

THE RADICAL HOPE OF PEACE EDUCATION

Peace education is a project of radical hope. Peace education aims to create new resources for peace – new narratives and new visions that forecast the creation of a different world from the troubled one we now inhabit. When it works effectively, peace education changes how children handle conflict, how they respond to their emotions and how they envision the future. Replacing the blunt instrument of violence with the more nuanced and creative tools of conflict resolution, peace education equips students to realise a culture of peace in their interactions with peers as well as in their families and communities. Child by child, family by family, community by community, peace education is intended to improve relational skills, prevent violence and reduce tensions between groups.

Given the scope of its aspirations, peace education is an eternally unfinished business. As long as children grow up in cultures that commit violence – in direct or structural forms – there is room for peace education to point towards alternative forms of organising social life and personal relations. As long as fists and bombs are used to solve problems, then there is room for peace education to bear witness to another way of living together.

In this chapter I continue to address critical questions that arise from comparative examination of peace education curriculum guidebooks. These questions include the following:

- Should peace education lessons be universal?
- What do children need to learn about peace?
- What concepts and experiences tend to be neglected in peace education programmes?
- What is the place of the inner life in peace education?
- How can peace education help children heal?
- What is the role of gender in peace education?
- How does a peace education programme produce meaningful change?

These questions are intended to be generative, that is, to open new ways of thinking about choices in the design and implementation of peace education programmes in a variety of contexts. This discussion builds upon the preceding chapter and illustrates points with references to specific guidebook lessons.

UNPACKING PEACE EDUCATION

Should peace education lessons be universal?

One of the surprising findings of this review of peace education guidebooks is that peace education lessons tend to be uprooted from their local contexts. Other than mentioning a few culturally specific objects or children's names, the guidebook for the programme in Montenegro seems almost interchangeable with the guidebook for a peace education programme in Cambodia. Despite the unique historical contexts of the Cambodian genocide and the ethnically divisive war in the Balkans, a page could be lifted from either guidebook written for those settings and used in a classroom anywhere in the world. The materials reviewed here suggest that the agencies sponsoring these curricula have emphasised the importance of portability rather than contextualisation.

Is peace education moving towards a standard packaged curriculum, like the controversial "school in a box" of emergency education, to be dropped in when needed?[1] How directly should peace education programmes address the problems of the context in which they are situated? Should local culture be added onto peace education activities only through supplementary songs and role plays? Is it wise for peace education programmes to sidestep direct engagement with problematic local issues?

Most peace education programmes provide opportunities for students to contextualise skills. Students often generate their own conflict scenarios and role plays. Such role plays are likely to be rooted in their experiences and thus highly contextual. As pointed out to me by M. Sinclair, an experienced international educator, the role plays done by young Afghan women about their concerns would look very different from those created by African teens about saying no to sex after drinking at a disco – yet the programme guidebook which facilitators use to generate such role plays would look exactly the same.

In the materials reviewed here, the Culture of Peace curriculum for the Philippines is perhaps the best example of how local issues and identities can be incorporated into training.[2] Oriented towards adults, this curriculum focuses intentionally on the local conflict as core content for participants' activities and dialogue. The curriculum cannot be exported elsewhere; it is specifically rooted in a place, and it is highly attuned to the social justice issues that the people of Mindinao are confronting. Thus, this training might be more appropriately understood as peacebuilding, rather than peace education training, because its goal is the creation of peace within a social context rather than within the behaviour of specific individuals. Furthermore, the guidebook intentionally incorporates religious/spiritual elements into the training, drawing on Muslim, Christian and indigenous ideals about peace and peacemaking to illustrate key points and motivate participants to commit to peace.

Contextually rooted stories – about the nature and history of one's own group and of other groups – are critical elements of peacebuilding. Especially in areas of protracted social conflict, children often grow up within cultural narratives designed to devalue a rival group and elevate their own. It may be naive to neglect such narratives. Ultimately, as Salomon argues (2002), peace education should help students to analyse their own narratives, to evaluate their own contributions to the conflict and to listen empathetically to the other group's narrative.

Although peace education curricula generally include lessons on exclusion and stereotypes, they may not do enough to address the particular stereotypes and discriminatory ideas which dominant groups hold about subordinate groups. The devaluation of a minority group, as pointed out by genocide scholar Ervin Staub (1989, 2002), can serve as a basis for violations of their human rights. Devalued groups can be easily targeted as scapegoats for problems experienced by the dominant group.

To counter this tendency, it is important for students to understand structures of devaluation in their own contexts, as well as their own patterns of devaluation. Devaluation refers to stereotypes or other cultural messages about the inferiority of a particular group. For students in a peace education programme, understanding the notion of devaluation leads to questions such as these: Which groups do they believe are dirty, lazy, ignorant, greedy, or dangerous? How are those patterns of devaluation built into the background of daily life in a particular place? For example, is it normal to see an indigenous person depicted in media as backward or a woman depicted as weak-minded?

From a global perspective, Salomon (2002) argues that peace education programmes should be differentiated according to the kind of conflict (or lack thereof) in a given region. In situations of enduring conflict, it may be necessary for students to analyse narratives of devaluation and begin constructing a different kind of identity. Educators in a Western European nation, in contrast, might wish to focus peace education efforts on building critical understanding of global environmental issues or to focus students' attention on less visible, yet locally pervasive, forms of violence such as racial discrimination, sexual abuse or peer bullying. Each context, each community will have different concerns. The point here is twofold: first, that the formation of peace education programmes should include analysis and dialogue on the nature of the peace challenges faced by people in that place; and second, that the design of peace education should be articulated with that analysis.

What do children already know?

The widely shared set of curricular objectives and activities in most peace education programmes reflects a series of assumptions about what children know and what they need to learn. While it certainly seems safe to assume that children do not have experience with structured problem-solving or conflict-resolution strategies, the exercises related to emotional understanding seem at times naive about children's capacities. Do children always need practice in understanding others' emotions? What skills do they already have in reading and responding to others' emotional cues? Do boys and girls need equal doses of training in empathy? Do children always need lessons in collaboration? Or in a given cultural context, have they already internalised values related to collective work and mutual responsibility?

Noting that children may already possess some of the desired skills and orientations associated with peace education does not lessen the value of a peace education's objectives; the more that peace education can promote, encourage and reinforce the habits of co-operation, trust and inclusivity, the better.

After all, most cultural environments in which children grow up are far richer in images and values related to war than those related to peace. Children's play reveals the underdevelopment of peace in their collective imagination: children know immediately how to "play war" but when asked to "play peace" they usually return blank stares (Raviv, Oppenheimer and Bar-Tal 1999). Children often have little experience with peacemaking strategies and few peace heroes to serve as the raw material which could generate peace-related play.

That said, it is worthwhile to challenge the assumption that children have not already developed some sophistication with the key themes of peace education, or that key topics must receive equal attention in all contexts. In different contexts the relative balance of topics within a curriculum might vary greatly depending on children's existing set of values, abilities and attitudinal orientations. There may be additional differences in the skills and capacities of girls and boys based on differences in socialisation and gender roles within a culture.

This leads to another argument for a participatory process of curriculum development, in which teachers engage children (and parents) in reflective conversation about children's existing communication strategies, the way they understand and work with emotions to meet their goals, cultural norms about authority and responsibility towards others, and so on. Such a process, in which children themselves would be engaged as key actors in defining their own learning needs, responds to the call for helping children become agents of transformation in their own communities.

What might be missing in existing curricula?

In a critical examination of peace education curricula it is important to consider what might be missing. One concept missing from peace education curricula is that of positive "bystandership." Extensive research in social psychology has found that bystanders have a key role to play in motivating others to help a person in distress (Staub 1989). In situations of potential violence, bystanders can also affirm the dignity of potential victims and thus prevent perpetrators from assuming that others condone their actions. By bearing witness to the humanity of potential victims and advocating for non-violence, bystanders can de-legitimise the use of force – whether on school playgrounds or in international relations. Peace education curricula might be strengthened by including dialogue about this concept and providing students with practice in being positive bystanders to conflict in their immediate contexts. An emphasis on positive bystandership would complement attention to bullying in school. The problem of bullying in schools is an immediate issue for children, and a discussion of bullying would naturally lead to concern for being a positive bystander in other instances of peer violence.

The importance of engaging students in concrete activities to benefit others is a further theme discussed by social psychologists interested in promoting peace education. Staub (2002) notes that conceptual learning is insufficient; children must have experiences of helping others and working collaboratively with members of other groups. Such experiences tend to make children more helpful and empathetic. Just as people's capacity for violent action evolves little by little, Staub argues that people's capacity for helping others evolves as we identify with our actions.

McCauley (2002) makes a similar point, advocating that peace education should be "feet-first" rather than "head-first," involving small commitments and opportunities to practise new behaviours with regard to excluded or devalued groups. Behavioural change does not necessarily result from changed ideas and attitudes, but rather from small actions in a particular direction. These insights from social psychology challenge the reliance in typical peace education curricula on a structure of weekly one- or two-hour lessons as a catalyst for behavioural change in students.

The notion of a "feet first" peace education programme suggests the following question for programme designers: In a particular local context, how can children be actively engaged in creating and sustaining peace? What are the first small steps that could lead to larger ones? Responses to these questions will necessarily be highly varied according to context. In Rwanda, youth might organise a commemoration event for Hutu families that protected or rescued Tutsis during the genocide; in Britain or the United States, children might organise a peace vigil in their school in response to their government's involvement in Iraq.

Some programmes encourage students to engage in a simple form of action research about local conflicts and constructive solutions. Such a community-action orientation contrasts with programmes that see peace primarily or exclusively at the level of interpersonal relationships. If peace education is only concerned about creating peaceful individuals, then learners may not be treated as actors within their community or family, actors with the power to help resolve interpersonal conflicts as well as to engage in dialogue/actions within the family and community to promote more inclusive, caring, non-violent approaches to collective problems. The point here is for curriculum developers to consider the role they envision for children as peacemakers and peacebuilders in multiple social settings. The roles for which programmes train students can influence the size of the role students are prepared to take on as they grow into public actors in their communities.

Helping students address real problems in their communities provides practice in peacebuilding. At the same time, supporting children's leadership can also support transformation at the community level, as children inspire their peers and even adults to take similar actions or to reconsider their own political and social commitments. By engaging students in concrete, community-based activities, peace education programmes can help students become models for others to follow. Students' actions can build new partnerships between youth and adults. These partnerships involve the development of shared understanding of complex problems and a sense of connectedness across generations and cultures.

Peace education curricula typically include a reflective dimension, particularly with regard to issues of emotions, personal qualities and group membership. Yet peace education curricula rarely include a deeper engagement with issues of inner peace. Just as many cultural and social environments fail to teach children the skills of non-violent conflict resolution, many environments also do not offer children resources for developing their internal capacities for peaceful being. Such capacities might include practice in calming the mind and body, in quiet reflection, and in cultivating resources for inner equanimity in the face of challenging events and emotions.

Children need a rich supply of metaphor and images to fuel their social imagination. They need support in opening up ideas about alternative futures, futures which fall outside the parameters which their societies may view as inevitable (Hutchinson 1996). In this sense peace education involves challenging socially accepted notions of the necessity of violence, of war, and of mass deprivation – notions which can colonise the future in young people's minds. Peace education involves the cultivation of new visions for other ways of living together. For Australian futurist Francis Hutchinson, to educate for peace means to liberate creative thought and action, to "nurture signs of hope" (1996, 20). In the long run, the "softest" aspects of peace education may be the most profound; that is, developing children's inner vision of peaceful possibilities builds the imaginative reservoir from which future action arises. One of the key goals of peace education, then, is the cultivation of what might be called an evocative peace vocabulary from which children can draw.

What is the place of the inner life in peace education?

At a spiritual level the aims of peace education overlap with the values of many religious traditions. Peace education programmes could potentially tap into traditional practices as complementary modes of cultivating the mind and heart of peace. The *Let's Talk* guidebook, for example, is effective in connecting conflict management processes with biblical messages. It invites learners to reflect on biblical models of conflict management, yet it does not place a heavy emphasis on the role of internal spiritual development in handling conflict constructively.

The strongest of the curricula reviewed here in terms of integrating spirituality is the Living Values programme. Grounded in the spiritual philosophy of the Brahma Kumaris, the Living Values programme incorporates a rich set of reflective/contemplative activities into its curriculum, complemented by many opportunities for artistic expression. One of the lessons in the peace unit, for example, guides children through a visualisation exercise in which they imagine themselves as a peace star full of light and good will. Through this and related activities, the programme cultivates an inner vocabulary of peace.

Peace education programme designers may wish to consider how a spiritual and/or religious dimension could be integrated in ways that would draw upon and complement traditions located in a particular context. Such an approach might involve inclusion of religious proverbs and lessons related to peace, as well as historical stories of exemplary peacebuilders in various religious or cultural traditions. On a more experiential level, it might also include activities drawn from contemplative spiritual practices such as yoga, meditation, prayer or sitting in silence. Such practices could provide children with additional skills – skills to be cultivated over a lifetime – that complement the more rational conflict-resolution skills while opening the depth dimension of inner peacebuilding.

How can peace education help children heal?

Peace education often takes place in settings in which people have endured violent conflict or severe social upheaval. The curricula reviewed here were designed for Cambodia, Montenegro, the Philippines and East Africa for groups that have suffered displacement and hardship. In such contexts development agencies may offer programmes designed to support children's recovery from traumatic experiences. However, peace education curricula appear to be separate and distinct from other programmes designed to help children heal from their painful experiences.

Such separation is ultimately artificial, because the two kinds of programmes are deeply related, in theory, if not in practice. In powerful ways psychosocial recovery programmes contribute to peacebuilding. They help children regain a sense of stability and safety, while enabling children to work with traumatic experiences through play and other forms of creative expression. Through such processes war-affected children can begin to reclaim their lives. Psychosocial healing processes, combined with efforts to rebuild economic opportunities for families and communities, increase the likelihood that children can escape the cycle of violence. They will be better able to meet their own needs in constructive ways. Through processes of healing, children can regain the capacities to trust and engage in positive relationships with others.

Like psychosocial programmes, peace education is intended to open new horizons of hope for children. Learning new skills of conflict management can give children and adults fresh confidence that violence is not inevitable, that there are technologies of peace, technologies that can be learned to open a way out of cycles of hostility. Peace education programmes, not surprisingly, incorporate many of the methods involved in helping children heal from social violence. Peace educators might encourage children to express their feelings about peace and draw images of a more peaceful world. Peace educators often use role plays that enable children to explore conflictual situations they have experienced.

Although there are methodological similarities, there are also differences. Typically, peace education curricula focus on role plays as vehicles for illustrating the application of communication or problem-solving skills; psychosocial recovery programmes, in contrast, use role plays and other artistic processes as avenues for children to come to terms with deeply disturbing experiences. In addition, psychosocial programmes rarely offer knowledge and skills related to the resolution and transformation of conflict in their environment. They provide a foundation upon which peace education can build, but they do not offer the kinds of skills available through peace education.

Unique among the curricula reviewed here, the Living Values programme has a special version written for educators working with war-affected children. The programme was first used in a Thai refugee camp and is intended to be adapted to any cultural context. Like other psychosocial programmes, the Living Values programme is designed to help children express the pain they have suffered and "develop a voice against what hurts" (Tillman 2001, 5). The programme incorporates many of the themes and activities found in the standard Living Values curriculum. It contains 60 lessons, with a focus on three of the values: peace, love and respect. Some of the material is unique to this programme. In the section on peace, for example, children are encouraged to think about the causes of war and to reflect on death.[3]

As suggested by the special Living Values curriculum for war-affected children, the practices of peace education and the practices of psychosocial recovery can be creatively synthesised. Making peace education more healing oriented would not necessarily require different methods or curricula. Peace education curricula, across the board, already emphasise the importance of creating a supportive social environment that models the values of co-operation and caring. In this respect peace education and psychosocial recovery programmes are very similar. They both appreciate the emotional and spiritual dimensions of the child, rather than treating the child only as a cognitive being. Creating an emotionally nurturing environment promotes learning generally and also helps create congruence between the official and hidden curricula children experience in peace education programmes.

To be more helpful for war-affected children, peace education programmes might provide more time for reflective and expressive activities in a more open-ended fashion than most structured lessons typically allow. Children might be invited to draw images or share stories related to themes of anger, fear, pain, or hope. Older children might also learn about the nature of trauma and its effects, so they can gain understanding of their experience and empathy for others. At a relational level, such programmes might focus more explicitly on supporting the development of positive relationships between children and teachers or care givers who can model constructive behaviours and positive orientations towards the future.

What is the role of gender in peace education?

In the curricula reviewed here, issues of gender are peripheral. Occasionally the instructions for an activity will include discussion questions that raise issues related to gender roles. The story booklet used in the PEP includes several stories about discrimination against girls, especially in regard to issues of male control of girls' education and their marriage choices. Advancing an empowerment agenda, the programme emphasises that tradition is dynamic and that changes are possible. Yet the curriculum is silent on issues of rape. Neither the curriculum for children nor the community workshops address sexual violence as a problem. According to Sommers (2001), rape is the most common violent crime in the refugee camps. Were the peace education programme more attuned to the needs of women, it is doubtful that rape could be excluded from peace education programming.

Indeed, a comprehensive evaluation of the PEP completed in 2001 found that there was insufficient attention to gender (Obura 2002). Even in lessons about inclusion and exclusion girl students were given far less attention than boys in class. In role plays the evaluators noticed that boys and men would rarely play women's roles, and thus they missed the opportunity to see social reality from a different perspective. In the refugee camps "women's work" often involves tedious and frustrating waits for water, a situation that easily sparks tension. An important dimension of peacebuilding in this context would be critical attention to male gender roles and a more equal sharing of household responsibilities.

Generally, issues of gender roles, the oppression of women and domestic violence deserve a more prominent place in peace education materials. In many social settings girls are subject to more structural and cultural violence than boys in terms of work expectations and power relations. To begin dealing with such issues in peace education curricula, more conscious attention could be given to having boys switch places with girls in role plays to increase awareness of inequities in gender roles. Several strong examples of gender-awareness activities come from the *Adventures in Peacemaking* guidebook, which includes, for example, the telling of fairy tales with the male and female roles reversed. It also invites children to discuss what challenges and opportunities they would face if they woke up one morning as the opposite gender. Of course, issues of gender are sensitive, yet a strong peace education programme should not neglect the concerns of women for fear of alienating men. To date, peace education curricula have not lived up to this challenge.

At another level the curricula reviewed here do not seem to have considered the curricular or pedagogical implications of gender differences in peace education's central themes. Given differences in socialisation and the construction of male/female identities within particular contexts, is it conceivable that peace education might look different for boys and girls? After all, violence tends to be a gendered phenomenon. If boys are socialised to prefer physical violence to meet their objectives and girls learn to rely on verbal violence or emotional manipulation, should they undergo different kinds of peace education to address those dominant modes of aggression? Furthermore, how are collaboration and co-operation between males and females understood in societies with strong cultural norms about gender segregation? Many challenging and complex questions arise once gender considerations are introduced, suggesting the need for feminist perspectives in the dialogue about the construction of peace education programmes.

What is the impact and scope of peace education?

From a global perspective, it is not clear how strong the impact of peace education has been. There is a general lack of evaluative insight into the quality and impact of peace education programmes. Out of 1,000 publications between 1981 and 2000 that touched on peace education, Nevo and Brem (2002) found that only 100 included an examination of effectiveness and only 79 provided some judgement about programme effectiveness. Of those, 51 were deemed effective, 18 partially effective, and 10 not effective. Although this finding is encouraging, the authors note that good programmes are the ones likely to be evaluated, while disappointing programmes may never be evaluated.

Nevertheless, there is strong evidence that some programmes have been successful. In a small study of several primary schools in an urban U.S. setting, Harris and Callendar (1995) found that the schools which used peace education curricula had students who were "more tolerant, compassionate, caring, cooperative, expressive of feelings, and caring than students in similar control classes" (1995, 142). Teachers reported similar observations in a preliminary review of the Creative Problem Solving programme in Montenegro (Slobig 2001).

Such hopeful findings are underscored by a more rigorous and extensive research agenda, undertaken over a 12 year period, on the Teaching Students to Be Peacemakers programme. In this programme all students in a school are trained in conflict-resolution and mediation skills, with the training supported by efforts to create cooperative classroom environments. In their review of seventeen studies conducted between 1988 and 2000, Johnson and Johnson (2000) found that students in their programme applied the conflict-resolution procedures they had learned in playground, neighbourhood and family settings. Also, the researchers found that, in situations in which either a win/lose or problem-solving strategy could be used, all untrained students used the win/lose strategy, while students trained in conflict resolution used the problem-solving, mutually beneficial approach.

In most peace education programmes, the child is positioned as the target audience, and success is understood in terms of changes in the individual's attitudes and behaviours. Helping children handle conflict in peaceful ways can be a great benefit to the children and to the larger society as the children mature. Successful peace education programmes can slowly build a cadre of individuals skilled in constructive conflict management and oriented towards non-violence.

But, as Sommers (2001) points out in his review of the PEP, children are not necessarily the most important audience for learning new peace-oriented skills. In the Kenyan refugees camps where the programme began, some of the most aggressive inhabitants are out-of-school youth – youth who tend not to participate in the programme. Sommers observes that people who attend the peace education programmes are, by and large, already peaceful. When only peaceful people participate in peace education, the degree to which even the best programme can actually ameliorate destructive conflict occurring in a community is questionable.

Even if peace education attracts people already oriented towards peace, it seems worth the effort. As suggested above, good programmes can make real differences in the tools young people have available to work with conflict. Moreover, to the extent that it reaches deeply into a community – including youth and adults, schools and non-formal spaces – peace education can strengthen participants' commitments to non-violent conflict resolution and give them practice in solving familiar problems in new ways. And, as M. Sinclair emphasised in a conversation with me, this is precisely the kind of learning that inoculates the community against violence.

In some peace education programmes, school-based components are complemented by a community-based programme. This approach respects the fact that school is only one social setting in which children learn concepts and values. For peace education to have a stronger impact, it must take into consideration the ecology of children's learning (Miller and Affolter 2002). Peace education, in this sense, is a larger project of building new skills of conflict resolution, new capacities to analyse the roots of local conflicts and unjust social structures, new attitudes and imaginative resources about the possibilities of non-violent futures among children and families, schools and mosques and churches, literacy centres and community workshops. Peace is a project that ultimately includes entire social networks and communities. For children to learn peace, they must experience and witness new ways of handling conflict in direct interaction with their parents, their peers, their teachers and their neighbours. This point echoes the recommendation advanced by Krech (see Chapter 2 herein), that World Vision (WV) develop a community-based approach to peace education that encompasses larger social environments and issues of conflict in children's lives. Peace education, if confined to children in institutional settings, is likely to have limited impact. School-based peace education programmes can help children understand themselves as partners in this larger effort. "A society that places peace education on its agenda has to spread its messages through other social institutions and channels of communication in order to show the pupils that they are part of a general effort to change society" (Bar-Tal 2002, 31). In the absence of such an effort, students may rightly conclude that peace education in school is disconnected from larger social priorities or even hypocritical.[4]

After all, it is quite difficult for individual students to become peaceful when surrounded by peers and a culture that valorises aggression. McCauley (2002) points to the problem of "re-entry" – people who have been changed by their experiences in an isolated programme return to an unchanged social context that demands that they behave in culturally familiar ways. This problem suggests the importance of a holistic, ecological approach that includes parents, teachers and community members in peace education, rather than treating individual children as the sole unit of change.

Individual change must be supported by change in the social context – institutions, policies and cultural narratives. For an individual to demonstrate inclusive, peace-oriented behaviour within an unchanged, exclusionary social context would require heroism beyond the reach of most people. McCauley points out that a challenge for peace education is to work in an action-oriented mode on multiple levels in order to "succeed with those of us who do not aspire to heroism" (2002, 257).

In any case, there is great value in thinking about peace education at the level of the school itself. A peace education programme with a school-wide scope might include the kind of training offered in typical peace education programmes but would also include concern for the whole environment of the school as a site of peacebuilding. From this perspective peace education involves bringing peace into the educational process itself (Harris 1988). To create more peaceful schools, educators might include the use of non-violent, conflict-reduction strategies in disciplinary procedures, support for peer mediation teams and analysis of the valorisation of violence in history texts.[5] There are powerful ways in which schools can contribute to peacebuilding even without instituting an overt peace education programme. Lessons in any subject which promote moral sensitivity and critical thinking also contribute. In general, efforts to create classrooms and learning environments that "draw out children's natural instincts toward peace" (Harris 1988, 123) can do much to promote the agenda of peace education, even in the absence of any peace education programming.

Beyond the school itself, peacebuilding involves complex issues of educational policy. Throughout the world education has served as a tool for the oppression of certain groups. Whether through limited access to education, assimilationist language policies or culturally demeaning learning materials, governments have used education as a powerful tool of suppressing the aspirations, talents and dignity of children from rival groups (Bush and Saltarelli 2000). Such oppressive policies may worsen the conditions that lead to violence, or they may directly fuel violent confrontation.

Helping children act non-violently is a vital step towards a larger agenda of peacebuilding. Yet that agenda should also include concern for how the school, and ultimately the educational system itself, can contribute to the realisation of a culture of peace. In this sense the agenda of peace education embraces concerns of allied movements for anti-racist education, environmental education, human rights education, and integrative or holistic education. All of these movements offer powerful critiques of existing structures and practices while providing creative alternatives that can reorient education towards the kind of goals espoused in WV's transformational development framework.

CLOSING THOUGHTS ON PEACE EDUCATION AND ITS FUTURE MANIFESTATIONS

Peace education can now be found throughout the world. As discussed in the preceding chapter, there is a consensus that topics such as co-operation and conflict resolution, appreciation of self and others and emotional management should be included in effective peace education curricula. As curriculum frameworks and creative activities are shared by educators globally, good practices can flourish. In many settings the very existence of a peace education programme, regardless of its quality, may be a triumph of educational courage in the face of scepticism and conservatism. In harsh circumstances any peace education initiative can be a symbol of hope.

Educators who aspire to peacebuilding face many constraints. In places with the greatest need for new modes of communication, conflict resolution, and problem solving, it may be quite difficult to introduce peace education. The political sensitivities around peace education, especially in fragile communities, may be enormous. For some groups, peace education may be too threatening to positions of power. For others, peace education may seem frivolous or simply too different from the work educators are accustomed to doing.

Clearly, effective peace education will not happen if students are simply copying words like *collaboration* and *tolerance* into their notebooks from the chalkboard. Peace education works best with a creative, activity-oriented pedagogy, a way of working foreign to the experience of most teachers throughout the world. Building capacity for such pedagogy requires sustained support for teachers and ongoing conversations with educational officials to ensure that the goals and processes of peace education are understood.

Designing and implementing school-based peace education programmes is no small task. The work is fraught with challenges and is likely to meet criticism from many sides. At this moment in history there is a certain audacity and faith that is necessary among those who believe that we can learn to live together differently.

Besides audacity, another virtue for peace educators is humility. Education cannot create and sustain peace on its own; that is a challenge to which every sector of society must contribute in some way. Educators should not expect their work to make all the difference, and even bold programmes may have limited impact in the short term. Much of what educational efforts achieve is at a subtle, long-term level. And much of what educators dream about is limited by the politics of the context.

Without forgetting the real constraints to the creation of new peace education programmes in the world, it is important to consider what the size and shape of peace education should be for our time. Given the opportunity to re-think peace education, we can ask – with an appropriate measure of humility and audacity – what is the kind of peace education we would want to create together? Is the formation of peaceful individuals the task at hand? If so, what activities and what kind of learning environments – in and beyond the school – do children need in order to turn towards peace? Is peace education about creating peace within the very structures and processes of education? If so, how can peace education engage teachers and ministry officials in the transformation of their work? Is the formation of peaceful families or peaceful communities the task at hand? If so, how can peace education attract the energy and aspirations of diverse groups? Furthermore, whose *peace* is being waged here? What of the larger vision of creating a just and non-violent world for children? If that is the purpose of peace education, then how does peace education ally itself with other social movements that promise the possibility of social justice and non-violent solutions to conflicts?

Keeping these questions in mind, I would like to close this chapter with an affirmation of the enduring positive potential of peace education in light of WV's commitment to transformational development. In its many manifestations peace education has much to contribute to the advancement of a transformative development agenda. At one level, peace education cultivates the inner resources of the child, building an enduring sense of self-worth and self-understanding. Peace education can also cultivate a vision for peace and enrich each child's experience of inner peace. In addition, peace education provides tools for students to create and sustain harmonious relationships with others. At a social level, peace education is a key to enabling children to become agents of transformation in their families and communities, especially if school-based programmes can be supported by community-based programmes for interested parents and community members. Instead of being victims of conflict, children can learn skills of constructive engagement with conflict, skills that will enable them to solve problems in new ways and help heal wounded relationships. In the end peace education can make a profound contribution to children's chance to live with dignity, justice and hope, thus building the kingdom of God.

NOTES

[1] The "school in a box" is a kit of educational supplies used to restart recreational activities and basic educational activities following devastating conflicts in which there has been widespread destruction of schools or teachers.

[2] The UNHCR Peace Education Program (PEP) does feature a rich collection of local proverbs, poetry and stories that can ground lessons in local realities. In this way it offers another model of how peace education can be contextually grounded. It should be noted, though, that the UNHCR materials make little explicit reference to the fact that the programme takes place within a refugee camp – a site of highly structured and power-laden relationships, especially between refugees and agency staff. The curriculum focuses on relationships among the refugees or on issues found in life outside the camp; it rarely overtly addresses the behaviour of agency staff or government officials as a source of violence, whether direct or structural.

[3] Curiously, no other peace education programme (not even the regular Living Values curriculum) includes any discussion of death. Presumably, death is a reality that most children will experience, whether in relation to a member of their extended family, someone in the neighbourhood or a favourite animal. Death may generate extreme emotions among survivors. Although understanding emotions is a standard element of peace education curricula, emotions related to death are never addressed.

[4] Any peace education taking place in the United States at the moment would inevitably run against the grain of government action against Iraq. A student might wonder if messages about the importance of non-violent conflict resolution are only "for kids," when what adults *really* believe in is war.

[5] Firer argues that the nationalist mythos that often valorises war should be replaced with the mythos of a peace culture: "That means introducing new heroes into historiography, literature, the mass media, and other reflectors of culture" (2002, 57). The challenge is producing new narratives in school curricula and popular media that are as exciting as war narratives, involving, for example, people who rescue others or people who resist totalitarian forces in times of government-sanctioned violence.

REFERENCES

Bar-Tal, D. 2002. "The Elusive Nature of Peace Education." In Salomon and Nevo 2002, 27–36.

Bush, K. D., and D. Saltarelli. 2000. "The Two Faces of Education in Ethnic Conflict: Towards a Peacebuilding Education for Children." Florence: UNICEF, Innocenti Research Centre.

Firer, R. 2002. "The Gordian Knot between Peace Education and War Education." In Salomon and Nevo 2002, 55–62.

Harris, I. 1988. *Peace Education*. Jefferson, NC: McFarland.

Harris, I., and A. Callendar. 1995. "Comparative Study of Peace Education Approaches and Their Effectiveness." *NAMTA Journal* 20, no. 2.

Hutchinson, F. P. 1996. *Educating beyond Violent Futures*. London: Routledge.

Johnson, D. W., and R. T. Johnson. 2000. "Teaching Students to Be Peacemakers: Results of Twelve Years of Research." Available online.

McCauley, C. 2002. "Head-first versus Feet-first in Peace Education." In Salomon and Nevo 2002, 247–58.

Miller, V., and F. Affolter, eds. 2002. *Helping Children Outgrow War*. Washington, DC: Africa Bureau, United States Agency for International Development.

Nevo, B., and I. Brem. 2002. "Peace Education Programs and the Evaluation of Their Effectiveness." In Salomon and Nevo 2002, 271–81.

Obura, A. P. 2002. UNHCR Peace Education Programme: Evaluation. Unpublished.

Raviv, A., L. Oppenheimer, and D. Bar-Tal. 1999. "Introduction." In *How Children Understand War and Peace: A Call for International Peace Education,* ed. A. Raviv, L. Oppenheimer, and D. Bar-Tal, 1–26. San Francisco: Jossey Bass.

Salomon, G. 2002. "The Nature of Peace Education: Not All Programs Are Created Equal." In Salomon and Nevo 2002, 3–14.

Salomon G., and B. Nevo, eds.. 2002. *Peace Education: The Concept, Principles, and Practices around the World*. Mahwah, NJ: Erlbaum.

Shapiro, S. 2002. "Toward a Critical Pedagogy of Peace Education." In Salomon and Nevo 2002, 63–72.

Slobig, J. H. 2001. "Peace Education in Montenegro." In *Children and Peacebuilding: Experiences and Perspectives,* ed. H. Elliott, 9-13. World Vision Discussion Papers. Melbourne, Australia: World Vision Australia.

Sommers, M. 2001. "Peace Education and Refugee Youth." In *Learning for a Future: Refugee Education in Developing Countries*, ed. J. Crisp, C. Talbot, and D. Cipollone, 163–216. Geneva: UNHCR.

Staub, E. 1989. *The Roots of Evil: The Origins of Genocide and Other Group Violence*. Cambridge: Cambridge Univ. Press.

———. 2002. "From Healing Past Wounds to the Development of Inclusive Caring: Contents and Processes of Peace Education." In Salomon and Nevo 2002, 73–88.

Tillman, D. 2001. *Living Values Activities for Refugees and Children-Affected-by-War, Ages 8–14*. Deerfield Beach, FL: Health Communications.

5

Teaching for peace

Helping people learn to live peacefully

James Olesen and Mavis Olesen

Education has the potential to provide people with alternatives. Without education, people repeat counterproductive behaviour because they lack knowledge of alternative ways of behaving. Education offers the possibility of change. The purpose of this chapter is to consider how peace can be taught so that behaviour changes. Five issues are explored:

- the goals and purposes of peace education
- the relationship between peace education and the moral, intellectual and physical development of young people
- the development of support among parents, community leaders, teachers and students for peace education programmes
- a rationale for defining a set of concepts, values and skills to be included in a peace education strategy
- effective methodologies for teaching peace education

THE CENTRAL GOAL OF PEACE EDUCATION

A significant goal of peace education in particular and education in general is to assist young people in learning to live peacefully. Societies offer a variety of values; some are peaceful, others are not. To live peacefully people must be able to choose those values that contribute to peace. Therefore, it is incumbent upon learning environments to help people learn to be independent thinkers with the capacity to make autonomous moral choices.[1] In 20 years the 10-year-old children sitting in a classroom will be 30-year-old adults beginning to be involved in the decisions of their society. What kind of decisions will they make? Autonomous moral choosers are able to argue that peaceful choices be made by society. Therefore, before young people can be effective leaders in the struggle for peace, they have to learn to be autonomous moral choosers.

Independent thinkers are the vanguard of social change. Autonomous moral choosers are independent thinkers whose thinking and behaviour are constrained by moral principles. For example, an autonomous moral chooser might decide any action or decision taken must do no harm to others. At the same time, such a thinker might seriously question existing social policies of society because they *do* harm people. Such thinkers need the courage and self-confidence to proclaim clearly and forcefully their vision of the future. Independent thinking is the ability to evaluate critically existing social policies and creatively imagine constructive alternatives. It is such thinkers who show a new and better way.

All change is risky and subject to heavy criticism by the forces resisting change. Independent thinkers also need to be courageous and firm in the face of opposition to their vision of peace.

Violent responses often seem simple, clear and quick. Peaceful responses seem complicated, fuzzy and time consuming. Because of this reality, education in general and peace education in particular have to help students understand and desire to practise the morality and ethics of peace. Students must realise that moral choices have consequences. They need to understand that the values each person adopts will play a role, however small, in creating a society.

NURTURING CHILDREN

Any subject being taught in a learning environment has the potential to incorporate an aspect of peace education. Therefore, teaching any standard academic subject can be a vehicle for teaching peaceful living. How subjects such as mathematics are taught says much to students about the relationship between those who have power and those who do not. Mathematics can be taught in ways that clarify or mystify reality. Meaningful teaching is much more likely to make students feel included and respected in the learning process. Mystification, on the other hand, demands that students conform to whatever way someone might decide to teach mathematics.[2] Such teaching contributes to fear, to a sense of incompetence and ultimately to powerlessness. When a teaching style forces students down the mystification road, they learn to hold themselves in disrespect.[3]

What role does respect and disrespect, inclusion and rejection, acceptance and scorn, and other attributes play in individual decisions about whether to resort to peace or violence? Children are born with a wide-ranging potential to be peaceful, violent or some mixture of both. The elements determining the personal behaviour of each individual is a complex mixture of personality traits (some of which may be inborn), societal treatment and individual choice.

THE BEST APPROACH TO PEACE EDUCATION

In societies where violence of various kinds is the norm, it seems reasonable to assume that existing indoctrination processes are biased toward violence. In these situations conceptual and moral alternatives to violence are needed to provide solutions to social problems. Since it is impossible to teach students a precise course of action to be followed in the future, it is necessary to equip students with those concepts, values and skills which make it possible for them to invent peaceful ways of living independently.

If unfamiliar (peaceful) concepts, values and skills are to become part of the students' thinking and reasoning processes, students have to be allowed to construct them in their minds. A personal reconstruction of reality is a critical piece in learning to live peacefully. Learning environments based on a "construction of learning" philosophy are more likely to provide opportunities for students to construct the concepts, values and skills that will allow them to take different approaches to living together and to solving conflict.

Learning to be an independent thinker is a delicate and easily discouraged process. It is not something achieved without specific teaching and encouragement. Instruction which forces students to learn (memorise) large amounts of information is not a useful approach to the creation of independent thinkers. Rote learning is not a route to independent thinking. It becomes too easy to memorise information rather than to think about it and to learn from it. This is particularly true when evaluation stresses memorisation to the exclusion of thinking.

Encouragement needs to come in the form of permission and reward for independent thinking. Lessons always need to be structured in ways which provide opportunities for students to be creative. The following pages and the examples of teaching methods in the appendices to this book attempt to provide some guidance in creating learning environments which stimulate independent thinking and learning.

The goals of the World Vision International peace education initiative are more likely to be achieved by a "construction of knowledge" (we will discuss this in some detail later) approach to education than through the standard forms of education practised in most societies.

VARYING PERSPECTIVES ON EDUCATION

There has been much controversy about the best approach to educating children. Proponents of traditional, modern and post-modern philosophies of learning are in conflict about the definition of learning (what children should learn), the best approach to teaching students (how children should learn) and evaluation (how we know what has been learned).

At this point we need to take a short digression in order to define traditional, modern and post-modern philosophies of education and examine how they work in practice. Education in early societies (which tended to be rural, hunting, farming, non-bureaucratic and egalitarian) was informal. Knowledge was transmitted through devices such as storytelling and modelling, ere whereby youngsters learned by copying adults. This form of education still exists in some parts of the world. In this chapter this is what we mean by the term *traditional*.

In most of the world *modern* education has been formalised into systematic levels (grades or standards) of education based on organised curricula and prescriptive teaching methods. Knowledge has been defined and compartmentalised into subjects. Subjects have been taught to students as organised, logical sequences of ideas to be memorised. Student success depends upon being able to convince examiners they know (remember) the information they have studied. This form of education was transferred by the colonial powers to those parts of the world they were colonising. Many colonised areas replaced their traditional systems with industrial (colonial) models of education.

Under modern systems of education the primary purpose of learning is to acquire quantities of information. Learning tends to involve the passive reception of information, most often through listening to a teacher. The standard evaluation for this form of learning is to test students' memories of what they have learned. If they can remember and express a set of information, it is assumed they can understand and apply the information. Many educational thinkers have become critical of this approach to learning.

We experienced a colonial model of education in a refugee camp where we were doing teacher training. Teachers and parents in the camp had uncritically accepted the British colonial model of education. They believed it to be superior to their traditional system and worked to maintain the British colonial model with few changes throughout the twentieth century.

Over the years it developed into a system of rote learning aimed at producing elite students. Not surprisingly, there were significant consequences resulting from this approach to education. The dropout rate was 97 per cent. For every 100 students who began their education in primary school, only 3 would graduate from tenth standard, the final year of schooling. Functional illiteracy among the majority of people remained unacceptably high.

The educational leaders with whom the authors worked intuitively understood the need for developing higher-order thought processes. They were motivated toward educational reform because they recognised their leadership had been ill prepared to deal with the complex politics of inter-ethnic strife that erupted after the British gave up control of their homeland. Many of the teachers admitted that they, as a people, had difficulty stating their case in public meetings, did not know how to resolve conflicts peacefully and generally had been unable to work effectively for peace. Their only alternative had been to resort to civil war. After 50 years of inconclusive civil war, they were searching for a better way of solving their problems. They believed a reformed educational system could help by creating more effective leaders.

THE PERSONAL CONSTRUCTION OF KNOWLEDGE

One perspective of *post-modern* education can be described as constructivism. In this view learners learn by "constructing" knowledge within their minds. Students have to re-create ideas actively before they can understand and remember them. Learning is more likely to be active when the student thinks about the subject being learned. Students are more likely to think when they have a reason for thinking.

Constructivist teaching responds by providing reasons for thinking; usually with a problem, situation, event, issue and so forth. The context of the problem should be concrete, so it will be real and meaningful to the student in some way.[4] Problems are most effective when they are described within the cultural context of the students. If they are not, students may not understand or see a purpose for what is being learned.

Many of the basic concepts and values inherent in peace education will seem unfamiliar to those who grow up in violent, often authoritarian societies. For example, the issue of power sharing is critical. In authoritarian systems power is jealously guarded. The belief is that power can never be shared because once it is gone, it is gone forever. Thus democratic systems of power sharing and power transfer from one group (political party) to another are strange and threatening.

This was certainly the case with the teachers in the refugee camp with whom we worked. The notion of power sharing, particularly in the classroom, was not easily understood or accepted. At the beginning stages of their educational-reform process, democracy and all of its related concepts were an intriguing mystery for the teachers in the refugee camp. They constantly asked questions about democracy. They had an insatiable curiosity about its "nuts and bolts." They spent a lot of time trying to understand how a democratic system might work in practice.

In their minds they were attempting to reconcile the authoritarian system with which they were familiar with an unfamiliar democratic system. Concepts like constituencies, representational democracy or federalism held very little meaning for them. They liked what they heard, but they had very little idea about how such systems operate. As a result, we spent many hours talking about different scenarios that might arise in a democratic society and how a democratic political system might respond to those scenarios.

Students react in similar fashion. This is why play is so important in the learning processes of children. Whenever children encounter a new situation, they want to play with it. In this sense play is the modelling, application, testing and evaluation processes described above. There is a story about a 2-year-old child who was making a mess while she happily dunked pieces of bread into her glass of milk. She was furious when her mother intervened. The mother saw a mess. The child saw a fascinating activity which was giving her new knowledge about how the world worked. The process of play continues into youth and adulthood. Adults give this play names like think tank, work, experimentation, recreation, empiricism, scientific method, reflection and so forth.

The teachers in the refugee camp were involved in an ad hoc think tank about power sharing and democracy. For those teachers, the purpose was to broaden and deepen their concepts of democracy. To a large extent the teachers were able to do that. For us, as teacher trainers, the objective was to introduce them to another style of teaching. These teachers had grown up in an authoritarian, rote-learning school system. This was all they knew about teaching. We wanted them to see that learning could be made problematic (What alternative ways are available to govern society?) and that through discussion and the sharing of ideas about problems much learning could be accomplished. To some extent we were able to illustrate constructivist learning to them. We say "to some extent" because when we suggested that classrooms could be made democratic, they were shocked and doubtful about such a "heretical" point of view. Authoritarianism dies hard.

The standard evaluation for the constructivist form of learning is to determine whether the student can perform the behaviour or operation being learned. The student has not mastered the learning objectives unless he or she can independently apply the ideas being learned to some novel situation. Understanding whether something has been learned (constructed) is determined by the behaviour of the learner. Can the student do something he or she could not do before? If so, something has been learned.

This is a demanding standard. Educational systems based on rote learning simply assume that the memorisation of information indicates the ability to perform a related behaviour. This is a very dubious assumption. A simple example such as learning to ride a bicycle illustrates this. Suppose someone is given a manual on bike riding, memorises it, receives 100 per cent in a test and attempts to ride a bike for the first time. It is not difficult to predict what will happen. It is not enough to tell people; they must be given direct practise in performing whatever behaviours are being taught.

Peace education involves understanding new ideas as well as developing the skills of independent thinking and moral thought processes. Teachers and students will not learn these objectives unless they are provided with opportunities to practise them as part of a learning process. In order to move away from a rote-learning teaching style, the teachers in the refugee camp required many hours of constructivist learning in which they developed strategies and practised using them in the classroom. There is no shortcut to this process.

ASSUMPTIONS ABOUT LEARNERS

The child is the parent of the adult. Children construct meaning from their life experiences. That personal construct of meaning becomes the "parent" of the future adult. The process of selecting and constructing meaning is the process of learning. Two major factors influence the child's choices: First, every child is born with a unique combination of genetic characteristics which influence future choices. Second, children are also influenced by their environment because it is the source of their experiences. But different children may select different things from similar environmental experiences and grow into different people. Within the framework of genetics and environment the child makes choices about what he or she will learn. A child's development is a complex interplay of nature and nurture.

The environment governs the choices available to the child. If children are forced to live in violent societies, if they are pressed into the army or if they are abandoned to the streets to be exploited, they will learn from those experiences.

Those experiences will in some way influence future adult behaviour. So long as children are brutalised, societies maintain the potential to be violent. Despite the complex resilience factors children may possess, the effects of mistreatment can be devastating.

Still, even within these extreme circumstances children can make choices. It is true their choices may be limited, but the desire for constructive human relationships based on dignity may survive. Children are born with dignity and aspire to grow into loving human beings. They may make mistakes along the way, but redemption is always possible.

The important question to consider is how should children be nurtured? Abusive behaviour is often justified as good discipline because parents mistake control for discipline. Many learning environments (schools) use violent practices (verbal and physical) to control rather than to discipline children. Abuse is problematic for peace education because children copy the models of social behaviour they find around them. It is not surprising, therefore, to see violence in the play of children. Because discipline and control are confused, children are nurtured to accept aggression as a way of life. When they become adults, they tend to use the control they received as a model for controlling rather than disciplining their children. There are other ways of nurturing children.

ASSUMPTIONS ABOUT EFFECTIVE PEACE EDUCATION

Positive nurturance

A peace education programme needs to break the cycle of abuse. Peace education has to help children, parents, leaders of learning environments, communities and others understand there are alternative methods of nurturing children. It is important to consider the elements of nurturing when thinking about the goals of a peace education strategy.[5] Nurturing means, at a minimum, caring for the child's physical needs (food, water, shelter, etc.);[6] it means socialising the child into a culture; it means giving the child an identity; and, above all, it means validating the child by giving him or her dignity. Peace education needs to advocate constructive and positive nurturance of young people.

Constructive socialisation

Parents and societies are highly concerned that children be adequately socialised. Their goal is to see their children constructively integrated into society. How this is done depends upon the way children are viewed and the purposes of the social integration of children. Children are often pictured as being selfish, lazy and disobedient. Childlike behaviour can be viewed negatively rather than viewing it as the child's way of learning. The purpose for integration may vary from self-centred reasons (viewing the children as future pension plans for their elders) to altruistic reasons (happy, developing children). Whatever the rationale for integration, it will affect the approach to integration. Peace educators need to consider their rationale so that social integration processes lead to positive and constructive socialisation of the child.

The attitude of the teachers in the refugee camp to the socialisation of students changed somewhat after they began to see another purpose for the integration of children into society. Under their authoritarian model they saw socialisation as a process for creating obedience and acceptance of one's station in life. From this perspective independence was seen as a threat to the social (school) order to be immediately struck down before it could spread. The role of teachers was to model an authoritarian figure who would not accept any questioning of authority.

When teachers accepted the notion that a better future involved power sharing in a democracy based on human rights, they began to understand the need to develop independent thinkers and autonomous moral choosers. They began to realise that conflict can be resolved through a process of constructive negotiation. From this realisation it was a short step to understanding they had to model the kind of behaviour they wanted the students to learn. If students were to have the intellectual tools necessary to allow them to integrate into a democratic society, then those skills had to be learned in the classroom. Discipline had to move from arbitrary teacher behaviour to a reasoned response to classroom relationships before any of this could happen.

Creating disciples

Discipline is an important part of the socialisation process. All too often discipline is narrowly interpreted as punishment. Discipline is mistakenly equated with social control and obedience. A broader approach to the word *discipline* is to consider its relationship to the concept of discipleship. A disciple is one who freely follows another because of feelings of respect and honour the follower holds for the leader. In healthy discipleship those feelings of respect and honour need to be mutual. A follower may go through difficult times with the leader. The path set by the leader may be difficult, and there may be disappointments and conflict. Yet, despite the troubles, the disciple and the leader maintain loyalty and respect for each other. In the process the disciple is moulded into something greater than he or she was at the beginning of the relationship. Successful peace education involves making disciples of its students.

Inherent dignity of the child

There is a high degree of congruence between the goals of peace education and good general education. Both education and peace education have to be about the dignity and well-being of the individual. It has been tempting for educational decision-makers to overlook the student in the educational equation. We have examined examples of that above. This is a critical issue for education in general and peace education in particular.

Should children conform to educational practices, or should educational practices conform to children? The assumption has been that children should conform. But respect for the inherent dignity of the child would suggest that the institution of education should conform to the needs of the child. A major tenet of democracy is that the individual is always an end and never a means. The tenet holds in democratic education as well. The child is always an end, never a means. Therefore, education is for the good of the child and not for some other goal of society. So long as goals other than the well-being of children hold primacy, children will be shortchanged by their education. The supreme irony of shortchanging children is that society will ultimately be shortchanged as well.

Discovering potential

Education should help students find and express their potential. Students need help with this because they may not know they have unexpressed potential. Often they are surprised and disbelieving at what they discover. Many students believe they are inferior to others; they need someone to validate their humanity. Peace education should work to place children in situations where they can discover the dignity of their potential.

Developing personal competence

Good education introduces students to the physical, social and cultural realities of their lives in ways that convince them they are competent and therefore can understand and cope with those realities. When students experience success, they see a true purpose for learning. Then they have a reason to become disciples of learning. Students who have learned to respect themselves and their capabilities are best equipped to lead the struggle for peace, wherever that might be. Peace education should work to develop personal competence.

CHILD DEVELOPMENT IS CRITICAL

Earlier we discussed discipline and the dignity of the child and emphasised their critical importance in encouraging children to adopt the basic principles of peaceful living. Another important factor in honouring the dignity of children is recognising and responding to their capacity to learn. The reality is that the child's intellectual capacity, like the child's physical capacity, is a slow, developmental process unfolding over many years. Children have interior timetables controlling their ability to respond to external stimuli. That timetable cannot be hastened or retarded without doing damage to the child. The timetable may vary somewhat from child to child, but in broad terms the timetable applies to all children. Intellectual activity which demands too much or too little from children is treating them in an undignified way. Such treatment is disrespect of the potential of children.

Patterns of growth influence human development throughout life (Brown 1991). Of course, the cultural and social contexts, and special intellectual, social-emotional and physical needs of each person influence development at some level. However, at a deep, basic, natural level human development patterns are universal across all cultures (Deloache and Gottlieb 2000).

This universality of child development or invariates of child development have been hotly debated by such notables as Vygotsky (1929) and Piaget (Wadsworth 1971). At present, as researchers strip away cultural and social contexts, no Eastern or Western basic pattern is found. Rather, general patterns of child development remain universal (Bowman 1994; World Bank 1996; Tobin, Wu and Davidson 1989; Kagan and Garcia 1994; Eve 1999; Bhavnagri 2001; Bredekamp 1997; Katz 1999; Eming-Young 2001).

Understanding and honouring the pattern of child development is important because it protects children from stereotypical, romantic, paternalistic or racist comparisons. It also protects children from nationalistic, ethnic, familial or private exploitative agendas that are intent upon using children beyond their capacity (World Bank 1996). Child development patterns provide benchmarks upon which the richness of culturally influencing concepts, skills and values can be built. From such benchmarks children can be regarded with respect in and of themselves, not as puppets to be manipulated for our pleasure.

CHILD DEVELOPMENT
PATTERNS

The learning potential of children is released slowly and in a reasonably or-
derly pattern. Sometimes the temptation is to rush this process. People are
tempted to believe that knowledge, skills and values can be learned faster if
teachers and children work harder. However, child development controls the
rate at which children can successfully learn information.[7] Hard work is useful,
but only when it coincides with the child's internal developmental timetable.
Education is one of those areas in life where the long way around the mountain
may turn out to be the shorter way. Children learn more when their developmental needs are recognised. A child whose needs have been respected is much
more likely to become a disciple of learning.

Returning again to the colonial educational system found in the refugee camp,
the major problem with that system was that it did not conform to the principles of child development. Children were expected to sit long hours with
little physical activity. The classroom environment could be quite punitive. The
intellectual expectations of the children bore no relationship to their intellectual capacity. Preschool children were expected to know and recite letters and
numbers long before those symbols could have any meaning for them. Children of 11 and 12 were expected to know and perform complex algebraic equa-
tions. Children at ages 13 and 14 were expected to understand and apply trigo-
nometric concepts. Children who failed mathematics in a particular grade were
expected to repeat the entire grade. The result was that children repeatedly
failed to pass a grade, leaving them in classrooms where they were significantly older than their classmates. The stress drove many children from the
schools, resulting in a very high dropout rate.

Children who are driven from schools are beyond the reach of the school
system to provide them with any kind of education, let alone peace education.
Of course, young people who do not attend school continue to learn. The question becomes what they learn. Young males who dropped out of school were
deemed to be good candidates for military training and a life fighting in the
ongoing civil war. It was interesting to observe that those few young people
who did graduate from the school system were much less likely to become
members of the army. They had other alternatives.

The principles of child development are not tangential to peace education.
They are critical issues that must be addressed if children are to have any opportunity of receiving some peace education.

Physical growth

The most obvious change in children is their physical growth. Adequate nutrition is absolutely critical. The brain is an organ like other organs. It must have balanced nutrition if it is to develop to its potential. Malnutrition, some diseases, drug and alcohol substance abuse during the prenatal and postnatal life of the child stunt mental, emotional, and social activity as well as physical activity.

As we learn more about stress, we realise that it has serious physical implications, particularly for children. The physical reality of learning in a stressful or fearful situation is brain cell damage as stress hormones flood the brain (Goleman 1995). Put the child in this situation often enough, and mental activity is affected. To avoid damage, learning must be pleasant and satisfying. It must contain sufficient novelty to attract a child's attention and focus, but it must not be so difficult that it creates stress. Children are not developmentally ready to endure large amounts of stress.

Children must also have physical activity to grow and learn. Large and small muscles grow more slowly without physical activity. Children develop from their heads downward and from the centre of their bodies outward. That is why children can control their eyes long before they can control their hands. It is also why they can draw before they can learn steps in a dance. There is a close relationship between physical activity and mental activity. Children first learn through their senses, for example, by physically touching things. Manipulation and experimentation all require some degree of physical activity.

Therefore, long hours of quietly sitting in classrooms are counterproductive to both mental and physical development. Learning which concentrates solely on physically passive intellectual activity misses many useful teaching opportunities. It is only when children have an opportunity to work actively with something that they begin to ask questions about what they are doing and begin to think for themselves. The learning process and curriculum design need to understand physical activity, make allowances for it and take advantage of it.

Cognitive growth

It is important to note here that many of the ideas (concepts) of peace education are highly abstract. Human rights, justice, equity, democracy, power, power sharing, negotiation, conflict resolution – these are concepts to be developed at the concrete level and then slowly expanded into the abstract as children become ready. A successful peace education strategy needs to consider carefully this reality and develop teaching materials to help teachers move their students along a continuum from the concrete to the abstract.

Learners of new information, particularly if it is complex and abstract learn more and faster when they can begin with the concrete. This applies to adults as well as children. Many of the ideas (concepts) related to peace education are abstract and may be unfamiliar to students of all ages. A peace education strategy will be more successful when abstract ideas are introduced to students as meaningful, concrete examples culled from the students' cultures. After older students have achieved a conceptual understanding of the ideas, they are able to think about these ideas abstractly.

Students learn in different ways. A peace education curriculum needs to allow students to use their strengths and their weaknesses to contribute to one another's learning. In this way learning environments can become communities in which students share and teach each other.

Emotional growth

One of the critical determinants of healthy emotional growth is a child's ability to form close personal ties (affectional ties) with a care giver in the first two years of life. Erik Erikson describes these learnings as trust versus mistrust and autonomy versus shame and doubt.[8] Children learn they can trust others to care for them. They also learn that when they are distressed by their own behaviour or the behaviour of others, they can resolve these feelings within a relationship. In this way children learn to accept authority, and they learn that relationships are essential.

To be successful, peace education has to develop within students an emotional commitment to its principles. Without that, the teachings of peace education will be ignored and forgotten. Learning to trust within institutions such as schools depends upon how children are treated. If they live in an arbitrary and punitive school system, the likelihood of them becoming trusting is very much lessened. They will also develop negative reactions to authority. Some become overly obedient in an attempt to conciliate arbitrary authority. Others become rebellious, based on the attitude that one must always have control and use it for one's personal aggrandizement. Whatever the case, these reactions are not conducive to the development of a constructive citizenry that is able to evaluate critically and contribute to the development of peaceful authority.

Erikson also argues that children need to develop an identity. An identity means knowing who you are and how you fit into society. It means you take all you have learned about life and yourself and use it to create a unified self-image, one that your community finds meaningful (1963). Erikson argues that a number of things can be done to make this process easier for young people. First, there should be a mainstream adult culture worthy of the adolescent's respect, one with good adult role models and open lines of communication. Second, society should provide clear rites of passage to help the child distinguish childhood from adulthood. In traditional societies there is a variety of milestones that must be passed, such as tests of endurance, symbolic ceremonies or educational events. The point of these rites is to make the distinction between the powerless but irresponsible time of childhood and the powerful and responsible time of adulthood (Erikson 1968). Without these cultural processes young people experience role confusion, an uncertainty about their place in society and the world. When confronted by role confusion, Erikson believes the adolescent is suffering from an identity crisis. In fact, a common question adolescents in our society ask is a straightforward question of identity: Who am I?

From a strong foundation children learn about values. For example, they gradually learn the difference between fantasy and lies, and the emotional consequences connected to their behaviour and the behaviour of others. They gradually learn to balance their need for being a unique individual in its various expressions (anger, fear, jealousy, joy, success) with the needs of the group (conflict, rejection, criticism, failure, empathy, inclusion). Children gradually establish their emotional independence, balancing interdependence with dependence.

Those designing a peace education strategy need to be mindful of children's emotional developmental sequence as well as the context in which the children live, including their cultural context. At this point pedagogy shades off into social development. For most young people education is seen as a means of integrating themselves into mainstream society successfully. Of course, child rearing practices are critical to the success of social integration. But, as Erikson points out, young people have to feel they can successfully fit into society (1968). If the society they are moving into is unaccepting for one reason or another, peace education will have to do what it can to ameliorate the situation. It will need to be a critical part of any peace education programme, because young people, particularly young men, will go where they feel appreciated.

Social growth

The early years of a child's life provide the primary experiences determining future social growth. Issues such as trust, self-confidence and self-worth determine the child's ability to build constructive social relationships. In addition, the physical health of the brain and the cognitive and moral environments also influence a child's ability to develop and sustain social relationships in various situations.

Children are first absorbed in their own person and needs (solitary play). As they encounter other children, they begin to interact by playing beside another child, although without much contact (parallel play). About the age of 4, children enter a stormy part of life as they begin to work out the various conventions of sharing, taking turns, compliance, individualism, rights and responsibilities (co-operative play). By age 8 to 9 their group play, rules and conventions are quite complex and demanding. Teams and same sex activity are critical to them. About age 12 cliques, conflicts, friendships and quarrels can be intense as the peer and adult codes are negotiated. At about age 15 adolescents are preoccupied with the opposite sex and are determined to be accepted as adults by succeeding at the various rites of passage offered to them by their culture.

Men and women react differently to life situations. This begins in childhood. There is still much argument about whether this is through a genetic factor or socialisation process. Carol Gilligan suggests that women are more interested in an "ethics of care," characterised by focus on responsibilities within particular human relationships, than in the male "ethics of justice," with its emphasis on rules and rights conceived in general terms (Gilligan 1982). A peace education strategy needs to be based on research in these issues as they are played out in various cultures so that young people may be helped with them.

Moral growth

Moral growth also appears to follow a developmental timetable. Lawrence Kohlberg, borrowing from the theories of Piaget, developed a series of stages of moral growth which he believed humans follow as they mature (1981).

Stages 1 and 2, typically occurring between ages 2 and 6, are part of the preconventional level of moral reasoning. At Stage 1 children obey rules in order to avoid punishment, while at Stage 2 their behaviour is mostly motivated by the desire to obtain rewards. Both phases are egocentric, and moral growth occurs as the children begin to understand that others have interests as well. Children can learn not to do physical damage to persons and property.

Stages 3 and 4 occur around age 10, when children enter the *conventional* level. Here their behaviour is guided by the opinions of other people and the desire to conform. At Stage 3 the emphasis is on being a "good boy" or "good girl" in order to win approval and avoid disapproval. At Stage 4 children have assimilated the concepts of doing one's duty and upholding the social order. These concepts become predominant in their moral reasoning. Respecting and obeying authority (parents, teachers, God) is an end in itself, without reference to higher principles. It is here that children develop mutual interpersonal relationships, conformity and expectations. Being good is important, as are trust, loyalty, respect and gratitude. Children desire to maintain rules but gradually learn to be more flexible if the rules conflict with other social duties. Children have a conscience, and they try to avoid any breakdown in institutions.

The post-conventional level of moral reasoning may develop sometime between the ages of 12 and 18. Capacity for post-conventional morality requires the ability to construct abstract moral principles which are obeyed to avoid self-condemnation rather than the censure of others.

At Stage 5 adolescents understand the "social contract" orientation toward the welfare of the community, the rights of others and existing laws. They are now capable of moral reasoning which attempts to balance conflicting rights. Stage 5 thinking attempts with difficulty to integrate individual rights and the social contract. At this stage people become aware of the possibility of pluralism. They can begin to accept that different people may have different but still legitimate ideas about a topic.

At Stage 6, the universal ethical principle stage, people become more committed to principles of justice and rely upon universal ethical principles to guide their moral reasoning. These ethical standards are thought to transcend the laws and mores of their society. Ethical standards might consist of such abstract concepts as freedom, dignity and justice.

The rate of progress through the moral stages and the number of stages achieved depends upon the surrounding social environment and cognitive, physical and emotional development of the child. Not all adolescents successfully find their way to post-conventional morality. Progress through the different stages depends upon the type of thinking a child or adolescent is capable of at a given point, and also on the negotiation of previous stages. In order to grow morally, young people need experience with moral reasoning.

Rote learning is not conducive to developing post-conventional morality. Memorisation leaves the impression that what has been memorised is truth and the only realistic interpretation of reality. Such an approach to interrelationships within society does not develop children's ability to deal with pluralistic reality. Pluralistic reality is a reality where there can be contradictory but valid interpretations of reality. There can be different religions with different conceptions of God. There are different ideologies that argue that society should be organised in different ways. There may be different ethnicities with cultures containing customs, values and mores that are quite different from one another. It is in such a pluralised, global world that future generations will have to live.

Peace education has to be dialogical. Dialogical reasoning is based on believing that it is possible to have situations in which there are contradictory truths. In such situations young people learn to be able to dialogue with difference in ways that maintain self-respect as well as respect for other points of view. Such thinking has to be nurtured. Children who grow up without coming into contact with dialogical thinking will find it difficult to develop the capacity later in life (Paul 1987). Learning environments have to foster an exchange of ideas based on respect for truth, morality and reason. Dialogical thinking cannot be taught successfully as a "one shot" learning experience sometime during the student's school career. It should begin in the very early years of a child's schooling and continue through to graduation.

A caution is in order here. Kohlberg discovered that growth in moral reasoning cannot leap across the moral stages. He suggests that for people to grow morally they need to encounter moral reasoning a half stage above where they are presently reasoning. Higher stages appear nonsensical and are discounted. Teaching moral development requires careful planning if instruction is to be successful. It needs to be culturally sensitive so the moral concepts being used resonate with students and their cultures. Despite these difficulties, curriculum designers need to provide the kind of learning environment which acknowledges and enriches the moral development of the children it serves.

It is also important to note Carol Gilligan's work on the stages of moral development from the perspective of gender. She argues that gender plays a role in moral reasoning (1982). As pointed out earlier, Gilligan believes women tend to view morality from an "ethics of care" perspective, while men focus on the "ethics of justice." However, Gilligan and Kohlberg agree that morality is a developmental process. It does not arrive as a finished product. Morality evolves over time as children mature. Gilligan and Kohlberg are also quite clear that moral growth is based on the social and cultural realities in which children find themselves. These realities may provide good opportunities for moral growth, or they may seriously limit the possibility of moral growth.

Peace education can respond to the need for moral growth. Moral (values) issues are very useful teaching tools. Children respond well to them, particularly if they are presented in some form of story or scenario. Obviously, major religious and philosophical structures have moral content which is useful as a basis for discussing various issues of interest to students.

Spiritual growth

Humanity has an inherent need to find a higher meaning and purpose for life. Children come quite naturally to this idea. As an example, our grandson, who is 2, loves us to say grace at meals. After grace he beams and raises his arms in celebration over his head. Often he will interrupt the meal and insist on another grace. This behaviour is his, not ours. Since his language is so limited, it is hard to know exactly what is going on in his mind and between him and the Lord, but something spiritual appears to be there. Spirituality and its related religious institutions help people find meaning and purpose for their lives. Most religions and their followers believe spirituality involves being on a path in which individuals gradually better understand the relationship between themselves and a greater power.

There are also developmental sequences through which children grow in their understanding of concepts fundamental to religions (Williams 1974). These are connected to children's cognitive growth. For example, in Christianity young children believe that God is a person; gradually they begin to understand what a spirit is and how they are a part of God's spirit. This development occurs apart from the kind of Christian religious instruction received or whether there was any at all. Curriculum designers must account for these developmental sequences in the particular faiths of the children.

PROFESSIONAL DEVELOPMENT

It is essential for those who work and teach children in any learning environment, including schools, to have a thorough knowledge of child development, how children learn and the cultural context in which children live. These factors must form the basis of any successful peace education strategy. Teachers need to understand the basics of a peace education strategy and be able to apply it in the classroom. All these factors are a necessary part of a teacher's professional knowledge.

Those who design and produce a peace education strategy may write with such knowledge, but those who apply it must also understand it. Otherwise, instructors may take shortcuts where slow careful development is needed. They may skip essential activities designed to support the developmental needs of children. They may not ask the community and the children those questions which will provide them with a cultural context for their teaching. Thorough and supportive teacher training is necessary to avoid a variety of pitfalls.

Any peace education curriculum adopted or developed out of a future World Vision International peace education strategy should not be an "add on." Changes in student attitudes toward peace will not occur unless the knowledge, skills and values fundamental to peace education are adapted to the developmental needs of children and integrated into the subject areas of all curricula, into all formal and informal instruction, into the discipline plan for the children and into the overall culture of the learning environment. On a broader level, the curriculum must be explained to and accepted by the community and the cultural leaders who influence families and the community. Families, especially, need information and understanding about what is happening in the learning environment (schools) before they can support their children's education. To do anything less is a waste of money, time and effort.

The experience of the authors in working for educational change among teachers in the refugee camp supports the need for a well-thought-out plan of professional and leadership development which emphasises community relationships. Without a careful plan, educational reform will lack focus. Unplanned reform can do more harm than good in terms of community relationships. So the question, taking into account the need for a thorough understanding of and a broad range of commitment to education reform and peace education, is not whether professional development is done, but how it is to be done.

The educational leaders and teachers in the refugee camp worked from a plan. At every step of the plan they both were decision makers in its application and received training in its use. They participated in a visioning exercise as their first step towards educational reform. In the visioning exercise they asked critical questions about how well their educational system was functioning in order to evaluate its strengths and weaknesses. From that thinking they developed a set of goals and a vision of what they would like their educational system to achieve. Essentially, they wanted to create an educational system that would produce critical and creative thinkers, effective leaders, good community members and proud members of their ethnic group. The fundamental goal of their educational system is to produce graduates from their schools who are willing and able to find a true and lasting peace to the civil war that plagues their lives and has made them refugees. A true and lasting peace is the great dream that drives their actions.

During the process of thinking their way through to their vision, the educational leadership began to realise that students, teachers, parents and community members had needs which were not being met by the educational system. Those needs would have to be satisfied before their vision for the future of society could be achieved.

A critical need was to involve the community as a willing and supportive partner in their reform initiative. While much of the cause for the very high dropout rate was the excessively difficult educational objectives, another cause was a serious lack of support for education by families. Families had to be convinced that children needed an education before children could be persuaded to stay in school.

A second major need was teacher training. Teachers had no experience with anything but rote learning. Most had received a limited basic education and very little teacher training. The teachers were willing to change, but they lacked knowledge of alternative educational objectives and the teaching strategies needed to achieve change. Unless teachers received more training and ongoing mentoring in implementing their training, the dream of educational reform would remain unrealised.

There is theoretical support for this view of educational reform. Michael Fullan, in *Leading in a Culture of Change* (2001), offers insight into professional development using local leaders as part of the change process. Change depends on training leaders to teach and influence their communities. Any peace education strategy needs to provide detailed information about how to access and develop leaders before it is introduced to the community and into the learning environments. Such a strategy helps local people develop their own moral purpose for peace education as well as developing relationships within the community. With these factors in place, Fullan believes, constructive change is more likely to occur.

During the course of our work in the refugee camp we developed an educational reform strategy called Ten Steps to Educational Reform in a Refugee Camp. The strategy is based on two fundamental assumptions. The first is that the people the educational system serves should be the final decision-makers about the nature of the reform. Educational advisers are needed to provide the people with new ideas about what might be useful educational reform, but those advisers must remain advisers.

The second assumption is that all parts of the community should be involved as much as possible in the process of reform. The Ten Steps strategy devotes time and energy to the development of positive relationships among parents, schools, leaders and others. This is an important factor, because teachers and educational leaders who have grown up in an authoritarian, elitist system often resist the inclusion of parents in educational decisions. They believe parents' lack of education disqualifies them from playing any role in the schools. Attitudes toward relationships between the school and the community need to be changed. Often a good place to begin building better relationships is with a discussion of the parents' dreams for the future of their children.

The Ten Steps represent a systematic strategy designed to take educational change from the visioning process to a point where educational leaders and teachers are professional enough to evaluate curriculum initiatives for themselves and determine whether proposed changes meet the test of their educational vision. A second critical point occurs when the parents, teachers and educational leaders are able to maintain and continue the educational reform. The teachers and leaders should also become trainers, so that they can continue the reform process after the educational advisers have left. At this stage the people of the community are behaving as morally autonomous, independent thinkers who are able to deal with differences in a constructive way. When this occurs, a basic objective of peace education will have been installed into the community culture. The values and skills of peace education will become an inherent part of the community culture and will grow with the community as the community grows morally.

THE LEARNING PROCESS

Before students (and teachers) can think independently about a topic such as peace, they need to be competent with three major categories of intellectual activity: knowledge, values and skills. Obviously, students need to have some basic knowledge about a topic before they can understand it. Less obvious is the need to understand the values (beliefs) and skills related to a topic. What one thinks about peace is highly determined by one's attitudes or biases. Without being aware of those biases and how they affect thinking, it is difficult to become an independent thinker. In like manner skills – the various intellectual processes used to think about something – are critical to understanding knowledge and applying it to various situations in life. In responding to issues of conflict and peace, people need to be able to use skills such as gathering and interpreting information and resolving conflicts with others.

Any peace education strategy has to be based on careful thought about what constitutes the knowledge, values and skills to be taught. Peace education has been accused of being somewhat nebulous and unfocused. Part of this problem results from an emphasis on instructional methodologies which attempt to relate to students' feelings and attitudes toward peace. While such objectives are valid and worthwhile, they do require that those who plan and conduct peace education experiences have a very clear idea of what they wish students to learn. If planners and teachers do not have a well-thought-out set of educational objectives, it is difficult to see how students will learn much from what is being taught. The first area that needs to be clarified is the conceptual basis of a peace education programme.

Understanding the role of knowledge in thinking

Knowledge can be defined as the information required to understand and to respond to some aspect of reality. Information can be divided into two fundamental components: facts or data, and concepts.

Modern teaching emphasises the accumulation of facts or data. Usually that involves storing geographical, historical, mathematical and scientific information in students' minds. The assumption is that understanding is not possible until students accumulate a broad range of information about a subject. That is true as far as it goes, but it does not go far enough.

The problem with the modern viewpoint is that memorising and storing quantities of information does not necessarily translate into understanding. It may, but only if there is a preexisting conceptual understanding of the information being studied. If there is no conceptual understanding, then students will be forced to memorise information as an alternative to understanding it.

Understanding higher-order thinking

Concepts stimulate higher-order thinking because concepts play a mediating role between information as fact and information as understanding. Let us return to the topic of societies and the concept of democracy while at the same time expanding thinking by adding related concepts to the thought process. The concept of democracy is complex, with many related concepts. Some people understand democracy based on a generalisation which holds that society should be ruled by the majority. As one studies democracies, it becomes apparent that majorities have the potential to be as arbitrary and dictatorial as authoritarian governments. That raises the question of what concepts might be applied to make critical distinctions between democracies and authoritarian governments. One concept might be human rights. Are meaningful human rights present or absent from the society? Another concept might be the presence or absence of meaningful elections. A third might be the presence or absence of meaningful accountability to laws and courts. After some thought, a new generalisation for democracy might be "a political system in which the individual is an end and never a means."

Before a topic such as peace can be understood, students must have an understanding of the fundamental concepts that define peace. For example, students need to understand concepts of human rights, political decision-making, rule of law, social justice, accountability, leadership and their roles in maintaining a peaceful society. These are complex and significant concepts which have to be accommodated within the students' intellectual framework. This process is known as concept attainment. Concept attainment takes time, but it is necessary if students are to understand topics like peaceful living.

The role of concepts in a peace education programme

There has been much discussion about the definition or lack thereof of peace education. Accusations have been made that peace education tends to be nebulous. The accusations may or may not be correct. Whatever the case, concepts can play an important role in defining peace education. A peace education strategy needs to be based on a set of carefully considered concepts. Some possibilities have been discussed, but many others should be considered.

A set of concepts defining peace education can be cross-cultural as well. First, concepts can be selected to suit the requirements of particular societies. But, more important, concepts are like empty containers which can be filled with information from different situations. So, a peace concept for one society will look somewhat different from a similar concept from another society.

Defining peace education conceptually is critical from a learning perspective. If students are to learn peace education knowledge in a way that can be retained for use in later life, then that knowledge will have to be conceptual. Memorised information is retained for a very short time. Also, memorised information does not easily transfer from one situation to another. Concepts have the potential to last for a lifetime and can be transferred from one situation to another.

Values in the learning process

Peace education, in one way or another, must help students think about the relationship between the individual and a social system inhabited by groups of individuals. There are a number of peace-related issues to unpack here. What responsibility do individuals have to the social system they inhabit? In what way should individuals conform to the system? Are societies capable of behaving badly? Does individual responsibility extend to criticising and changing the system? How should the social system respond to criticism and demands for change? Ultimately, who has the best handle on truth: the individual or society? Responses to these questions involve values.

Values are the second critical component to the learning process. There is much about life that is uncertain. Life requires decisions from us even when the consequences of those decisions may be unclear. Decisions have to be made, because the consequences of not making a decision may be worse. People learn to rely on sets of beliefs to guide them in situations of uncertainty because in other situations those beliefs have resulted in positive consequences. These beliefs are called values.

Goals of the values component of peace education

Before a peace education programme is implemented, the fundamental moral positions people tend to take in the society need to be examined. This is an important exercise for a couple of reasons. It defines the kinds of moral choices and the responses students are expected to make throughout their lives. This is where students reside morally, and this is where they will need help. If they grow up in a society dominated by revengeful, violent values, then they will need help in understanding that less violent values can be practised without sacrificing self-worth. The second reason is that many of our value responses are habitual and occur with very little thinking. New values may feel uncomfortable. Students will need practice in learning to respond to issues and confrontations with more peaceful values. All of this means that peace education has to look at real life scenarios and find ways of helping students develop and practise alternative responses to them.

In many authoritarian societies people are conditioned to be obedient and to accept the status quo. The overriding goal of values education has to be to help students move from moral heteronomy (the notion that the various moral and ethical beliefs of society are what one should believe) to moral autonomy (the notion that individuals have the capacity and responsibility to evaluate and select a personal set of values to follow).

It is important to note that moral autonomy does not mean an individual would divorce himself or herself from religious traditions or other sources of values. Nor does moral autonomy mean discounting or dismissing all significant values (secular or religious) of society. Rather, what it implies is that morally autonomous people carefully consider religious or other values and adopt them on some reasoned or spiritual basis that seems morally acceptable, even if this may contradict widely held values of the larger society.

There are many examples of thinkers who have found themselves in a position of having to question the values of the society in which they lived: Martin Luther, Voltaire, Dietrich Bonhoeffer, Ghandi, Martin Luther King and Nelson Mandela, to cite a few examples.

Independent learning from the values perspective should result in young adults who are able to make independent moral judgements about their behaviour and about the society in which they live. They do not need to be lectured about "good" values and "bad" values. Rather, they should have the opportunity to evaluate values in discussion and, based on those discussions, make a judgement about the consequences of selecting certain values over other values. It is this kind of values or moral education that is likely to give young people the motivation, skills and knowledge necessary to make good moral judgements. Since all of us often find sorting out moral issues confusing and complex, it should not be surprising that young people also have these difficulties.

A second goal for peace education is to create an attitude of sceptical open-mindedness (what other commentators refer to as critical consciousness) among students. Students who are sceptically open-minded are willing to think about values-related issues, unwilling to make up their minds about an issue too early and willing to test their conclusions before accepting them. This is a path to autonomous moral reasoning.

Moral reasoning occurs when students find themselves in a learning environment where it is modelled and where they have an opportunity to practise it. Such an environment requires teachers who are comfortable with moral reasoning and are willing to create situations which stimulate discussion about significant moral issues.

It is important to consider the context in which teachers and school systems operate. It can be complex and contradictory. Many teachers have grown up in authoritarian school systems that reflect authoritarian societies. Initially, they will be reluctant to get involved in what they perceive to be controversial issues. To some extent that was true of the teachers whom we were training. But it was not the complete story.

The families of the teachers had been in a 50–year struggle for cultural survival against a brutal military dictatorship. Many of the people we worked with had been leaders and soldiers (or married to them) in the struggle for autonomy. They had undergone great suffering and privation. These teachers had a vision of freedom and peace they wished to see implemented in their schools and society. Despite this background, the teachers' society was itself quite authoritarian and conforming.

The first year we conducted teacher training sessions we were told by the military we could not teach history and geography because they considered them to be dangerous and inflammatory information. During the course of our training sessions with the teachers, we were periodically visited by the army colonel in charge of the refugee camp. He would descend upon our classrooms with his retinue and ask pointed questions about the teaching we were doing. This was the kind of environment in which the refugee teachers existed.

The response of the teachers to this situation was somewhat contradictory. The visits and questions by the military tended to make them more disobedient than obedient, because they considered the army's behaviour somewhat ridiculous and all too familiar to what they had experienced in their homeland. Ironically, it was the conforming nature of their society that exerted a stronger restraint for them then did the military.

For these reasons it was not surprising that the teachers were initially hesitant to discuss moral and ethical positions which might be contrary to the traditional educational system and society in which they lived. In the first year of our discussions we talked about many issues related to a democratic society, as noted earlier in the chapter. The teachers were curious about the relationship of Canadian teachers to educational authorities (school boards and so forth). When it was explained to them that sometimes the relationship could be difficult and that teachers occasionally went on strike, their reaction was quietly rejecting of such behaviour: We would never form a union and treat the leaders of our society in that way.

As the educational reform process continued, many more discussions of social issues occurred. Over the course of three more years, one could detect a shift in attitudes if not behaviour. In the fourth year some dissension developed between the Camp Educational Committee (equivalent of a local school board) and the teachers. A well-liked administrator was fired. The teachers were upset about the possibility of misadministration over the next school year. They began seriously to consider forming a teachers' union. They wanted to know how to form a union which would help them exert pressure upon a governing school committee that they felt did not understand education and was not interested in listening to the advice of teachers.

Values change comes slowly and from a variety of sources. It is important to remember this in terms of peace education. This was the case for the refugee teachers. An early problem that really shocked them was the change in attitudes toward obedience by their students. They were used to teaching students who lived in isolated mountain valleys. They now had to deal with students who lived in a community of 9,000 people. Student attitudes toward authority had changed, and the teachers were finding their teaching methods had to respond to the social changes. They now had to learn to discipline based on a discussion of values rather than resorting to force. As a result, we had discussions about how teachers, schools and parents should respond to the behaviour of students. One example was the issue of responding to pregnancy among students. School policy required expulsion of the female student. The teachers began to wonder whether this was an appropriate course of action. They asked how Canadian schools would respond. A long discussion ensued with no specific resolution, but response to the issue was now problematic rather than just being assumed.

Should these issues be considered part of a peace education strategy? We would argue they should, because they establish a climate of dialogue that will eventually lead to a discussion of issues more traditionally considered to be peace education issues. If peace education is to be successful, a social climate must be established that resorts to dialogue rather than various forms of coercion. In working toward the development of an effective peace education climate, it is important to remember that values change takes time. The refugee teachers needed several years to become comfortable with dialogue about values issues.

Instruction in the form of teacher training can also be very helpful in the development of dialogue. At the beginning of the training sessions we discussed the use of teaching strategies involving the use of simulation games to analyse social issues within the refugee community. Initially, as we have noted, teachers were doubtful and reluctant to approach these issues at all. Three years later they willingly and creatively participated in simulating a constitutional conference where the constitutional issues involved the creation of a democratic, federal homeland for the refugees. The following year they were involved in simulating an environmental conference where environmental issues related to a major river system were discussed. They had become much more willing and able to discuss values issues related to peace education. They also exhibited the ability to argue forcefully and passionately for their points of view and still be able to find creative solutions for the environmental problems they faced. It is only when teachers have had these kinds of experiences that they can visualise themselves doing something similar related to peace education in the classroom.

As illustrated with the refugee example, teachers need permission and guidance before they will be willing to move toward an honest and open dialogue on peace education issues. Permission needs to come as part of an educational reform process that involves the community as well as the school. Guidance needs to come in the creation of situations in which teachers actually see themselves conducting a peace values dialogue in their current learning environment. Active, hands-on training is required to provide teachers with permission and then guidance in using the tools to lead a learning environment. Teachers need modelling in their training so that they can see and participate in activities that create dialogical discussions around peace education issues. All of this takes time and mentoring. What teachers are able to do in the first year of their training is quite limited in comparison to their abilities after three or four years. Admittedly, this is a slow, labour-intensive process, but a lifetime of teaching experience is not overturned by one or two short sessions on peace education theory.

We found that under appropriate circumstances teachers were willing, even eager, to participate in activities which were values oriented. Teachers of young children used theme-based role plays and activity centres to stimulate values through the incorporation of play into the learning activities. We experimented with simulation games with both teachers and adolescents and experienced good results. The teachers needed the opportunity to try activities such as simulations and receive guided practice in using them in the classroom. Teachers had opportunities to create learning activities and observe children as they played and learned from them. Given this kind of in-service support, many teachers gained the potential to become effective leaders in developing peace education values.

Skills and abilities in the learning process

There is an important bridge to be made between values education and skills education. For purposes of educational analysis and discussion, the two are often separated, but in reality they complement each other. Students need a reason to use the skills of critical thinking. Consideration of values, particularly in some form of dialogue, provides that purpose. It is important to realise that dialogue, itself, is a skill which uses many of the skills outlined below. If teachers are not prepared or are unable to explain and model the skills of thinking, then the level of thinking exhibited by the students will remain limited.

The same observation can be made for teachers who have grown up in an authoritarian, rote-learning educational system. They will be unfamiliar with dialogical thinking and its related skills. We have noted how the refugee teachers needed time to become familiar and comfortable with some of the critical thinking skills outlined below. When they reached a certain comfort level, one could see them beginning to use some of the skills in the classroom debates we held. At that point the teachers would be more comfortable in using (modelling) them in a learning environment.

Critical and creative thinking

Some examples of intellectual thought processes are the ability to summarise information, to draw inferences from information, to predict consequences and to evaluate results. Figure 5–1 shows a set of skills selected because they are basic to thinking. This is not an exhaustive set, but it does represent a minimum set of skills necessary for effective critical and creative thinking.

The column on the left are analytical skills and those on the right are synthesis skills. One theory of thinking suggests that people work back and forth between the two columns as they deliberate. Critical and creative thinking also work in tandem. Critical thinking involves unpacking and analysing a situation, while creative thinking involves reformulating (synthesising) the factors derived from critical thinking into new (creative) forms which can then be evaluated. This process continues until the thinker is satisfied with the conclusion.

The skills in this model represent a basic set of skills found in most types of critical and creative thinking. The skills in and of themselves are not sufficient to create the autonomous moral thinking described in the values section above. More is needed. The following sections describe some of the more global thinking skills student will need to become comfortable with if they are to pursue peace education issues successfully.

Figure 5–1. A model of thinking skills

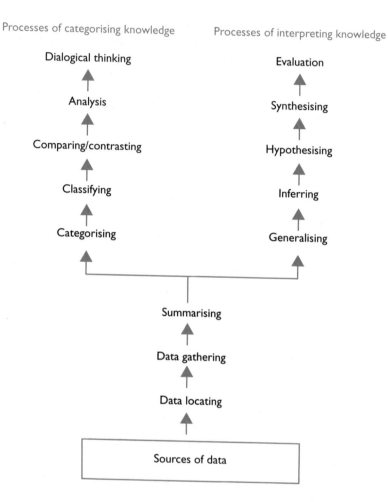

Processes of categorising knowledge   Processes of interpreting knowledge

Dialogical thinking   Evaluation

↑   ↑

Analysis   Synthesising

↑   ↑

Comparing/contrasting   Hypothesising

↑   ↑

Classifying   Inferring

↑   ↑

Categorising   Generalising

Summarising

↑

Data gathering

↑

Data locating

↑

Sources of data

Source: Figure 5–1 is adapted from L. Hannah and J. Michaelis, *A Comprehensive Framework for Instructional Objectives: A Guide to Systematic Planning and Evaluation* (Menlo Park, CA: Addison-Wesley, 1977).

Communication skills

Living together peacefully and settling conflicts peacefully require the ability to communicate well. In order to do that, students need to learn some basic communication skills such as logical argumentation; effective rhetoric, both verbal and written; and the ability to listen well. Again, a skill such as the effective use of language may seem tangential to peace education, but it is not. The refugee teachers recognised this when they insisted that their students be able to express themselves effectively in public. They realised that the ability to negotiate well depends upon the ability to use language well. Conflict can be resolved through negotiation, or it can be resolved through force. Language provides an alternative to force. Learning to use language for the purpose of negotiation and reconciliation depends upon accepting negotiation as a primary value and developing the skills to make it a viable alternative.

The creative resolution of conflict

Peace is not the absence of conflict but rather the creative resolution of conflict. There must be awareness and acceptance of the significance and the inevitability of conceptual and values-based misunderstandings. Different understandings of aspects of reality lead to disagreements which are very difficult to resolve. The conceptual understanding of power is an important example. Some conceptualise power as a zero-sum process. Others conceptualise it as a process of empowerment?[9] There are many such misunderstandings. Ideological conflicts thrive on these types of conceptual ambiguities. Coping with ambiguity requires dialogical skill and empathy in order to understand and react constructively to differing points of view. Students must understand that conflict is inevitable and learn to expect it. The real issue in peace education is learning to resolve conflict well.

Conflict resolution

There is a wide range of skills and abilities directly related to resolving conflict. Conflict resolution requires knowing and, most important, accepting those skills and abilities which enable one to respond to the needs of others in positive ways while being able to express constructively one's own needs. Conflict-resolution skills include being able:

- to confront the opposition to discover whether something can be done about the conflict
- to define with the opposition what the conflict is about so that misunderstandings are not taken into the conflict-resolution process

- to communicate during the conflict-resolution process an intention to co-operate with the conflict-resolution process
- to look at the other person's perspective accurately and fully during the conflict-resolution process
- to communicate clearly and honestly any changes of position and feelings during the conflict-resolution process
- to work to negotiate an agreement that achieves a balance between the goals of both sides
- to seek creatively one's good in ways that are not at the expense of the opposition's good

Mediation

Often the parties to a conflict are unable to resolve the dispute without help. A third party who can mediate the dispute is often invaluable in finding a resolution. Effective mediation requires one to be able:

- to listen and observe (the feelings, body language, interpretations, vocabulary and so forth of others as well as yourself)
- to paraphrase the viewpoints of others
- to find solutions
- to select solutions

Dialogical (dialectical) thinking

It is not unusual to find a dispute between parties who have taken valid but narrow positions on an issue. As the dispute grows, each party becomes less able to appreciate the point of view of the other or to concede that there may be some inadequacies in its own viewpoint. Dialogical reasoning is the process of resolving contradictory but acceptable points of view in some way. Students need practical experience in using dialogical thinking skills:

- making an initial value claim expressing what is good, right or worthwhile concerning an issue
- providing supporting arguments for taking that particular position on the issue
- being able to define a value claim opposing the first value claim
- providing supporting arguments for the opposing value claim
- creating a dialectic by acknowledging the existence of opposing value claims, pointing out some aspect of the opposing value claim that is worth

noting, and pitting the first set of supporting arguments against the second set

Negotiation

Another highly significant part of effective conflict resolution is the ability to negotiate well. There are many skills involved in negotiation. A peace education curriculum might consider some of the following skills as important for students to understand to and be able to apply in their lives. One is the ability to define the underlying stances being adopted as a negotiation strategy. Stances may be win/win, win/lose, and lose/lose.

Values and the processes of resolving conflict

Conflict resolution, mediation, dialogical thinking and negotiation share similar skills and values. They all require an appreciation and acceptance of a set of ethics which involve respect for the dignity of those who disagree with one's position and willingness to search for truth rather than scoring debating or power points. They also require personal values such as being flexible and reasonable in one's demands. Success in reaching a negotiated bargain is knowing when the possible resolution to a negotiation is good enough.

Negotiation/political skills

Learning experiences can be constructed to give students practice in understanding and using political procedures constructively (*political* is being used here in the broad sense of negotiation between individuals and individuals and groups). Some examples of the processes that might be taught in this way include:

- gathering accurate information
- forming consensus
- influencing others
- negotiating
- presenting and defending a point of view
- interest-based bargaining
- decision-making procedures
- understanding that all decision-making ultimately has moral and ethical implications
- decision-making

- conflict-resolution procedures
- creative problem solving

It is not realistic to expect to teach all of these skills at one time. They require a lifetime to master. Still, it is possible by the end of secondary school to make a good beginning. These skills can also be taught in a variety of learning environments as well as in the classroom. What is required is some knowledge of teaching strategies that can present concrete activities to students so that they can practise these kinds of thought processes.

It is important to remember that most societies and cultures have developed variations on the conflict-resolution processes described above. For example, aboriginal cultures in North America use the Talking Circle as a technique to provide people with a structured environment in which they can speak without being interrupted and to encourage everyone to listen attentively to the views of other members of the circle. Any peace education strategy which is concerned with furthering conflict-resolution procedures would do well to research the traditional techniques of the culture and begin with them.

The culture of the learning environment

Learning environments are miniature societies, each with a personality and culture which can be labelled a learning culture. The teacher plays a large role in establishing the norms and relationships that prevail in the learning culture. However, the teacher is not the only player in a learning culture. Various student personalities present in a learning environment synthesise themselves into a small society. Students are able to exert power in the society, even if it is only through passive resistance. Often they can have a much more active influence. As we noted earlier in this chapter, parents and the community may also have a powerful effect on a learning environment.

Learning environments are based on conceptual understandings about what people should learn, how they should learn and how they should relate to one another. A teacher's concept of discipline strongly determines relationships within a classroom community, for example. Related to this concept are powerful values concepts about how people should relate to one another. The concepts of obedience and conformity are two examples. Finally, there will be a well-established set of tactics employed to resolve conflict and maintain order within the learning environment. Those tactics are often punitive, with corporal punishment playing a large role. A major issue for any peace education programme is how to deal with the systemic violence of learning environments. A "do as I say and not as I do" philosophy based on force will contribute little to a successful peace education programme.

The culture of a learning environment is never educationally passive. Children learn many things (besides formal objectives) from a school culture. The mechanism that makes this possible is informal learning. Formal learning is the planned, structured activities carried out in a learning environment. Informal learning is the personal learning that occurs as students react to the events of the learning environment. Formal teaching inevitably results in some kind of informal learning. The irony is that informal learning will be retained long after the formal lessons have been forgotten by the students. The critical issue is what kind of informal learning should be left in the minds of students. The student may have forgotten the history lesson but will remember for a lifetime the boredom that accompanied it. A major opportunity and problem for peace educators is that formal teaching results in unintended informal learning.

Discipline can be a major determinant of the kind of informal learning students do. The attitude of the teachers to their power has much to do with students' informal learning about the use of power. If discipline is arbitrary, disrespectful and self-serving, the implicit message is that people in power have the right to behave this way. Alternatively, if discipline is consistent, respectful and serves the well-being of the learning community, students will come away with a different vision of the exercise of power. Students learn about power relationships between the weak and the strong by watching the behaviour of the powerful in their lives.

Implications of informal learning for peace education

The effect of informal learning on students will depend upon the assumptions of the peace education curriculum. If the curriculum assumes that democracy is an important prerequisite to peace, then building democratic learning environments would be useful, because students could observe firsthand a community administered under democratic values. From this perspective the discipline of learning environments should be considered a process of building disciples where the teacher is the "first among equals" rather than some kind of all-powerful figure. Such a learning environment might be characterised as a community of scholars.

Learning environments as communities of scholars

In a community of scholarship, students are encouraged to work independently and co-operatively with other students on self-guided work projects. Students have the freedom and responsibility to make choices about how they learn. Students learn to draw upon the resources of the teacher and other students as they learn. They are encouraged to be self-evaluative and self-adjusting so that as adults they know how to take responsibility for their lives and personal conduct. The role of the teacher becomes more a facilitator of learning and a coach who works with individuals and small groups in a problem solving mode.

It takes time and patience to help students learn to move from an authoritarian learning environment to a democratic environment. Based on past experience, students have learned a set of values appropriate to authoritarian situations: never take initiative, do not ask questions, do not take responsibility, learn passive-resistance strategies, sabotage whenever possible, take advantage of weakness whenever you see it and so on. It takes strong and courageous teachers to turn this around, but it can be done if teachers systematically and overtly begin to conduct their classrooms according to a different set of values. Teachers must be overt in the sense that students must clearly know what the teachers' objectives are. One way of doing this is to begin the class with a concept-attainment lesson on human rights. Help the students to understand what human rights are, how they protect people and how they act as guides (values) for the administration of a community. Emphasise that all students because of their humanity have human rights. Also remind them that teachers are human and, as such, have human rights as well.

Initiate a discussion with students about the human rights needed in a learning environment. Brainstorm a list of human rights and place them on a chalkboard or paper. Ask the students to consider carefully which human rights they are prepared to support and live by in their learning community. Make a list of the human rights the students have selected. When the list is finished, ask the group to reconsider the entire list from the point of view of a code by which they agree to conduct themselves. Are they willing to live this way? When there is agreement, have some students make a poster of the group's human rights code and post it in some prominent place in the room. In the future whenever there is some kind of discipline problem, it is both the teacher's and the students' responsibility to make sure that discipline is administered consistently and humanely in accordance with the human rights code.

VARIOUS TEACHING METHODOLOGIES WHICH MAY BE EMPLOYED BY THE PEACE EDUCATION CURRICULUM

An understanding and appreciation for the power of informal learning leads one to consider which teaching techniques are most appropriate for a peace education classroom. Discipline and teaching techniques work together to establish the kind of informal learning achieved by students. By creatively combining the two, teachers can achieve a high level of formal learning while creating a learning environment that contributes to a constructive informal learning.

Child-centred education

Child-centred education is a set of teaching methodologies aimed at making the child an active participant in learning environments. Teaching activities are active and centred on concrete experiences meaningful to students. Students are encouraged to ask questions and to take some responsibility and some control of the learning process. The goal of this approach is to encourage children to become self-confident, self-reliant, independent, and capable of working constructively with others.

Discovery learning

Discovery learning is a set of teaching methodologies intended to encourage students to ask questions and develop answers for themselves. Discovery learning is also active, child centred and concrete. Usually these activities begin with some kind of problem, mystery, or need that requires a solution, decision or the like. It is the role of the student to find the answer(s), not the role of the teacher. It is not unusual for contradictory answers to be discovered and to spend time discussing and evaluating the best possible answer(s). The teacher's role is to create problems suitable for the students, prepare materials and act as a guide as the children work through the problems. For very young students, structured, rich play environments are prepared by teachers to accomplish the same ends.

Concrete learning

Young people (and adults) learn better by starting with the concrete and moving to the abstract. Teachers have a tendency to begin teaching in the abstract too early for most students. This is true for all students from preschool to university. Many ideas to be explored in a peace education curriculum can be highly abstract and removed from the experience of students. It is important to find meaningful situations students can relate to as a starting point for any discussion.

IMPLEMENTING A PEACE EDUCATION STRATEGY

Teacher support

Teachers need more than a curriculum on peace education. Teachers will not have much experience with the kinds of teaching activities being described above. An activity guide that provides specific examples and guidance in their use would be a useful aid. It would help teachers of young children learn to create a rich, play-based classroom. Teachers need support in designing and using teaching methodologies in the classroom. It is important not to assume that teachers know how to use these approaches without guidance and in-service training. Simulations are relatively easy to create, provided one knows some of the basic principles. An activity guide can provide samples and guidance in how to create activities related to local situations. In this sense an activity guide can be an in-service tool for teachers who are motivated to look for different teaching methodologies.

The role of the teacher

The teacher is highly significant in establishing the culture of a learning environment. There are two important realities about teachers: they tend to teach the way they were taught, and they are the gatekeepers to the learning environment. Educational change will not happen unless teachers are willing to introduce new ideas and methodologies into their learning environments. Teachers cannot change until they understand how to use alternative methodologies in their learning environments. Teachers need ongoing support and encouragement because change is risky.

IMPLEMENTING PEACE EDUCATION STRATEGIES

Developing a peace education strategy is one thing; putting it into practice is another. Teachers cannot implement educational practices they do not understand.

Teachers need concrete examples of what curriculum developers envision. As teachers become more familiar and secure with an activity, they can innovate. One approach to providing support to teachers is to prepare activity guides which give teachers specific direction about how to teach certain objectives. However, even with explicit direction, many teachers will hesitate to experiment with these teaching strategies. They will perceive a high level of risk on many fronts. If these fears are not allayed, teachers will ignore the curriculum and continue to follow the teaching practices with which they are comfortable.

The ultimate goal of the learning process is to provide students with experiences which give them the opportunity to apply the knowledge, concepts and values they have learned to real, meaningful situations using the skills they have learned. Teachers and students alike need direction and support in achieving these objectives.

CONCLUSION

The purpose of this chapter has been to define a set of optimal educational approaches to be taken in creating an effective peace education programme. Education is considered effective when behaviour changes in constructive ways. A subject like peace can appear to be taught, but if behaviour has not become more peaceful, it is difficult to argue that peace has been successfully taught.

In terms of behavioural change nothing can be guaranteed, but there are approaches which increase the probability of peaceful behaviours being learned. The following list contains principles any peace education strategy could usefully adopt:

- The overriding purpose of education in general and peace education in particular is to help students understand and practice the morality and ethics of peace.
- Since it is not possible to teach a precise course of action to be followed by students in their future lives, the only alternative is to teach them how to apply the concepts, values and skills of peace in their present lives.
- A peace education programme needs to break the cycle of abuse flowing from generation to generation by advocating the constructive and positive nurturance of young people.
- Both education in general and peace education in particular have to respect the dignity and well-being of all individuals involved in the learn-

ing process. Students must always be viewed as ends and never as a means.

- If a peace curriculum assumes students need to learn and practise the values, concepts and skills related to human rights, then a democratic learning environment is necessary so that students have firsthand experiences with democratic communities operating under assumptions based on human rights.

Students are ultimately autonomous in determining the basis on which they live their lives. Teachers using peace education programmes can attempt to influence that autonomy, but in the future – away from teachers and learning environments – students must personally decide what their behaviour will be. Students as adults are more likely to adopt peaceful behaviour if they have experienced positive, constructive learning experiences that clearly demonstrate a peaceful way of life.

NOTES

[1] The term *learning environment* is used here to categorise a whole range of teaching and learning environments. Learning environments include classrooms as well as a variety of other formal and informal learning situations.

[2] Mystery can be both a positive and a negative motivator. *Mystification* in the sense used here creates helplessness and frustration that ultimately destroys motivation and independence. Mystification can also have the effect of creating curiosity and wonder, but that occurs in different circumstances and for different purposes. We describe some of those circumstances later in the chapter.

[3] It is important to note here that mathematics is not the only subject that can be taught in this way. It is also important to note that mathematics teaching is no more prone to this style of teaching than other subjects.

[4] *Concrete* here refers to ideas that are real or tangible in some way. There may be aspects of a context that are abstract (morality, ethics, etc.), but the situation being discussed is real and meaningful to students in some way. For young children situations must be concrete before they can deal realistically and meaningfully with them. Young children need to use their senses in learning: seeing, hearing, tasting, smelling, and touching. Play is an important vehicle to learning.

[5] This may well broaden the definition and goals of peace education. When considering this, it is important to remember that children are whole beings and that education is most successful when all the needs of the child are being met.

[6] It is important to distinguish between needs and wants here. Needs are defined as those things humans must have if they are to have healthy physical and psychological lives. Wants are those things people would like to have but are not necessary to their well-being. Needs and wants are often confused. Sometimes we substitute unnecessary wants (certain

foods) for needs. Other times we deny needs (love) because we view them as unnecessary wants. Higher-order needs (social and esteem needs) are often confused with wants.

[7] Learning and memorisation are often confused. Here, learning means understanding and performance. A child may memorise something but not understand it or be able to apply it to some other situation.

[8] For a brief discussion of Erik Erikson's personality theories, see C. George Boeree, "Erik Erikson: 1902–1994" (1997). Available online.

[9] A zero-sum concept of power holds that power is a limited commodity. If power is shared, the person who shares automatically loses power while the power of someone else increases. The empowerment conception holds that the co-operative sharing of power increases the power of everyone involved.

BIBLIOGRAPHY

Bhavnagri, Navaz Peshotan. 2001. "The Global Village: Migration and Education" [special issue]. *Childhood Education* 77, no. 5.

Blackwell, C. 1994. "The Problem of the Cultural Development of the Child." In *Vygotsky Reader,* ed. R. van der Veer and Jaan Valsiner. Cambridge, MA: Blackwell, 1994.

Bowman B., and F. Stott. 1994. "Understanding Development in a Cultural Context." In *Diversity and Developmentally Appropriate Practice*, ed. B. Mallory and R. New, 119–34. New York: Teachers College Press.

Bredekamp, Susan, and Carol Copple, eds. 1997. "Developmentally Appropriate Practice in Early Childhood Programs." National Association for the Education of Young Children no. 234. Washington, DC: NAEYC.

Brown, D. E. 1991. *Human Universals.* Philadelphia: Temple Univ. Press.

Deloache, Judy S., and Alma Gottlieb. 2000. *A World of Babies.* Cambridge: Cambridge Univ. Press.

Eming-Young, Mary. 2001. "Early Childhood Development: Investing in the Future." Washington, DC: The World Bank Group.

Erikson, Erik. *Childhood and Society.* 1963. 2nd ed., rev. and enl. New York: W. W. Norton.
———. 1968. *Identity: Youth and Crisis.* London: Faber and Faber.

Eve, Marie Arce, ed. 1999. *Perspectives in Early Childhood Education.* New York: Houghton Mifflin.

Fullan, Michael. 2001. *Leading in a Culture of Change.* San Francisco: Jossey-Bass.

Gilligan, Carol. 1982. *In a Different Voice: Psychological Theory and Women's Development.* Cambridge, MA: Harvard Univ. Press.

Goleman, Daniel. 1995. *Emotional Intelligence: Why It Can Matter More than IQ.* New York. Bantam Books.

Hannah, L., and J. Michaelis. 1977. *A Comprehensive Framework for Instructional Objectives: A Guide to Systematic Planning and Evaluation.* Menlo Park, CA: Addison-Wesley.

Kagan, S. L., and E. E. Garcia. 1994. "Educational, Cultural and Linguistic Diversity Perspectives: Moving the Agenda." *Early Childhood Research Quarterly* 6: 427–43.

Katz, Lillian G. 1999. "International Perspectives on Early Childhood Education." *Early Childhood Research and Practice* 1, no. 1.

Kohlberg, Lawrence. 1981. *Essays on Moral Development, I: The Philosophy of Moral Development: Moral Stages and the Idea of Justice.* San Francisco: Harper and Row.

Paul, Richard. 1987. "Dialogical Thinking: Critical Thought Essential to the Acquisition of Rational Knowledge and Passions." In *Teaching Thinking Skills: Theory and Practise,* ed. J. B. Baron and R. J. Sternberg, 127–48. New York: W. H. Freeman.

Tobin, Joseph, David Wu, and Dana Davidson. 1989. *Preschoolers in Three Cultures: Japan, China and the US.* New Haven, CT: Yale Univ. Press.

Wadsworth, Barry J. 1971. *Piaget's Theory of Cognitive Development.* New York: Davis McKay.

Williams, Mavis L. 1974. *Children's Concepts of God and Self: Developmental Sequences.* Doctoral diss., Univ. of Texas at Austin.

World Bank. 1996. "Early Childhood Development." World Bank Group/NAEYC Position Statement.

Selected Sources with Original Authors' Comments

Berman, Sheldon. *Children's Social Consciousness and the Development of Social Responsibility.* Albany: State Univ. of New York Press, 1997.

> This book is an effort to synthesize the research in these diverse fields, explicate a new theoretical framework, and answer the questions: What are the processes by which young people develop a sense of social responsibility? And, what are classroom and school practices that effectively support this development? In answering these questions, I hope we can begin to build the base of knowledge and research in the field of social responsibility and use that knowledge to guide our future efforts.

Bigelow, Bill, and Bob Peterson. *Rethinking Globalization Teaching for Justice in an Unjust World.* Milwaukee: Rethinking Schools, 2002.

> We began this book with the intention of focusing on sweatshops and child labor around the world. . . . It was impossible to separate our teaching about wretched conditions for workers around the world from all the factors that produced the desperation that forces people to seek work in these conditions. . . . This book is an argument for the necessity of holding, in our minds and in our classrooms, the big global picture.

Derman-Sparks, Louise, and Carol Brunson Phillips. *Teaching/Learning Anti-Racism: A Developmental Approach.* New York: Teachers College Press, 1997.

> Anti-racism education is not an end in itself but rather the beginning of a new approach to thinking, feeling and acting.

Kivel, Paul. *Uprooting Racism.* British Columbia: New Society Publisher, 1996.

> This is a book about racism for white people. It is not another book about how bad racism is, filled with facts and figures about inequality and justice. In this book I want to talk to you personally about what is means to those of us who are white, and how we can make a difference in the struggle for racial justice.

Lee, Enid, et al. *Beyond Heroes and Holidays: A Practical Guide to K-12 Anti-Racist, Multicultural Education and Staff Development.* Washington DC: Network of Educators on the Americas, 1998.

> In *Beyond Heroes and Holidays* we attempt to expose race and racism as they operate in schools by including lessons that help students, parent, and school staff pay attention to race.

Mertz, Gayle, and Carol Miller Lieber. *Conflict in Context Understanding Local to Global Society.* Cambridge: Educators for Social Responsibility, 2001.

Educators for Social Responsibility has developed this resource to provide middle and secondary educators, and their students with inquiry-based tools to support their exploration of emerging local, national, international, and transboundary security issues.

Reardon, Betty A. *Comprehensive Peace Education Educating for Global Responsibility.* New York: Teachers College Press, 1988.

This book contains my own, necessarily subjective, reflections on the evolution of peace education and my hopes for its future. . . . It was time to become much more self-conscious about both the pedagogical purposes and the political goals of peace education. We need to go beyond the immediate aim of preparing for nonviolent politics and investigate the root causes of the violent conditions we face so that we can determine how education can be used to interrupt the cycle of ever-increasing violence in which we are now swept up.

PART III

ENCOUNTERING THE EDGES

*Extending peace education to embrace child
protection and inner beliefs*

6

Peace education in the context of family and community

Peace education and child protection

Heather MacLeod

INTRODUCTION AND OVERVIEW

Developing effective peace education curricula in the diverse contexts in which NGOs' work is complex. This chapter focuses on the family and community contexts in which children live and face violence. It identifies and discusses the types of violence children face in their day-to-day lives around the globe, the impact that violence has on them and then considers this knowledge of the child, family and community in the light of peace education programmes.

In the humanitarian and development community, peace education is generally thought of as an intervention for children living in war or post-conflict situations. This chapter argues that the influence of peace education could be much broader. Education on peace is needed in every community.

One need only read the newspapers or watch TV to be alerted to the problems of violence in schools, on the streets and in families. The World Health Organization's *World Report on Violence and Health* states that "more than a million people lose their lives, and many more suffer non-fatal injuries, as a result of self inflicted, interpersonal or collective violence each day" (WHO 2002, 1.3). A study covering over 30,000 young people by the Johannesburg Metropolitan Local Council and a local NGO, the Community Information Empowerment and Transparency foundation (CIET) found one in four of the men interviewed claimed to have had sex without the girl's consent. At least half of those interviewed - male and female - believed that forcing sex on someone they know is not sexual violence, but just "rough sex."

Violence in the home is not a problem confined to the developing world; it also exists in the so-called developed world, which, despite numerous studies on violence and the introduction of a wide variety of programmes to address violence, still struggles with the impact of violence in communities. In 1995 the U.S. Federal Bureau of Investigation (FBI) "reported that 27% of all violent crime involves family on family violence, and 48% involved acquaintances with the violence often occurring in the home" (National Incident-Based Reporting System, Uniform Crime Reporting Program, 1999, cited in Perry 2005). Children are often witnesses to or victims of these violent crimes.

Why is peace education needed?

Violence in families and communities is a complex issue. It affects the social, political, cultural and economic development of communities and individuals around the world. It results in population displacement, reduced productivity, increased health costs, reduction in educational opportunities, increased crime and unhealthy communities. Addressing violence towards children is also complex and requires a wide range of tools. Peace education offers one of many tools.

The strength of peace education is that it offers community-based relief and development organisations and civil society groups a very practical tool to address their concerns related to the protection of children from situations of violence. Peace education offers a programme with an intentional focus on teaching practical skills for reducing conflict and supporting peaceful living.

As we consider peace education as a child protection tool, a reflection on philosophy and consistency of approach forces a discussion of who should "own" peace education. Should it be a stand-alone programme or should it be integrated into existing relief and development programmes?

This chapter suggests that where peace education belongs depends on each environment. In some places it may be an activity that is integrated into a broader health or peacebuilding programme; in others it may be a separate sectoral programme. Factors of cultural, political, economic and social diversity affect these decisions, as do the strengths of the particular group or NGO that introduces the programme.

This chapter argues that the links between child protection and peace education should be strengthened. Child abuse prevention is the goal of child protection, and the knowledge gained from years of research in this field could also assist peace educators in their work. In addition, child protection–related research gives valuable insights into the effect of violence on the developing brain. It should be noted that while there are some effective tools already available for the prevention of child abuse, many developing countries still lack resources for effective prevention of abuse at the community level. Peace educators and child protection professionals would do well to collaborate more closely.

Why should an NGO be involved specifically in peace education? Peace education programmes support social sustainability, emergence of hope and community participation – WV's standards for transformational development. In relief and CEDC (children in especially difficult circumstances) settings peace education is able to address the need for alternative models of behaviour for children who are at risk of facing further violence or perpetrating violence themselves. It also has potential to offer support to existing interventions such as emergency education, health, separated children in transit care, agricultural recovery programmes and so on.

WV has articulated its framework for child well-being with the clear message that programmes for children must be created in the context of family and community (WVI 2002a). This provides a solid reason why peace education must intentionally involve parents, care givers and community members.

J. Boyden and G. Mann argue that child protection is compromised by "the lack of coherent objectives and consistency of approach, generally reflecting high levels of professional and institutional specialisation and the absence of an overarching philosophy of child wellbeing" (2000, 1). NGOs may have an overarching philosophy but generally struggle to find coherent objectives and consistent approaches to the protection of children. Peace education provides one approach that moves WV closer to the creation of these coherent objectives.

There are many other compelling reasons why NGOs should be involved in peace education. First, most NGOs endorse the 1989 U.N. Convention on the Rights of the Child (CRC), which states that children have the right to be free from violence and have the right to education. The convention's articles refer to the purpose of education as preparing children for a responsible life, which includes learning how to live peacefully and to have the ability to reduce conflict.

Second, from a child development viewpoint, V. Varma notes in a discussion on emotional abuse that children's developmental needs "span both the need for a good enough parent and the need for place in society where they can work, respect themselves and have access to education, material comfort and freedom. We need to teach children to be more critical and more observant and to criticize and challenge abuses of power and inequalities of opportunity"

(Varma 1997, 21). Peace education has the potential to criticise and challenge abuses in non-violent ways.

Finally, peace education provides a practical tool to support the implementation of child protection policies whereby "plans for rehabilitation of children who have been abused and exploited are developed in the best interests of the child by enhancing and maintaining safety and security, and reducing the risk of further harm" (WVI 2000). Figure 6–1 illustrates the mutually supporting functions of child protection and peace education in the interest of creating a safer and better world for children.

Figure 6–1. A safer world for children

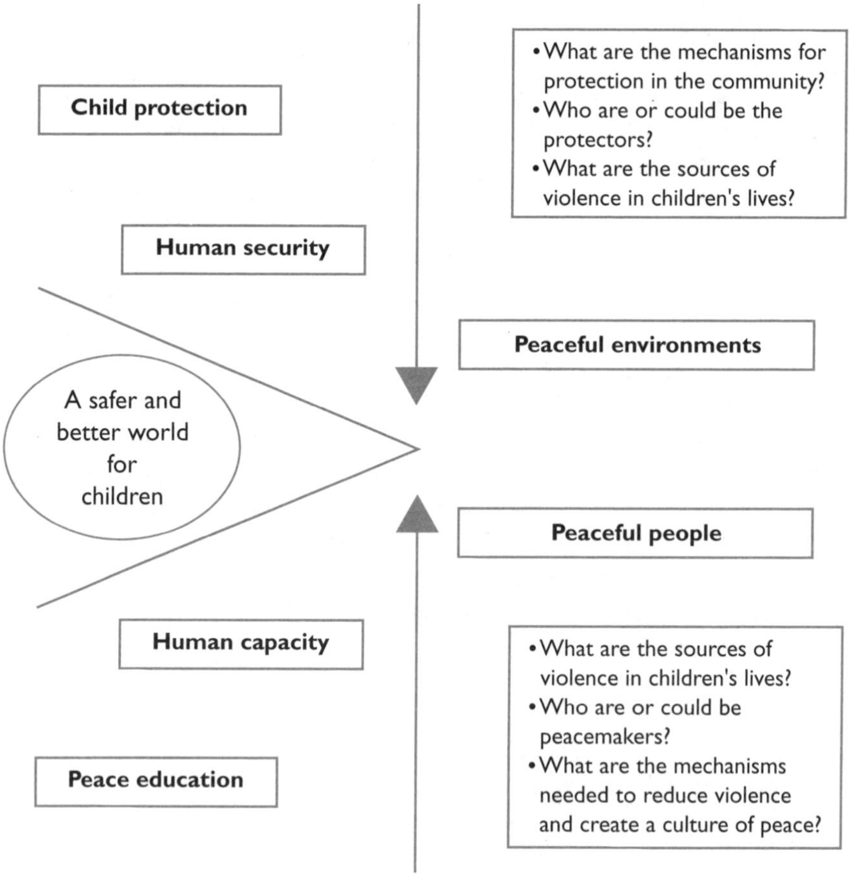

Child protection

- What are the mechanisms for protection in the community?
- Who are or could be the protectors?
- What are the sources of violence in children's lives?

Human security

Peaceful environments

A safer and better world for children

Peaceful people

Human capacity

- What are the sources of violence in children's lives?
- Who are or could be peacemakers?
- What are the mechanisms needed to reduce violence and create a culture of peace?

Peace education

But peace education is not only for child-focused NGOs. The humanitarian imperative compels all NGOs to examine the real impact of violence on their relief and development activities, to consider seriously their role in reducing violence and perhaps to refocus their interventions to find ways to reduce the impact of violence on half the developing world's population – children.

Overview of the paper

This chapter draws on the knowledge and experience of both child protection professionals who have documented research and practice over fifty years and WV experiences in its programmes and responses to violence. These experiences offer peace educators valuable insights into the role peace education programmes might have in effectively responding to violence experienced in the family and community today.

In the "Violence" section below, five children are introduced. They reflect children in many situations in the developing world and are intended to help readers consider the practical realities of peace education for the child in the context of family and community. The chapter considers how peace education might be most effective for them. Each of these children faces different types of violence and lives in very different circumstances.[1]

There are four main sections to this paper. Following the introductory first section is a section that focuses on the child and the impact of violence on a child, with particular attention given to the broader issues of culture, violence and peace in communities. The third section examines the role of peace education in protecting, healing and upholding the rights of children, focusing again on culture but also the main actors who could be involved. The fourth section concludes with summary statements and directions for application. Boxes at the end of each subsection contain key points and/or questions for review and discussion.

Definitions of key concepts

Peace is defined by J. Large as "more than the absence of war, just as health is more than the absence of disease. Peace is a condition is which individuals or groups do no damage to each other and can develop their potential in growth, creative forms of productivity, or change" (1997, 4). Johan Galtung, a world-renowned academic, refers to two aspects of peace: the absence of personal violence, which he calls "negative peace," and the absence of both personal and structural violence, which he calls "positive peace" (in ibid., 4). These are two of many definitions.

Violence also has many definitions. For example, WHO defines violence as 'the intentional use of physical force or power, threatened or actual, against oneself, another person, or against a group or community, that either results in or has the high likelihood of resulting in injury, death, psychological harm, mal-development or deprivation" (1996, 2). The Collins English Dictionary defines *violence* as "an unjust, unwarranted, or unlawful display of force, esp. such as tends to overawe or intimidate."

Child protection means creating safer homes and communities for children who are at risk of violence. This incorporates the broad range of responses to nurture and promote the well-being of children. Responses that reduce the impact of or prevent violence on children are often described in terms of protecting children. Others refer to child protection more narrowly in terms of prevention of abuse, usually in the context of family (Reppucci, Britner and Woolard 1997).

Child sexual abuse is the involvement of a child in sexual activity that he or she does not fully comprehend, is unable to give informed consent to, for which the child is not developmentally prepared and cannot give consent, or that violates the laws or social taboos of society. Child sexual abuse is evidenced by an activity between a child and an adult or another child who by age or development is in a relationship of responsibility, trust or power, the activity being intended to gratify or satisfy the needs of the other person. This may include but is not limited to the inducement or coercion of a child to engage in any unlawful sexual activity, the exploitative use of a child in prostitution or other unlawful sexual practices and the exploitative use of children in pornographic performances and materials.

Physical abuse occurs "when a person purposefully injures or threatens to injure a child or young person. This may take the form of slapping, punching, shaking, kicking, burning, shoving, or grabbing. The injury may take the form of bruises, cuts, burns or fractures" (Child Wise Australia 2001).

Emotional abuse is most frequently used to describe "sustained, repetitive, inappropriate responses to a child's expression of emotion and emotional needs" (Child Wise Australia 2001). F. Briggs and R. Hawkins (1997) refer to the types of behaviour that can constitute emotional abuse. They include rejection of the child; punishing positive, normal social behaviour; lacking or discouraging care giver–infant attachment; discouraging children's self-esteem; punishing and preventing the child from developing interpersonal skills; isolating a child; depriving a child of security; exhibiting indifference to or ignoring a child; corrupting a child; or depriving children of opportunities to develop as individuals.

Neglect is the omission on the part of the care giver to provide for the development of the child in all spheres – health, education, emotional development, nutrition, shelter and safe living conditions. It causes, or has a high probability of causing, harm to the child's health or development. Neglect includes the failure to supervise properly and protect children from harm as much as is feasible.

Peace education refers to "the process of promoting the knowledge, skills, attitudes and values needed to bring about behaviour changes that will enable children, youth and adults to prevent conflict and violence, both overt and structural; to resolve conflict peacefully; and to create the conditions conducive to peace, whether at an intrapersonal, interpersonal, intergroup, national or international level" (Fountain 1999, 7). More simply stated, peace education is the process of learning skills for peaceful living in a structured environment.

Addressing such complex issues in a brief chapter has limitations that need to be mentioned:

1. There is a lack of detailed evaluation of peace education programmes to back up this chapter's claims about the utility and effectiveness of peace education. This limitation enables us to reflect only on what is known about violence, reduction of violence, and the healing of the survivors of violence and to compare that with the curriculum available. It highlights areas that need to be evaluated in the future.

2. Statistics and studies on violence have generally been completed in Western environments with limited consideration to the wide variety of cultural, social, economic and political differences that exist among and within different communities in the world. Therefore, not all findings from research are relevant for all situations. On the other hand, this research cannot be considered to have no relevance whatsoever for developing countries. In fact, some of the research findings could provide developing countries with opportunities to rediscover the existing strengths in their culture and avoid some of the mistakes made by Western countries. They may also provide alternative models that are very relevant for the new global world in which we live.

3. The broad range of contexts in which NGOs work around the world, from community development programmes in rural and urban settings, to CEDC projects, to emergency programmes, makes it difficult to give specific recommendations.

4. As this chapter examines each issue in detail, there is no doubt that new questions will arise. This chapter cannot cover such complex issues of

poverty, gender, the media, religion and violence in depth without leaving unanswered questions. Nevertheless, there is an attempt to provide a context and highlight some key areas for further consideration in the development of effective peace education programmes.

VIOLENCE

Violence and the child

In order to illustrate the situations facing children around the globe, this section introduces five children and their experience of violence. The following sections illustrate the impact of violence on their lives and the role parents and other key actors in their lives could play through a peace education programme.

Joff, a 9-year-old boy, loves school and has been participating in peace education class for the past three weeks. But things on the farm are not going well. The crops are bad this year, and there is not enough food to eat. Joff's father tells him he will have to work on a neighbour's farm to supplement the family food supplies. Joff desperately wants to attend school, but when he and his mother question his father's decision, he beats them severely.

Manta, a 12-year-old girl, is sitting in class. Her mind is not on the teacher or her studies but on what happened to her at home the night before. She feels sick to her stomach and is trying to decide what she will do. A new lesson begins. The topic is peace education. With her mind on her abuse, she misses the instructions the teacher gives. This is not the first time. Her teacher tells her in no uncertain words to stop daydreaming and to pay attention.

Senti is 7 years old. She is the middle of four children. Her older sister died in a house fire two years ago, and her father was killed in the cross-border conflict that has been going on for 10 years. Senti does not attend school regularly and often cares for her 2-year-old brother. She is supervised by her older brother, Reyi. Sometimes she does work for neighbours to earn some food, but it is tough to care for children for little reward. She is often told she is like her mother: useless. Her mother began working as a commercial sex worker three years ago, after increasing political violence forced the factory where she worked to close down. Recently, Senti's mother died after a long illness. There have been aunts and uncles who have died in the few years too. One uncle drops in from time to time, but he appears more interested in the house than the children. He does not listen to their problems but talks about his problems. Senti often acts like a little mother. She does not have friends her age, but she acts very adult with men who visit the house.

The older boy in Senti's family is Reyi. He is 13 years old and spends a lot of his time on the streets in a nearby town. He is not interested in school. He hangs out with his friends. They have a system where one of his friends distracts a person who appears wealthy while Reyi robs the person. He does this partly for fun and partly to earn some money to help the family. He is experiencing peer pressure to become more involved in criminal activity.

Pris is a 3-year-old girl. She has three older sister and no brothers. Her father works away from home, so he can come home only every three months. He provides the family with enough money to feed and educate the children. Pris's mother had not wanted any more children when she became pregnant with Pris, but she decided that if she had a boy, then maybe her husband would be pleased. When Pris was born, her mother was very disappointed. Pris did not breastfeed well and cried a lot. Her mother started to drink to cope with her fussy baby and fell into drunken stupors frequently. This often led her to beat the children, particularly Pris. There is no extended family in the area, and when Pris's father is home her mother's behaviour changes.

The types of violence children face

These children are survivors of three main types of violence: (1) interpersonal violence both within the family and within the community; (2) collective violence between social/political/ethnic groups; and (3) structural violence.

Interpersonal violence

Children begin to understand peace in the home and in their relationships with parents and siblings. It is in the home that children first learn about appreciating themselves and others, about co-operation and communication. Unfortunately, home for many children is a place where stress and violence is the norm, where the word *love* is used to justify acts that crush self-esteem, where co-operation is another word for coercion, and where secrecy abounds and truth is avoided.

Accurate global statistics on familial abuse are impossible to obtain due to the diversity of contexts and cultures. However, an estimated 57,000 children were victims of homicide in the year 2000, which implies that the numbers of survivors must be significantly higher. In addition, available data suggests that about 20 per cent of women and 5–10 per cent of men suffered sexual abuse as children (WHO 2002). In sub-Saharan Africa between 40 per cent and 80 per cent of women report verbal and physical abuse, with 46 per cent reporting abuse in the presence of their children (Advocates for Youth 1997). There is evidence that children who witness domestic violence also contribute to the cycle of violence, and so the statistics are very concerning (Varma 1997, 112).

Children who are neglected by their primary care giver face significant challenges for their future. According to R. Karr-Morse and M. Wiley:

> The foundation of empathy is laid from the beginning. When the early months of an infant's experience include consistent, sensitive interactions in which the care giver accurately assesses the child's needs and responds quickly in a soothing manner, and when a child's sadness or joy is mirrored in the face of the parent the child experiences comfort and trust with the care giver. But when the baby instead experiences unpredictable or dissonant emotions from a key adult, or no response, or a harsh overwhelming response to efforts to engage the adult, the attachment to the care giver may be characterized by distrust, fear, or a disorganized combination of conflict feelings. (Karr-Morse and Wiley 1997, 189)

WV's child abuse and neglect study highlights the level of violence in the family. The study was carried out in 10 Area Development Programs (ADPs) in five countries and four continents. In all communities taking part in the study (apart from Romania) more than 60 per cent, and up to 80 per cent, of respondents (care givers) said child abuse was a serious problem. Over 70 per cent of respondents regularly use hitting with the hand or a stick or a belt as a primary means of discipline. More severe methods were used in some of the study countries with great frequency. In addition, men were reported to be abusive to both their wives and their children, and alcohol is seen as a major contributor to this behaviour (Dorning 2002).

Most development practitioners and community members agree that the level of interpersonal violence in families and communities is too high and must be reduced.

Collective violence

The concept of collective violence was initially described in the 1930s. It refers to the behaviour of groups, such as the youth gangs dedicated to vandalism, drugs and extreme violence in the cities of Guatemala (WVI 2002b, 42). Collective violence also reflects the many conflicts that devastate lives around the world in Sudan, Sri Lanka, Democratic Republic of Congo, Burundi, Colombia, West Bank and Gaza. Collective violence tends to escalate in rapidly changing societies and is particularly affected by the urbanisation process. The issues of urbanisation will be discussed also in relation to changing culture and inter-generational violence. Another example of collective violence is situations of armed conflict. Where children are devastated by armed conflict and/ or recruited into armed forces, the physical, psychosocial and spiritual damage is significant.

Structural violence

"The term *structural violence* is used when damage to an individual or group occurs because of an unequal distribution of resources (or access to them) in a given society. . . . For structural violence to exist, damaging inequalities are the result of relations between groups" (Large 1997, 1).

Deborah DuNann Winter and Dana Leighton explain further why perhaps we identify interpersonal and collective violence more easily: "Direct violence is horrific, but its brutality usually gets our attention: we notice it, and often respond to it. Structural violence, however, is almost always invisible, embedded in ubiquitous social structures, normalised by stable institutions and regular experience. Structural violence occurs whenever people are disadvantaged by political, legal, economic or cultural traditions. Because they are longstanding, structural inequities usually seem ordinary, the way things are and always have been." (DuNann Winter and Leighton 1999, 1).

There is a relationship among the three types of violence. "Structural violence is problematic in and of itself, but it is also dangerous because it frequently leads to direct violence. Those who are chronically oppressed are often, for logical reasons, those who resort to direct violence" (DuNann Winter and Leighton 1999, 1).

The types of violence faced by Joff, Manta, Reyi, Senti and Pris can be categorised as:

- interpersonal violence
  domestic violence - Joff
  sexual violence within the family – Manta and possibly Senti
  emotional abuse and exploitative labour by community members -Senti
  neglect – Pris, Senti
- collective violence
  armed conflict with the threat of expansion – Reyi, Senti
  gang violence – physical and emotional violence and potentially sexual –
  Reyi (victim and perpetrator)
- structural violence
  inequality in economic, political, education, legal and cultural structures
  that seriously disadvantage these children and increase the potential levels of other types of violence – Senti, Manta, Joff, Reyi.

KEY POINTS
Children face three types of violence:
- interpersonal (physical, emotional, sexual; neglect)
- collective (physical, emotional, sexual)
- structural (economic, political, legal)

The impact of violence on children

What may be observed

Children who are survivors of violent acts experience, to various degrees, the interruption of normal child development – physical, intellectual, social, psychological and spiritual. The effects of violence on a child depend on the type of violence, the developmental age at which the child is exposed to the violence and the duration of the violence. Violence may result in a few or many of the signs and symptoms[2] noted below:

- *psychological signs and impact on ability to think:* low self-esteem, sadness, depression, anger, hyper-vigilance, withdrawal, poor concentration, anxiety, numbness, overwhelming tiredness
- *social impact:* hyperactivity, opposition or defiance, social isolation, pseudo-mature behaviour, involvement in gangs, runaway, avoidance of places or people, sexual exploitation, risk-taking behaviours, poor relationships
- *physical impact:* broken bones, gun-shot wounds, severe bruises, hearing loss, blindness, brain damage, landmine injuries, burns, vague physical health symptoms, sleep problems, self-mutilation, sexually transmitted diseases, unwanted pregnancy, abortion, alcohol and drug abuse, suicide, a child becoming the mother of a child
- *spiritual impact:* questioning, confusion, anger

Among the five children introduced above, we can observe a number of these signs and symptoms of violence.

Sexual abuse: Sexual abuse survivors, like Manta, could probably relate to the statement expressed by a therapist, "Feeling dirty becomes part of her character rather than the response to an event that happened to her" (Sands 1999, 40). Manta is showing some of the symptoms above. She is not concentrating at school, she is distracted, and she is anxious. Senti also is showing some of the symptoms that raise concerns about possible sexual abuse.

Emotional abuse: Senti, a child who has to cope with the grief of losing parents, is also a survivor of emotional abuse. She may reach the point where she is extremely sad and feels she is not coping as she tries to fulfil the role of mother. At times she may also be angry at her world. She is not able to enjoy her childhood, and the combination of many factors could lead her to abuse the children for whom she is responsible.

Manta probably worries about contracting diseases or becoming pregnant because she is so vulnerable in her community and may face early marriage.

As an adolescent, Reyi seeks to attach himself to his peers and the older teenage boys from whom he seeks affirmation. His main source of socialisation is a criminal group, where he has access to small arms and is at risk of being recruited into a militia group. Like his sister, Senti, he too is grieving the loss of his parents. Significant and unresolved loss may be a precursor for later violence (Varma 1997, 78). Reyi is not experiencing healthy social development and is the child most likely to be violent, unemployed for a long time or be killed before he reaches adulthood.

Physical abuse: Joff is challenging authority. He may have bruises from his beating, and if he is regularly beaten, he may suffer long-term effects. The symptoms, however, particularly psychological ones, may not be obvious to those around him.

Neglect: Pris and Senti both have experienced neglect. No adult has given attention to their basic need for sustained care. Pris has not formed a strong attachment to her mother, and Senti has had to take an adult role, violating her right to play, to be educated and to socialise with peers.

Violence and a child's development

Violence is bad for the development of a child's brain. "It has been shown that there are considerable changes in brain structure and function in association with both the traumatic abuse and severe neglect" (ISPCAN 2001).

Brain development is at its peak in the foetal stage and the first few years of life. The importance of this information is that peace education will have significant limitations if children with potential for violence are not provided with appropriate guidance and support when they are young. Waiting until they are school age will be too late for the most effective violence prevention.

"There is strong evidence that conduct disorders at preschool age predict similar disorders in middle childhood. Additional studies have confirmed that where such behaviors are strongly in place in grade school . . . approximately 80% of children go on to delinquency, adult crime and alcohol abuse" (Karr-Morse and Wiley 1997, 111).[3]

To explain in more technical terms the actual effect on the brain B. Perry explains:

> Exposure to violence activates a set of threat-responses in the child's developing brain; in turn, excess activation of the neural systems involved in the threat responses can alter the developing brain; finally, these alterations may manifest as functional changes in emotional, behavioral and cognitive functioning. The roots of violence-related problems, therefore, can be found in the adaptive responses to threat present during the violent experiences. The specific changes in neurodevelopment and function will depend upon the child's response to the threat, the specific nature of the violent experience(s) and a host of factors associated with the child, their family and community. (Perry 2005; see Perry and Azad 1999)

KEY POINTS
- Violence can affect the developing brain permanently.
- The long-term impact will depend on many issues related to the violent act(s).

Q. How does this knowledge about brain development and violence impact our expectations of peace education?
What other activities/programmes need to be included in addition to peace education for peace to be a reality in a community?

Impact of violence on the education of a child

When considering the impact of violence on the education of children, we need only look at the list of possible signs and symptoms to realise that if a child attending school has many or even a few of these symptoms then his or her education will be affected.

Manta is a good example of how a survivor of violence may have difficulty at school. School actually has the potential to make her situation worse. While she is at school she is focused on what has happened at home. She is not able to concentrate and is often chastised by her teacher. Children in her situation generally have poor self-esteem, and they tend to isolate themselves from others. Their vulnerability can increase the amount of teasing and bullying at or on the way to school. The other impact that sexual abuse can have on girls is that their self-loathing can lead to promiscuous behaviour and has all sorts of potential unhealthy consequences. It often results in poor attendance at school and other unhealthy coping mechanisms. Further, physical punishment by teachers usually is condoned by parents, which suggests that children who are survivors of violence at home may be abused again at school. This results in increased difficulties at school.

The impact of violence on children out of school

Children who are not in school are affected by their environment and often learn new skills. These are not usually the skills that promote healthy living. Research from Casa Aliansa, a street-children's NGO, highlights one of the reasons why children take to the streets: abuse in the home. Once on the streets, Human Rights Watch points out, they are vulnerable to further abuse from police, criminals, and other adults who should protect them.

M. Straus (2001), J. Garbarino (1999) and K. Browne (Browne et al. 2002) indicate that children who are survivors of child abuse have higher levels of violence as they develop. In addition, they are also more likely to become involved in criminal activity, and they often enter the juvenile justice system.

But street children represent only one group of children out of school. What is the impact of violence on other children who are not in school? The first point here is that often children who are out of school are further isolated from their peers. This places them in even more vulnerable situations, or they become connected to a peer group that is rejected or marginalised from the general community.

Most children report their abuse to their peers. This may be difficult for children who are at home caring for family members or are orphans being moved around the extended family (Parton and Wattam 1999, 73). Family stress due to poverty can increase levels of violence, and if the child is working around the abuser(s) all day and not having a break at school, he or she is at even higher risk of abuse and exploitation (Browne et al. 2002).

Children who live in institutions cannot escape violence if the abuser is a worker in the centre or if the centre does not create a space where "telling" in a situation of abuse is nurtured. The institution is their home. Normally, links with family have been broken. Where would they run? Most institutions are isolated units where outside social and cultural contacts for the child are weak (Tolfree 1995). Some anecdotal evidence also suggests that street children and children not in school are at higher risk of being recruited into fighting forces.[4]

Children with disabilities are at higher risk of all forms of abuse and often are not in school. A World Bank report states that "disability may be the single most important factor excluding children from schooling" (World Bank 2003). If they *are* in school, many times it is a residential school, which often elevates the risk of abuse (Tolfree 1995). Sadly, the placement of children in institutions often leads to further social and psychological developmental delays. Children with disabilities are also often excluded from cultural, social and education opportunities. Those with more severe disabilities, who are unable to communicate verbally, have no voice to speak about their violence and are often dehumanised by community members. Romania is the most widely known example of this type of abuse. All these reasons create a strong rationale for concentrating efforts for the protection of children and empowerment out of the school setting in order to reach the most vulnerable.

KEY POINTS
- Children affected by violence are less likely to succeed at school, more at risk of absenteeism, and anti social behaviour in the school setting.
- Abused children are likely to be further impacted by the condoning of physical punishment in schools.
- Children out of school are more vulnerable to the effects of violence.

Culture and violence

Introduction

John Bodley uses the term *culture* to refer "collectively to a society and its way of life or in reference to human culture as a whole" (Bodley 1994). In general, culture is defined around the theme of the distinctive practices and beliefs of a society.

Many cultural practices can be extremely positive, such as the care of a child by the extended family; the role of the elders; non-violent practices for entry into adult life (rites of passage), in which adolescents are taught about the history of the tribe, skills for living and being an adult in a particular community; the use of traditional herbs for healing; and some of the cleansing ceremonies. The cause of violence is often couched within a cultural understanding, and this is important to understand in the context of violence against children and peace.

While there are many positive cultural practices, there are certain harmful cultural practices that are violent in nature such as female genital cutting and, indirectly, early marriage. Another negative cultural norm holds that children "must be seen and not heard," which renders children who are in situations of potential or actual abuse very vulnerable. This practice empowers the abuser and not the survivor of the abuse – the child.

A community's proverbs about children are an interesting indicator of how it views them. In WV child protection workshops discussion about the participation of children starts with the question of how to define *child*. Participants raise issues about whether a child is an incomplete adult, a dependent person or someone who is innocent. All these definitions and others indicate the cultural norms that influence how these adults relate to children. As one thoughtful colleague asked, "Why do we define an adult hitting an adult as assault, but an adult hitting a child as discipline?"

The culture of celebrations, while strongly linked with food, unfortunately is also strongly linked with alcohol. WHO has alerted readers of their report to the high levels of alcoholism in Latin America, and especially Ecuador. The reasons include recent economic crises coupled with local cultural traditions encouraging the consumption of alcohol during celebrations. This behaviour, however, can be changed. in Ecuador the Inti Raimi celebration, involving rites, ceremonies, dances and intense alcohol use, was challenged and the event became alcohol free in 2003. Alcohol use resulting in violence is well documented. One can only imagine how many children are victims of violence as a result of this and other "celebrations."

Also in 2003 the *Washington Post* reported about "Liberia's rebel fighters, clutching AK-47 assault rifles, New Testaments and the belief that the rubber bands in their hair signal possession by demons." This is another indication of how beliefs influence a society's views of violence. Consequently, a peace education programme must address directly these cultural beliefs.

The culture of "not telling" is evident in many societies where sexuality is simply not discussed, leaving children who are survivors of sexual abuse more at risk. "Telling" an appropriate person who will be supportive and provide protection is critical. N. Parton and C. Wattam discuss this in detail in *Child Sexual Abuse*.

Some cultural practices are more dominant in certain regions of the world than others. For example, while the WV publication on violence in Latin America and the Caribbean highlights the wide variety of violence, it also points out the violence of sexism and patriarchy that is reflected in the region and places priority on addressing *machismo* in the prevention of violence. While the issues of gender are global, *machismo* has particular relevance in Latin America (WVI 2002b).

Culture is not static; it changes. The impact of armed conflict in Central and East Africa is affected by cultural practices as well as having an impact on culture. For example, the intense tribalism that exists in Democratic Republic of Congo is used to manipulate the population and has enabled the recruitment of children to take up arms and fight. Convincing children to take certain drugs or to drink specific water to give them strength or to protect them from bullets endangers children's well-being.

Conflict forces women to take on traditional male roles, as it did in the West after World War II. Men return to find their role in society changed. Trying to fit back in is difficult and increases stress. It increases in many cases the already existing problems of alcohol-related violence.

With many deaths due to disease (often as a result of structural violence) or conflict, men and women remarry, creating new step-parent relationships. It is documented in the West and is anecdotally reinforced in developing countries that step-relationships increase the likelihood of abuse and exploitation (Browne et al. 2002). The large number of fatherless households reduces the possibility for girls and boys in such families to form a positive male attachment and have readily available male role models.

Cultural practices of the extended family taking in children who are orphaned is a healthy traditional protective practice. With the large numbers of orphans and vulnerable children as a result of HIV/AIDS in Asia and Africa, this cultural practice and coping mechanism is breaking down and placing children in situations of violence, exploitation, early marriage and abuse.

Changing culture has the potential for good or bad, depending on perspective. For example, the Internet is a wonderful tool that can be used to provide educational opportunities. However, the negative side to the Internet culture is the escalation of and easy access to child pornography as well as much easier access for pedophiles to children previously isolated from such practices.

Referring to our earlier definitions of peace and child protection, the decisions about which particular cultural practices are encouraged surely must be based on the nurturing qualities of the practice that support the healthy development of the child.

KEY POINTS

- Cultural norms can increase or mitigate violence. A positive nurturing culture that supports the well-being of children should be encouraged.
- Cultures are not static, and changes are not always for good.

Q. What cultural practices in your community positively contribute to protecting children from violence?

The individual and the group

The culture of the individual versus the culture of the group is an interesting one. While there are many exceptions to the rule, in general Western societies highlight the rights and the well-being of the individual, whereas in many indigenous societies around the world social cohesion or the interests of the group (extended family, clan or village) override the individual rights. The needs of an individual, such as a child who has been badly abused within the family, may be of less value than the need of the family to stay together. The needs for honour in the community will result in silence about the abuse of a child. Contributing to this are the "socially organized rules attached to the exchange of information" (Parton and Wattam 1999, 73). A child well-being perspective would state that the culture of "not telling" is unhealthy.

In terms of collective violence, violence against one of the group is viewed as violence against all of the group. For example, in Kosovo in 2000, being a Serb or an Albanian was the deciding factor in whether a person was a friend or an enemy. The social pressure was such that individual positive experiences of inter-ethnic caring did not override the collective damage to the group.

In Bolivia three indigenous groups have had a long history of violent clashes over land and property. WV's *Faces of Violence in Latin American and the Caribbean* recounts the story of one child who experienced this violence. The child's words highlight the issue of the individual versus the group: "The Laimes [one of the tribal groups] killed my mother, my father and my grandparents. . . . I don't understand why they're always fighting. . . . The elders say it has always been this way, so we have, to be brave and if they attack, we attack back, to make them regret it" (WVI 2002b, 78).

KEY POINTS
- A cultural understanding of the individual and the group affects the levels and continuation of violence.

Q. In what situations in your community does the individual good versus the good of the community affect issues of violence to children?

Inter-generational differences in culture

In addition to other links between violence and culture, inter-generational differences often exist and are sometimes a source of violence in the home and the community. This is particularly of concern with the increase in urbanisation. The family support systems tend to break down, and a clash of cultures between the old rural life and the new life in the city increases family tensions, especially during the adolescent phase. An example of the effect of inter-generational differences is in the immigrant Pacific Island community in New Zealand. At home, children are expected "to be seen and not heard," while at school the same children are taught to challenge and to question ideas. If a child comes home from school and is unable to make the shift to the home culture and challenges authority there, he or she is often physically punished.

The same situation arises when children and youth are sent to cities from rural areas for educational opportunities. They often come home with new ideas, practices and beliefs that clash with the beliefs and practices of their parents and elders. This can lead to an increase in stress and tension that in turn leads to physical and emotional abuse.

KEY POINTS
- Inter-generational differences in the context of changing cultures can increase violence.

Q. What particular inter-generational issues exist in your communities and how might peace education address them?

Culture, poverty and violence

Poverty is highlighted as a cause of violence by many researchers and practitioners (see, e.g., WHO 2002). Browne et al., in reference to the prediction of abuse, note that "several studies have indicated that the prevalence and severity of child maltreatment are correlated with poverty related stressors, such as unemployment, overcrowded housing, geographic mobility, low levels of parental education, large family size, poor child spacing, and single parenting" (2002, 226). Families who have no food will sometimes send their girls to wealthy men who will give money for sex, a practice highlighted in the 2002 UNHCR/ Save the Children Fund–UK report on sexual exploitation in West Africa. Or young girls are targeted for early marriage in order to provide a dowry for their family. The lack of good nutrition affects the development of the brain, creating the possibility that a child may be developmentally delayed and thus more at risk of abuse (Daniel, Wassel and Gilligan 1999). The breakdown of extended family supports due to unemployment and other factors results in increasing mobility of family members, placing children more at risk of violence. Children who live below the poverty line often cannot attend school regularly, if at all.

Gabriel Garcia Marques also refers to the stress factors of poverty: "Our history of violence is a dynamic of our ongoing war against adversity. Perhaps we have been perverted by a system that urges us to try and live like the rich, while 40 per cent of the population lives in misery" (in WVI 2002a).

KEY POINTS
- Poverty is a significant factor in violence towards children. The social and economic impacts of poverty increase stress.
- Survival needs and lack of education override protection needs.

Q. How does economic hardship contribute to violence in the families in your community?

Gender-based violence

The majority of perpetrators of violence are men. The UNHCR emphasises that in refugee situations "unaccompanied women, lone female heads of households, unaccompanied children, children in foster care and those in detention or detention like arrangements [both male and female]" are most likely to be victims of sexual violence (1995, 2). Children with disabilities are also at serious risk for the reasons discussed above.

Boys have been ignored as victims of violence, particularly sexual violence (Dorais 2002). Most discussion and research around issues of sexual abuse are focused on girls, and, while the impact on girls is significant, sexual violence by men against boys is believed to be significantly underreported. The cultural and media pressure that reinforces the notion that "big boys don't cry" makes reporting abuse even more difficult for boys than for girls. Boys who are victims of sexual abuse can struggle with their sexuality; they wonder if they may be homosexual or bisexual, because, as with girls, there may be aspects of the abusive relationship which are not completely negative (Dorais 2003).[5]

Discussions about child soldiers tend to focus on boys; often the impact on girls as child soldiers is ignored. Girls associated with fighting forces are often the "wives" of soldiers, some of whom have multiple partners, placing the girls at high risk of STDs and unwanted pregnancies. This is in addition to the psychological and social impacts on such girls. It is important, therefore, to be inclusive as we describe particular types of gender-related violence.

Girls and boys also view the impact violence has on the opposite sex differently. For example, in a recent community discussion in Somalia, young women ranked verbal abuse, physical assault, and rape as their three major concerns, whereas young men did not put these issues on their list of concerns at all! While this was a small sample, it does indicate gender differences and the need to consider them in any peace education curriculum.

Finally, a practical reality for girls throughout the developing world is that they are less likely to be sent to school. The reasons may be religious, social or economic. If peace education programmes focus on schools alone, then in certain societies most girls will not benefit.

KEY POINTS
- Gender is a significant issue in violence.
- It is important to be gender inclusive when referring to types of violence (for example, boys are victims of sexual violence, but most sexual-violence programmes are focused on girls, leaving boys marginalised).
- Girls are less likely to attend school.
- Girls are more vulnerable than boys in many situations.

Q. How have the needs of children who are sexually abused – both boys and girls – been acknowledged in your community?

Religion, violence and spiritual development

When considering the impact of violence on the spiritual development of a child, there is a paucity of literature; in general, the impact of this type of violence is also poorly understood. Perhaps one area where there is relatively more literature is with survivors of incest (sexual abuse within the family) who express their difficulty in responding to the idea of God as a loving father (Sands 1999, 56). Their experience of "love" is linked with violence, and the concept of a loving father is not one to which they are naturally drawn. This issue is captured well in psychiatrist Leonard Shengold's book entitled *Soul Murder* (1989). While this notion may create theological debate, it certainly highlights the depths to which the soul of a child is plunged when the child is abused. This should never be underestimated.

When violence occurs in the context of religious institutions and spiritual or religious teachings, one can speak of spiritual violence. The concept is not well defined, but it addresses violence that results in the child's spirit being damaged.

It affects how children view themselves and the world, and in many cases, how they come to understand spirituality.

An example of spiritual violence is the expulsion from the church of an unmarried young girl who has become pregnant. This damages the girl's spirit and is an emotional form of violence. Another example is extensive beating of a child justified as an appropriation of the biblical teaching to "spare the rod, spoil the child," when in reality the child is being beaten because the adult cannot control his or her anger. In the same way, a child may observe a mother being abused because the father says he is the "head of the household" and thus women must obey him in all things. Enticing children to commit acts of violence, even to kill because of religious beliefs, is another form of spiritual violence.

These situations are often explained as an integral part of culture, and acts of violence are justified as obeying the teachings of the faith. J. Garbarino explains this type of violence: "The emotions of children are manipulated in such a way that children feel incredible pressure to adhere to certain rituals which they may not feel comfortable with and where rationalization for injustice and abuse creates confusion" (1999).

Alternatively, it has been argued that some children can be sustained by their beliefs. S. Vanistendael reports that children who have discovered meaning in life are more likely to be resilient than children who have not (1995). Robert Coles has written a number of books related to the development of children. A children's story he wrote about Ruby Bridges highlights the positive influence spiritual beliefs can have when children face violence. Ruby was one of the first African American girls to be integrated into a multiracial school system. She was verbally and emotionally abused by adults and her classmates. But she was able to remain strong because of her faith and her supportive family (Coles 1995).[6] She was a true model for peace.

Child-protection professionals infrequently refer to the role of religion and spiritual beliefs. However, James Garbarino, because of his experience with extremely violent adolescent boys, some of whom have been convicted of brutal murders, refers to research linking religious and spiritual experience to adolescent behaviour and development. He has found that a religious or spiritual experience may buffer children from the cultural and social poisons of modern life (Garbarino 1999, 143). He writes: "When spiritually grounded and supportive rather than punitive, religion can make a big difference, particularly in adolescence" (ibid., 155). Garbarino also points out that the environment for this religious experience must be caring, not punitive. This can assist in the creation of a spiritual anchor as part of the positive behaviour changes encouraged in these violent youths. It is important to note here that these spiritual experiences are only a *buffer;* they do not protect the child completely from the impact of violence.

KEY POINTS
- Violence can affect all areas of a child's development, physical, emotional, social, intellectual/cognitive and spiritual.
- The long-term impact of violence depends on many issues related to the violent act(s).
- Inconsistency between deeply held religious beliefs that condone violence while at the same time promoting non-violence is very confusing for children.

Q. In what ways is the spiritual development of children affected by violence?
In what ways could a peace education process be a tool to reduce the impact of spiritual violence?

PEACE EDUCATION AND CHILDREN
IN THE CONTEXT OF FAMILY AND COMMUNITY

The child

Potential for peace education to strengthen children

Often we cannot remove children from situations of adversity. In the past decade discussions amongst child workers in the humanitarian field have focused on building stronger children, that is, building resilience. Studies on resilience have identified some key issues related to "the capacity to do well when faced with difficult circumstances" (Vanistendael 1995, 2), and peace education appears to offer a perfect "space" in which such skills can be taught and supported. Vanistendael identifies five building blocks for resilience:

- social support
- capacity to discover meaning in life – this is related to the spiritual life and religion
- skills and a sense of having control over what happens in life
- self-esteem
- sense of humour

Three of these form the basis of most peace education curricula, which aim to build self-esteem, create social support and enable children to find skills which will allow them to have a sense of control over their lives. Creating opportunities for laughter and learning to laugh are also found in the creative learning environment of peace education. The capacity to discover meaning in life is less tangibly visible in peace education, but the open learning environment certainly allows for discussion of this issue. Even if peace education does not have an immediate effect on levels of violence, children develop skills that help them be stronger in the difficult situations they face now and will face in the future.

In their paper on resilience J. Boyden and G. Mann identify the participation of children and the ability to solve problems as two additional factors in building stronger children (2000). These insights offer opportunities for the formation of peace education programmes. The ability to solve problems is very important in assisting children (and adults) to find non-violent solutions when conflict arises. Formal education systems in many countries tend to be very authoritarian and oriented toward imparting information and data. Such education does not prepare children well for adapting to new situations. The changing world in which children live and the conflict situations they face vary so much that children need to be able to adapt. If the learning environment has encouraged discovery, practical application of skills and making mistakes as learning opportunities, children will be better problem solvers and more flexible. While personality, family situation and genetics play a part in resilience, opportunities exist to strengthen all children to varying degrees. "Resilience however is not absolute; some settings can overwhelm human capacities" (Garbarino 1999, 116). Caution is required to ensure that children are not overwhelmed by events and that children who are resilient over a long period of time do not develop unhealthy coping mechanisms.

A focus on strengthening children must be combined with advocacy to change the situation for the child.

KEY POINTS
- Peace education can assist in strengthening children to face situations of adversity.
- Humour is a building block of resilience in children, so fun as a part of the peace education curriculum makes sense.

Q. How can humour be introduced that is uplifting for all and is also culturally sensitive?

Potential for peace education to contribute to healing

V. Varma states that "even though most writers about war consider it to be 'normal' it is time to reconsider the myth and realise that few, if any, children experience war without some psychological residual effects" (Varma 1997, 21). We could say the same about children who face other forms of violence. Children can definitely learn skills to reduce some types of violence. They can, for instance, learn to scream for help when someone is touching them inappropriately and they can learn to advocate for change as a group. But what happens when prevention does not work, and they are left to survive abuse and violence on their own? What do we know about their healing process after the act(s) of violence or while they are in the midst of violence?

The process of psychological and social healing is not as visible as physical healing. Peace education could provide a setting where healing can be supported. For example, the Interagency Working Group on Psycho-social Care of Children wrote in 2003 that children affected by violence often

- need to feel safe (the term *feel* is important here)
- need positive adult support
- need opportunities for play
- need a routine in their lives
- need to regain a sense of control in their lives

Peace education programmes that are facilitated in the same safe place on a regular basis, that encourage play, that provide the nurturing support of adults, and that actively involve children meet the essentials of a good psychosocial activity. They do not exclude the need, in some cases, for specialist support for victims of violence.

The situation at school or in the community could be a positive and healing experience, with peace education offering specific skills for coping that will assist Manta or others like her. The foundation of many peace education programmes is recognising the dignity of each person and empowering children (Miller 2002). Manta needs to hear that she has dignity. She also would benefit from having relationships with her peers strengthened, and many peace education programmes highlight trust building and strengthening social skills. Over time, these skills may help her speak out to someone she trusts about the abuse she is experiencing, usually a peer (Parton and Wattam 1999, 73). Trusting relationships is a critical factor in preventing child abuse and healing the abused.

KEY POINTS
- Peace education can be effective for the psychological and social healing of a child survivor of violence if it is facilitated in a place/space that is felt to be safe by the participants.

Q. How safe are children at or on their way to school in your community?

Peace education giving a voice to children

Children have amazing capacities and abilities that are not always recognised by adults. Since the introduction of the CRC in 1989, child participation – also called giving a voice to children – has been highlighted in the international child and development community as a key success factor for effective development.

The participation of children in the design of peace education programmes is not highlighted in any research. However, WV encourages involving children in the formation of peace education curricula, believing that those who are affected directly have the greatest credibility on an issue." A. James and A. Prout state: "The predominant (Western) discourse of the notion of childhood sees children as 'adults in training' and, therefore, not totally capable of informed thought or decision-making. . . . Children must be seen as active participants in the construction of their own social lives, not passive subjects of social structures and processes" (1997, 8).

There are several key challenges. One is identifying what children are capable of doing at any given period in their lives in relation to the social and cultural contexts in which they live. Another is recognising that children, like adults, must not be treated as a homogenous group; they reflect the diversity of the population, particularly children who are marginalised. WV supports the argument for participation by children: "Children are considered active participants whose hopes and aspirations are respected" (WV 2000, 2.4). Child participation is a new and emerging field, in which WV is involved, and there is still much to learn, but this does not discount the argument that the participation of girls and boys in peace education development, implementation and evaluation is non-negotiable.

KEY POINTS
- Children's participation in the design, monitoring and evaluation of peace education programmes will enhance the quality of programmes offered.

- Inclusion of marginalised children is critical.

Q. How open would your community be to the participation of girls
   and boys in the development of your peace education curriculum?
   How do you ensure child participation does not become an
   excuse for adults to neglect their roles as role models, mentors
   and parents?

The role of the family and peace education

In families where there has been abuse, both the abusive and the non-abusive
parent are frequently depressed, have substance-abuse disorders or have anti-
social personality characteristics (Browne et al. 2002). Research conducted
in WV projects in Rwanda (war affected) and Uganda (HIV/AIDs affected)
found that over 20 per cent of care givers in both countries were suffering
from what the developed world would call clinical depression (Bolton and
Ndogoni 2000). These parents were unable to function effectively in their
day-to-day tasks, including caring for their children. Thus, there is a need to
address family issues and not just the child in isolation. Unfortunately, these
parents are least likely to be involved in community gatherings, especially
school PTAs.

As children learn skills for peaceful living, they will come up against many
cultural and other barriers that may disappoint them and overwhelm them.
Consequently, all children need the support of adults, preferably family members. Research supports a focus on parent education to allow parents to learn
more about child development and, in particular, non-violent forms of discipline, which are critical to reduce the levels of family violence (Janko 1994;
Dorning 2002; Varma 1997). Research on brain development also suggests that
early intervention and support of parents in positive child-rearing are critical.
The challenge will be to find ways for these parents to be supported in a parallel process as their children learn skills for peaceful living.

Parents also have primary responsibility for their children and therefore have
a right to be actively involved in the education of their children (UN 1989, Art.
18).

Caution is necessary, however, not to have too narrow a definition of *parent;*
children take a parenting role for siblings, grandparents are parents to their
grandchildren and neighbours or members of the extended family take on

parenting roles. One child development specialist recommends that all members of the family be involved in a parenting programme (Janko 1994, 38). This again argues for involving the wider range of care givers that children in developing countries often have in peace education.

One concept that is associated with the role of the child as a family member is that children can learn the skills of self-discipline (Varma 1997, 167). The aim of most parents is that their children will develop skills of self-control, motivation, persistence, and that they will have goals. An example of self-discipline is a child learning a positive statement about self, such as "I am not going to be an idiot and get in trouble with my parents just because my friend expects me to do this." Thought patterns such as this can help an aggressive youngster avoid situations of violence. A child acknowledging the wrong he or she has done and suggesting appropriate punishment – "I'm sorry. I know I came home later than I promised. I guess that means I cannot go out tomorrow" – is more likely to reduce tension that an argumentative response – "I was only a few minutes late." If peacebuilding can teach self-discipline to children, particularly in the area of self-control, this could reduce familial stress and reduce potential violence.

However, in addition to the more general sociocultural factors that may prevent a child from putting new skills into action, a child at risk or a survivor of abuse may use inaction as a survival mechanism. Maintenance of the status quo may be based on the fear that any challenge to the abuser(s) may increase and not decrease the levels of abuse. A child's apparent inaction in relation to peace education may reflect a negative situation in the home or community setting.

KEY POINTS
- Peace education without parent education related to child-rearing will have a limited impact in the family.
- The term *parent* needs to be kept broad.
- Members of abusive families are less likely to be involved in community meetings; creative ways to connect with these families need to be found.
- Peace education can help children learn self-discipline techniques.

Q. WV has a history of working in CEDC projects. How do CEDC projects connect with parents and families of children at risk?

Culture and peace education

Introduction to culture and peace education

Because culture plays a decisive role in both the perpetration and the mitigation of violence, it is critical that peace education curricula include attention to local cultural strengths. Appropriate translation of materials is important because language is very much a part of culture. Rewriting certain sections to make them culturally understood is just as important. For example, terms to describe different types of violence, grief and reactions to the violence cannot always be directly translated from English. This is important ethnographic material to collect as part of preparing for peace education work. The healing processes in many cultures involve specific rituals, for example, healing and restitution ceremonies for child soldiers to be accepted back into their communities in Sierra Leone and Northern Uganda. How will peace education acknowledge such practices?

Despite the necessity for harnessing strengths inherent in the culture, the aspects of a culture being promoted need to be supervised. For example, an anecdote from Rwanda relates that some "children were performing for government visitors. A child confidently read a poem he had written. Translation of one line highlighted the challenge ahead: 'We are brave and we are strong and we will fight the enemies at the borders'" (Slead and Janz 2000, 41). Staff members were encouraging the children to express their ideas, but they had firm views themselves. The question arose as to how many of these ideas came from the children and how many from the adults. While the project management was expatriate, without adequate local language skills the potential for national staff members in a very tense period to use children to promote their own views was high.

This leads to a critical concern with peace education; that is, how do we protect children from further violence when they challenge cultural beliefs and practices in order to promote peace? Children may decide that they should not have to tolerate beatings at home or school and speak out against it. This could result in a violent reaction from the perpetrators. In a similar vein, children speaking for peace and resisting the local teen culture of being recruited into local gangs may have negative results for children, including being killed.

Cultural differences can provide strength to the argument against a universal peace education curriculum. However, the basic principles of peace education do not need to differ. Provided the curriculum allows for different emphases and examples focused on the local culture, it is possible to design a curriculum that allows for and gives guidance to making local adaptations. For example,

Susan Fountain, an internationally known expert on peace education, notes that "the choice of language used to describe peace education programmes in UNICEF is determined by local cultural and political sensitivities, as well as by the scope and objectives of the programme" (1999).

Some practical examples of cultural differences are found in Joff's situation. If Joff lived in a community in Sierra Leone, or indeed in any number of West African countries, his father might well state that "our wives don't know we love them unless we beat them." The focus of the programme discussion on skills for peaceful living would likely be very different if Joff came from a community where wife beating is against the law and not an acceptable practice. How can positive cultural practices be valued while challenging harmful cultural practices?

Fountain identifies this challenge by stating that "an inherent risk in the promotion of a values-oriented activity such as peace education lies in the possibility that it will be seen as culturally biased, or as an imposition of one culture's values upon those of another. And in some contexts, the word 'peace' itself may carry political connotations" (1999).

KEY POINTS
- Positive cultural practices related to peace and child protection must be incorporated into peace education curricula.
- Negative cultural practices related to peace and child violence must be well understood and explored.

Q. What regional differences may influence the peace education curriculum?
   At what point do we allow children to make decisions about what steps they want to take to resist violence, and at what point should adults intervene to protect children who want to put their lives at risk of more violence or even death?
   How can we reduce the risks that peace education will be viewed as an imposition of one culture's values upon another's?

Gender and peace education

Gender is such a critical issue in relation to violence that it must be intentionally addressed in peace education curricula. But, in fact, peace education curricula tend not to acknowledge gender issues (Miller 2002). One need only watch groups of children to observe that boys and girls are different in their play and in their relationships. Their learning styles are also different. For example, boys tend to learn more by doing and girls by talking.

Do programmes therefore need to separate girls and boys at different times to allow for these differences? In societies where girls have very different roles from boys, WV has achieved more success by first talking about issues of violence to boys and girls separately, then bringing the girls and boys together.

The fact that peace education focuses on both girls and boys is a strength. However, because fathers are often the perpetrators of violence against children, peace education will have limitations on its effectiveness if there are not complementary programmes that involve men to teach them how to be protectors and not perpetrators of violence and giving them skills to be more effective parents. This returns to the question of how to involve parents, care givers and extended family in peace education.

J. Scourfield draws attention to this even further by pointing out that women are the focus of interventions by most social work agencies (and humanitarian agencies) and are often placed in very difficult situations where they are under considerable pressure (Scourfield 2003). How can peace education be designed to support fathers and mothers, girls and boys?

KEY POINTS
- To ensure that gender issues are addressed both in the style of teaching and the curriculum itself, an intentional process of looking through a gender lens must be an integral part of peace education development.
- Peace education programmes are more effective when the learning styles of girls and boys are integrated into the curriculum.
- There are times when girls and boys benefit from being separated to discuss issues, then brought together to share perspectives.
- In societies where girls are less likely to attend school, school may not be the best place to introduce peace education.
- Both men and women need to be involved in peacebuilding and peace education initiatives.

Q. Does the gender of the educator need to be considered in peace education?
  How might gender be integrated into a peace education curriculum?

Urbanisation issues for peace education

Urbanisation often increases tensions due to frequent competition for space and a mix of cultures; also, hoped-for economic gains from living and working in a city often are not forthcoming. "Living in a city is as much about negotiating relationships with other human beings as it is about living in material places and spaces" (Christensen and O'Brien 2003, 1). Because urbanisation often results in a separation from the support of the extended family and increased poverty as well as unhealthy attractions such as drugs, the focus of peace education in urban settings makes good sense. One need only look at the number of gangs to suggest that peace education in urban settings is relevant. The global increase in the numbers of street children has also alerted child-focused NGOs both in post-conflict and more stable environments to consider a more urgent response to street children. An examination of why children are on the streets suggests that domestic violence is a significant factor. Children exposed to domestic violence are more likely to respond violently, so the question is whether NGOs that respond to the needs of street children provide peace education as a tool for these youth and use peace education as a "prevention of abuse" tool.

KEY POINTS

- Urban living and the lack of opportunity for economic mobility can lead to an increase in violence. Peace education in urban programmes therefore makes sense.

Q. Does peace education in urban and rural settings need to be different?
Knowing that the influence of violence on the brain begins in the foetal and preschool years, how might this affect the target audience for peace education in an urban setting?

The roles of other key actors

The ethical issue

The first question that needs to be asked is related to ethics. When NGOs focus peace education efforts towards children, are adults "let off the hook" by placing the responsibility for peace more on children? J. Boyden and G. Mann from the Refugee Study Centre at Oxford University, England, suggest that adults need to be challenged when they adhere to the notion that "rehabilitation implies that it is the child rather than society that needs changing" (2000, 1). Children should not be burdened with the adult responsibility for peace in their community. Children need time to meet all their developmental needs.

Is it unethical to create peace education for children without a similar process of peace education and peacebuilding for the adults in the same community? These are critical questions to be answered. While it can be argued that children are more open to new ideas and change, family and community members must be involved in any programme design and implementation.

In addition to the family, Miller points out that " peace education requires the support and engagement of multiple actors and institutions" (2003). Also, children facing violence have so many burdens that care needs to be taken that peace education does not place an additional burden on them. Also, children need mentors who model peaceful responses to violence to inspire them. Drawings by children affected by war most often depict war heroes. There need to be peaceful heroes to counteract this focus on violent solutions.

So, who are these key actors and institutions, and how can peace education activities involve community actors and institutions? What roles do or should politicians, teachers, members of the police force, NGOs and other members of civil society (including religious leaders) and community opinion leaders play in peace education?

In most situations where children face familial violence there are essentially three groups of adults: the passive bystanders, the protectors and the perpetrators. The majority of adults take the role of bystander, usually due to their own fear or ignorance. If peace education focuses on empowering the parents and adults in the community to find non-violent alternatives to punishment, the assumption is that there will be more involvement in reducing violence by those who were once passive bystanders. This is of critical concern to the child-protection worker, because children need adults who can protect them effectively and who will create an environment in which children can talk about the issues affecting them. All the scenarios of the children in this chapter show a need for supportive adults to reduce the violence. Child survivors of abuse who in turn become perpetrators of violence need adults to help them develop empathy and to protect them from degrading and dehumanizing images.

Adults who will listen to children, who will model preferred behaviours and who will stop violence when it happens must be present in sufficient numbers to take the responsibility for peace in the community.

KEY POINTS
- Peace education is a community responsibility, and therefore key actors must be involved in planning for peace education for children and adults.
- Children need adults to help them reduce violence; when they face violence, they need adults whom they trust to communicate with and be assured of their support.

Q. What are the ethical issues related to introduction of peace education to children when there are no peacebuilding interventions with adults?

Teachers, schools and peace education

Peace education can make a significant contribution to the rights of children to the "preparation of the child for responsible life in a free society, in the spirit of understanding, peace, tolerance, equality of sexes, and friendship among all peoples" (UN 1989, Art. 29).

Unfortunately, teachers in many countries have been poor role models of peace and tolerance because they are often authoritarian in their approach and use corporal punishment. Some are exploitative of children – particularly girls. Therefore, schools may not be the most appropriate place to start peace education. Perhaps advocacy to address the right to education as described by the CRC needs to be the starting point. Only when there is a clear commitment from education ministries at the central and local levels to a change in policies that will support more collaborative teaching methodology should peace education be introduced in a school setting. Even with changed policies in place enabling schools to create such learning environments, a realistic number of well-trained teachers is still required.

Consider Manta for a moment. It will be especially critical that the teaching styles allow her to hear the same message repeated often and in a variety of ways – written, spoken and visually – because she finds it difficult to concentrate. Good learning environments allow for different learning styles, but they are not typical in many formal school situations where there may be only one teacher for as many as 150 children.

Manta needs a patient and caring teacher to support her to learn and put into practice the necessary skills for her to consider changes in her situation. Not all teachers have the skills required for facilitation of peace education; it is necessary to identify the most appropriate educators (just as it is with community-based programmes).

KEY POINTS
- There are many hurdles to jump before schools are the best environment for peace education.
- Teachers must be selected carefully; not all teachers may have the skills needed.

Q. What are the competencies required for a skilled peace educator?
Can all the required skills be taught?

NGOs, poverty reduction and peace education

While peace education, as such, will not have a direct impact on structural violence, attention to structural violence is critical to creating a peaceful environment for children. The consequences of structural violence provide the rationale for communities introduced to peace education to be supported with poverty reduction strategies and vice versa. Where WV and other humanitarian organisations already support poverty-reduction strategies, this must be continued and indeed further strengthened by focusing on families and communities with a higher risk of violence. Limitations of sponsorship have prevented funding less accessible or highly mobile populations of vulnerable children and their families, so recent attempts within the partnership to creating new funding streams for CEDC children are commendable.

If an NGO is to introduce a peace education programme, surely it must look at its strengths. As most countries have centralised education departments responsible for curriculum development, the U.N. and bilateral government donors are well placed to invest time and energy at this level. NGOs, on the other hand, tend to be more effective in working with communities with vulnerable children and with civil society. This suggests that NGOs, such as WV, should build on their relationships with groups such as community committees, faith-based organisations, women's organisations and existing projects to explore the most appropriate involvement in peace education. This does not exclude NGOs from being involved in school-based peace education, if the environment allows it, but a better role for NGOs may be to advocate with governments for the integration of peace education curriculum in all schools. Let NGOs focus on their strengths and build on their existing relationships with communities.

KEY POINTS
- Poverty-reduction programmes can address structural violence.
- As structural violence affects the levels of collective and interpersonal violence, there is good rationale for a combined approach of peace education and poverty reduction in terms of other sectoral inputs within a community.
- NGOs should build on their strengths in community relationships.
- U.N. agencies and the like are better placed to influence education department curriculum development.
- NGOs can have a key role in advocacy with governments on peace education.

Q. What roles should NGOs have in peace education?

Religion, the leadership of faith-based organisations and peace education

Despite placing a high value on peace, in practice many religious leaders model values and practices contradictory to those espoused in peace education. For example, authoritarian, controlling structures create a dilemma for the collaborative styles and inclusive decision-making valued in peace education. In addition, punitive disciplinary practices justified by religion presents a challenge for both peace educators and children. The condoning of physical punishment by religious leaders reinforces violent rather than non-violent approaches to child rearing. How many children grow up misunderstanding the loving nature of God because they are beaten and have it explained as "being obedient to God" or "I do this because I love you"? The recent public exposure of the involvement of church leaders (both Catholic and Protestant) in the abuse of children has eroded the confidence of victims of sexual abuse in the church as a safe place. When values and practices in the religious context put children at risk, a dilemma is created for the appropriate involvement of religious and faith-based organisations in peace education,

Religious and faith-based organisations involved in peace education development need to address in detail the issue of religious foundations for certain violent practices in a world where physical violence is damaging thousands of children every day. In such contexts a complementary, parallel process of examining religiously supported practices and values which put children in danger is called for. Part of the rationale for such action is that having the staff of a faith-based organisation also involved in leadership positions in their own churches may be the first step towards creating discussion in the church about the impact of beliefs and practices of leadership on the well-being of children.

So, what can peace education offer and how best can it have a real and lasting impact on the holistic development of a child in his or her context of family and community? Faith-based organisations should put into place measures that clearly communicate that violence is unacceptable to the leadership. Peace education can help achieve consistency between beliefs and practices of religious leaders and the non-violent values of peace education. Resources from most religious and faith traditions are available for reference to prepare to introduce issues of religion in any discussion of violence and religion.

KEY POINTS
- Religion has an important place in peace education discussions
- Inconsistency between beliefs and practices condoning violence and promoting non-violence is confusing and puts children at risk.
- Religious leaders and leaders of faith-based organisations need to bring the discussion of inconsistency to the table before initiating peace education initiatives.

Q. How does one introduce the issues of religion into a peace education programme without exacerbating tension?

Lawmakers and law keepers

The role of lawmakers and law keepers in reducing violence and complementing peace education cannot be overstated. If there are no laws or government policies including social safety nets to address the types of violence that children experience, this too contributes to the structural violence they experience. For example, if there are no laws to cover the sexual abuse of boys, then abusers will continue with impunity. A street child like Reyi, who is being harassed by militias, is not likely to report this if the police who manage juvenile justice are unaware of laws to protect street children. If Manta appears at a health clinic, will she be treated with care and attention or will she be treated solely for physical symptoms? Will her abuse be identified, and will she be referred to appropriate agencies that can address the social and justice issues?

WV's experiences in the area of child rights promotion highlight the potential that exists to engage these actors and institutions (such as police force training) in child rights, child protection and juvenile justice. This suggests that the involvement of lawmakers and law keepers in peace education is relevant in many situations. As key stakeholders they should be among those who are included in any orientation to planning peace education programmes. One outcome of peace education may be that children will choose to challenge the structures that have the responsibility to create and enforce peace in a community. This is not without risks. Children who do challenge structures may find that without adequate preparation they face additional conflict that may or may not be in their best interests in the long term.

KEY POINTS
- Lawmakers and law keepers need to be involved in peace education programmes in some way.
- Training for law keepers can support peace education efforts.
- The result of peace education may be that children and adults may be challenged about some of the structural violence issues, but the risks associated with addressing structural violence need to be assessed by children and adults together.

What type of violence is best addressed by peace education?

Interpersonal violence

The impact of violence on the healthy development of children, on their dignity and self-esteem, is substantial. The focus on respect, dignity and building self-esteem in most peace education curricula has the potential to provide a base for survivors of interpersonal violence and to rebuild their life. However, healing and support come from a social group. The integration of group work and joint problem-solving within peace education is critical.

Collective violence

Can peace education actually address collective violence? It can, but only to a limited extent. For example, many peace education curricula teach children negotiation skills. Perhaps on an individual level this may enable a child to challenge an elder or to negotiate with a peer to make non-violent choices, but the pressure of the group and the need to belong often will prevent an individual from challenging a group. The Maras in Guatemala, for example, provide "acceptance, companionship and money"; this legitimises violence for the youth involved (WVI 2002b). As WHO observes, "Gangs tend to proliferate in places where established social order has broken down and where alternative forms of shared cultural behaviour are lacking" (2002, 215). Peace education could provide the venue for an alternative form of shared culture.

However, in many cases of collective violence the need to reduce the violence may be more effectively met by addressing the structural violence and challenging the underlying causes of marginalisation and poverty. As already mentioned, peace education will not directly affect structural violence.

KEY POINTS
- Peace education offers opportunity to address issues of interpersonal violence.
- In many cultures interpersonal violence is often interpreted as violence that affects the group, and so solving the problem is a group process. Peace education has the potential to develop the social skills to strengthen effective non-violent problem-solving.
- Peace education does not directly affect structural violence, but it may provide skills to give children confidence and to empower them to challenge systems and structures.

Q. Gang violence is a tough culture to dismantle. Can peace education provide a realistic alternative form of shared culture?

Where should peace education be facilitated?

This is a critical question to consider in terms of types of countries as well as locations within those countries. Until now, most peace education programmes in the developing world have focused on countries affected by armed conflict of a political nature, such as Liberia, Colombia, Sri Lanka and Sudan, excluding other "more peaceful" countries. But might a focus on more stable environments be a more active approach than the reactive approach in the post-conflict environments? As mentioned in earlier sections, violence is a global problem; yet, peace education has not focused on societies where violence is "invisible," where violence is accompanied by a code of silence, as in the case of familial abuse.

Children not in school need peace education as much as school children. Preschool children need peace education activities too. Reyi, Joff and Sendi are all examples of children who are not in school. Is it possible for a peace education programme to provide child care so that Sendi can safely attend a peace education programme? Can Joff attend peace education activities in a community setting when the agricultural season is less busy? He would not be considered in many communities to be at risk as a perpetrator of violence, but he would benefit from peace education initiatives. Certainly there is potential that his resentment at not being able to go to school could boil over into other areas of his life. Can Reyi be drawn away from gang life by being included and accepted in a supportive learning environment that caters to street children or children at risk of taking to the streets? Peace education could offer Senti and Reyi negotiation skills to reduce stress in the family and reduce the likelihood of Senti physically punishing younger siblings. And Pris would benefit from opportunities to learn discipline in a caring environment with other preschoolers. In most situations there is good reason to focus on children who are not in school because they are often more likely to be exposed to violent situations and be perpetrators of violence in the future. Other children not at school may include children with disabilities, children whose parents are in prison, children in the juvenile justice system, children in institutional care and children who live too far from school to attend regularly. These children are found in the community. Thus, peace education should start in the community.

There may be one exception to this. In immediate post-conflict situations in which all children have been affected by war, it makes practical sense to start by targeting schools for peace education. Schools in these settings are usually viewed by the adults and children as safe and secure settings.

KEY POINTS
- Be more active than reactive in peace education.
- Peace education should not be confined to schools.
- Peace education may well be more effective in reducing violence if it targets children who are not in school.

Q. Do NGOs that have a history of working in child-focused projects see potential for peace education within their groups of children?

Conclusion

This chapter has identified the types of violence children have experienced, explored the relationships between violence and cultural issues and then related these to peace education programmes. It also has highlighted the strong connections that exist between child protection and peace education and encouraged peace educators to learn from the knowledge and experience of child protection practitioners and incorporate that learning into peace education programme design. It has argued that a parallel parent education programme must accompany any peace education work with children if the desired outcomes for peace in the community are to be realised.

Of course, care givers need support to develop positive social networks and improve parenting skills as well as programmes to reduce poverty.

Some factors have not been explored. For example, what role could the media have in peace education? At this point the media plays a significant role in the perpetration of violence. The area of health and the training of health practitioners as peace educators has not been discussed, and neither has the role of the Internet. There is much to learn.

However, despite the fact that the issues of violence against children in the context of family and community appear overwhelming at times, by no means does this chapter suggest that all is hopeless. It has suggested some key contributions peace education can have in assisting the most vulnerable children – both those who are already survivors of violence as well as those at risk of becoming victims or survivors of violence. As a child-protection advocate and practitioner, I see great potential for peace education to support other efforts for the protection of children.

A multilevel approach to the prevention of violence is needed. One standalone project is not sufficient. We need to pay more attention to the design, monitoring and evaluation of any programmes we introduce, and to do this while providing quality programming for the children involved.

One final word of concern: If peace education programmes are going to address the issues of interpersonal violence, then it is likely that personal abuse stories will emerge. A strategy to address this immediately needs to be incorporated into the design of programmes to ensure that a child who reveals such information does not endure further violence. In addition, caring people in a community who support peace and child protection need support themselves as they absorb the pain of listening to the stories. Caring for the care givers should not be ignored. NGOs should have child protection policies. And, ultimately, each government and each community has the responsibility to protect children. For all, it is important to keep this in mind: Do nothing for us without us.

NOTES

[1] These children are not based on any specific living persons but reflect the lives of children the writer has met. Any apparent likeness is purely coincidental, and the names are fictitious.

[2] There may be additional signs and symptoms, and the above signs and symptoms can also be due to other issues. A child showing these signs needs further follow up and investigation before saying a child has been a victim of violence.

[3] *Conduct disorder* is "a complicated group of behavioral and emotional problems in youngsters. Children and adolescents with this disorder have great difficulty following rules and behaving in a socially acceptable way. They are often viewed by other children, adults and social agencies as "bad" or delinquent, rather than mentally ill" (American Academy of Child and Adolescent Psychiatry 1997).

[4] There are some exceptions to this pattern. In Northern Uganda, for example, boarding schools have been targeted by the LRA for the abduction of children, who are then forced to become child soldiers.

[5] It should be pointed out here that most homosexuals are *not* victims of sexual abuse. Nor do all those who have been abused abuse others.

[6] Robert Coles was Ruby Bridges's psychiatrist.

BIBLIOGRAPHY

Advocates for Youth. 1997. *Fact Sheet about Sexual Abuse and Violence in sub-Saharan Africa.* Washington, DC: Advocates for Youth.

American Academy of Child and Adolescent Psychiatry. 1997. "Facts for Families" series, no. 33.

Bodley, J. 1994. *Cultural Anthropology: Tribes, States, and the Global System.* Available online. A third edition of this book was published in 2000 by Mayfield Publishing (Mountain View, CA).

Bolton, P., and L. Ndogoni. 2000. *Cross Cultural Assessment of Trauma-Related Mental Illness Report.* August.

Boyden J., and G. Mann. 2000. "Children's Risk, Resilience and Coping in Extreme Situations: A Background Paper to the Consultation on Children in Adversity." Oxford. September.

Briggs, F., and R. Hawkins. 1997. *Child Protection: A Guide for Teachers and Child Care Professionals.* St Leonards, NSW: Allen and Unwin.

Browne K., H. Hanks, P. Stratton and C. Hamilton, eds. 2002. *Early Prediction and Prevention of Child Abuse: A Handbook.* Somerset, NJ: Jossey-Bass.

Child Wise Australia, 2001. *Choose with Care.* Melbourne: Child Wise.

Christensen P., and M. O'Brien, eds. 2003. *Children in the City Home, Neighbourhood and Community.* London: Routledge Falmer.

Coles, R. 1995. *The Story of Ruby Bridges.* New York: Scholastic Books.

Daniel B., S. Wassel and R. Gilligan. 1999. *Child Development for Child Care and Protection Workers.* London: Jessica Kingsley Publishers.

Dorais, M. 2002. *Don't Tell: The Sexual Abuse of Boys.* Quebec: McGill-Queens Univ. Press.

Dorning, K. 2002. *Crying Out: Children and Communities Speak.* Milton Keynes, UK: World Vision International.

DuNann Winter, D., and D. Leighton D, 1999. "Structural Violence Section Introduction." Draft. 1 June. Available online.

Fountain S. 1999. *Peace Education in UNICEF.* Draft of UNICEF staff working papers. New York: UNICEF.

Garbarino, J. 1999. *Lost Boys: Why Our Sons Turn Violent and How Can We Save Them?* New York: The Free Press.

Karr-Morse, R., and M. Wiley. 1997. *Ghosts from the Nursery: Tracing the Roots of Violence.* New York: The Atlantic Monthly Press.

IRIN (U.N. Integrated Regional Information Networks). 2003. "New Project in South Africa Trains Teachers on Gender-based Violence." Report no. 596. 31 July.

ISPCAN (International Society for the Prevention of Child Abuse and Neglect). 2001. "The Brain and Its Relationship to Child Abuse and Neglect." *Quarterly Newsletter* 10, no. 1.

James, A., and A. Prout, eds. 1997. *Constructing and Reconstructing Childhood: Contemporary Issues in the Sociological Study of Childhood.* London: Falmer Press.

Janko, S. 1994. *Vulnerable Children, Vulnerable Families: The Social Construction of Child Abuse.* New York: Teachers College Press, Columbia Univ.

Large J. 1997. "Considering Conflict." Concept paper for First Health as a Bridge for Peace Consultative Meeting, Les Pensières, Annecy, 30–31 October.

Miller V. 2002. *Assessment of Peace Education Curricula.* Unpublished paper for the World Vision Peace Education Consultation, 2003. Draft.

Parton N., and C. Wattam. 1999. *Child Sexual Abuse: Responding to Experiences of Children.* Chichester, UK: John Wiley and Sons.

Perry, B. 2005. "Violence and Childhood: How Persisting Fear Can Alter the Developing Child's Brain." Available online.

Perry B., and I. Azad. 1999. "Post-traumatic Stress Disorders in Children and Adolescents." *Current Opinion in Pediatrics* 11 (1999): 121–32.

Reppucci N., P. Britner and J. Woolard. 1997. *Preventing Child Abuse and Neglect through Parent Education.* Baltimore: Paul Brookes Publishing.

Sands C. 1999. *Learning to Trust Again: A Young Women's Journey of Healing from Sexual Abuse.* Grand Rapids, MI: Discovery House Publishers.

Scourfield J. 2003. *Gender and Child Protection.* New York: Palgrave MacMillan.

Shengold, L. 1989. *Soul Murder: The Effects of Childhood Abuse and Deprivation.* New Haven, CT: Yale Univ. Press.

Slead, J,, and M. Janz, eds. 2000. *Complex Humanitarian Emergencies: Lessons from Practitioners.* Monrovia, CA: World Vision International.

Straus, M. 2001. *Beating the Devil out of Them: Corporal Punishment in American Families and Its Affects on Children.* Somerset, NJ: Transaction Publishers.

Tolfree, D. 1995. *Roofs and Roots: The Care of Separated Children in the Developing World.* Hants, UK: Arena Ashgate.

U.N. 1989. *The Convention on the Rights of the Child.* New York: United Nations.

UNHCR. 1995. *Sexual Violence against Refugees: Guidelines on Prevention and Response.* Geneva: UNHCR.

Vanistendael, S. 1995. *Growth in the Muddle of Life: Resilience.* Geneva: International Catholic Child Bureau.

Varma, V., ed. 1997. *Violence in Children and Adolescents.* London: Jessica Kingsley Publishers.

World Bank. 2003. "Education Notes." August. Available online.

WHO (World Health Organization). 1996. *Violence: A Public Health Priority.* Global Consultation on Violence and Health Document WHO/EHA/SPI.POA.2. Geneva: WHO.

———. 2002. *World Report on Violence and Health.* Geneva: WHO.

WV (World Vision). 2000. *World Vision Partnership Required Standard for Child Protection.* January 21. Available online.

WVI (World Vision International). 2002a. *Disability Fact Sheet.* WVI Disability Taskforce. Unpublished.

WVI. 2002b. *Faces of Violence in Latin American and the Caribbean.* San José, Costa Rica: WVI Regional Office for Latin American and the Caribbean. Available online.

Additional reading

ANPPCAN. 1998. *Challenges of Caring for and Protecting Children in Kenya in the Next Millennium: Report of the National Conference on Child Rights and Child Protection in Kenya.*

Briggs F., and R. Hawkins. 1997. *Child Protection: A Guide for Teachers and Child Care Professionals.* St Leonards, Australia: Allen and Ulwin.

Cairns, K. 2002. *Attachment, Trauma and Resilience: Therapeutic Caring for Children.* London: British Association for Adoption and Fostering.

Coles, R. 2003. *Children of Crisis.* Boston: Little, Brown and Company.

Cousins, L., and J. Jennings. 2003. *The Positive Behaviour Handbook: The Complete Guide to Promoting Positive Behaviour in Your School.* London: PFP Publishing.

Fowler, J. 2003. *A Practitioners' Tool for Child Protection and the Assessment of Parents.* London: Jessica Kingsley Publishers.

Johnson, J., E. Ivan Smith, G. Gordon, P. Pridmore and P. Scott. 1998. *Stepping Forward: Children and Young People's Participation in the Development Process.* London: Intermediate Technology.

Jones, D., and P. Ramchandani. 1999. *Child Sexual Abuse: Informing Practice from Research.* Oxon, UK: Radcliffe Meidcal Press.

Kellerman, J. 1999. *Savage Spawn: Reflections on Violent Children.* New York: Ballantine. Available as a download from Adobe eBooks.

Strand, V. 2000. *Treating Secondary Victims: Intervention with the Nonoffending Mother in the Incest Family.* Thousand Oaks, CA: Sage Publications.

7

Inner beliefs as foundational to peace education

Bill Lowrey

INTRODUCTION

I am a peacebuilder and a peacemaker. Working for a just peace is like a driving engine within me. I remember the passion, anger and pain I felt at age 19 when my local church pastor would not allow me to bring a black friend to our all white church. There are vivid memories from my 30s of joining with pulpwood cutters in Mississippi to stand against a system of abuse and economic manipulation. I found myself in my home state confronting international paper company officials, appealing to politicians and the public, organising hearings so that the poor could share their stories and working to resolve deeply ingrained societal conflicts. Among my friends and family I was often drawn into interpersonal conflicts as a mediator. And when the conflict was personal between others and me, I felt a deep need to work for resolution and to search my own soul to identify my failings. By the time I reached my early 50s I was shuttling between warring parties in the midst of tribal conflicts in southern Sudan, taking risks for peace and reconciliation that in earlier years would have been impossible for me to imagine. But what has made me this way? What are the inner beliefs that shape my life and how were they formed over the decades? It didn't happen overnight. I am acutely aware of how much I need to learn. But I have also become convinced that many of my core beliefs were shaped in my earliest years and that those beliefs have been influential in my transformational process of peacemaking.

During the past couple of years of intensive consideration of peace education I have been on a personal journey of reflection. This chapter reveals the journey and the initial results. But it is an unfinished chapter, even as our lives are unfinished. However, I have become convinced that this type of journey is a valuable part of the process of understanding our contexts and designing and implementing peace education programmes that can make significant contributions to peaceful and just communities.

My journey has taken me inward and outward – to explore what I believe about myself and others, the physical world around me, the spiritual world that is both within and outside of me, and the institutional world that is both local and global. In the process I have identified a set of affirmations that is at the core of who I am and has shaped my values and behaviour.

I have used an *elicitive* approach to develop the substance of this chapter. Such an approach draws from within a person or a community that which is already there. It assumes that there are beliefs, values, skills, experiences and wisdom. John Paul Lederach has made this term well known by using it to describe an approach to peacebuilding and peacemaking that starts with what the people know rather than what outsiders may introduce.[1] I used a similar approach, but with different terminology, in my work among the Nuer people of southern Sudan. I studied the indigenous peace methodologies and wisdom of the Nuer people and facilitated peace processes that were built on their inner beliefs.[2] For this chapter I first have elicited from within myself the beliefs that seem to be at the core of my understanding of peace education. Second, I have elicited from the Christian faith a framework for these inner beliefs. Finally, I have sought out from other religions, traditional cultures and international conventions data that speak to these inner beliefs. This personal journey has produced a set of affirmations that has a direct bearing on peace education.

Ian Harris and Mary Lee Morrison contend that peace education is both a process and a philosophy. The process focuses on developing knowledge, skills and attitudes. The philosophy expresses values that embrace life and relationships.[3] When Harris and Morrison speak of philosophy, they expect a fairly well articulated set of beliefs and values. However, there are times in peace education literature that this seems to be assumed and remains implicit rather than becoming explicit. It is important to develop an explicit philosophy in order to teach the philosophy as well as the process of peace education. I have become convinced that one step towards articulating a philosophy of peace education is to examine and explore the inner beliefs held by community members that have a direct bearing on peace formation.

Most of this book has focused on the *process* of peace education with a weaving of *philosophy* throughout. In this final chapter I am looking behind the philosophy and exploring the inner beliefs that shape our lives, our organisations and our philosophies or approaches to peace education. Our inner beliefs drive what we do and shape who we are, whether we are consciously aware of those beliefs or not.

NGOs are institutionally shaped by core values, beliefs, philosophies of relief and development and their commitment or lack thereof to engage in advocacy for a more just society. For World Vision (WV), as a Christian NGO, there is a stated mission to follow Jesus in service to the poor with a special focus on children and a holistic approach to relief, development and advocacy. These values and mission statements are carefully formed and publicly declared. However, no institution perfectly practises what it professes. There are tensions within every institution, just as there are tensions within individuals. Recognising this disparity between professed and practised beliefs and values, it is helpful to explore the inner beliefs that undergird these values and that shape both staff and communities in their approach to peace education. To create a peace education programme that contributes to transforming people and communities we need to understand the beliefs that are deep within the people. In a very real sense those deep inner beliefs are the baseline on which peace education must build.

In this chapter I identify a set of inner beliefs, or affirmations, and wrestle with the implications of these beliefs for peace and peace education. I do not argue that the twelve affirmations are exhaustive. It is to be hoped that this engagement will bring other beliefs to the surface that can be articulated, debated and applied to peace education. These affirmations are drawn from and rooted in religious teaching, cultural and traditional wisdom and traditions and international conventions and laws. These twelve affirmations may carry universal messages, but they will need to have culturally appropriate ways of being applied in particular contexts. I will root these inner beliefs in the Judeo-Christian Sacred Scriptures, relate them to the multifaith context of our world and the teachings of other religions, and give them a global context through reference to international conventions and thought.

Inner beliefs are manifested in behaviours. Consider two teachings, one from the Abrahamic sacred writings common to Jewish, Christian and Muslim faiths, and another from a current writer who is from the Bahá'í faith.

In Abrahamic religious thought every human being has the God-given capacity to make constructive contributions to the rest of the human community. The concept is rooted in the religious belief that all people are created in the image of God. In Christian teaching this means that while sin has marred or damaged the image of God in humanity, the *imago Dei,* or image of God, is never completely lost. Every human being has the potential for good. Life is filled with illustrations of this belief. Some stories are heroic in nature, as when a person lays down his or her life to save another. Other examples are mundane and can go unnoticed. These include the common sacrifices that parents make for their children on a daily basis and the diligent work that many people engage in as a part of their vocation.

Peace education is built on this inner belief in human potential, however differently religious communities may express it. It is a belief that every person, child or adult, male or female, wealthy educated person or poor illiterate individual, warrior or peacemaker, politician or common citizen has the potential to make a contribution to the common good. Peace education depends on this belief being held to and nurtured. But, as recounted later in this chapter, there is an opposing belief. People not only have the ability to contribute, but they also have the ability to destroy. These two beliefs must be held together in tension. In the same crisis event some people will act heroically to save others while others seek their own interests and will inflict pain and suffering on their neighbours.

The second example is drawn from Brian Lepard's *Rethinking Humanitarian Intervention.*[4] Lepard seeks to reframe humanitarian intervention so that it is based on fundamental ethical principles in international law and world religions. At the heart of his work is the principle of "unity in diversity," which he describes as the "pre-eminent ethical principle." He argues that this principle is present in all the major religions, traditional religions, the major charters and documents of the United Nations and international law.

"Unity in diversity" sounds complex and philosophical. And it can be. However, it can also be simple and straightforward. Experiencing diversity creates discomfort in many people. It is easy to slip into a belief that uniformity is superior to diversity. Such a belief can lead to attitudes and behaviours that seek to suppress diversity and enforce uniformity. What happens in a family when the adults believe that a girl child is less valuable than a boy child or that a child with a physical disability is less valuable than the child who is a physically fit athlete? What happens in a community or nation when one ethnic group is considered superior and believes that another ethnic group should be subdued economically and politically or that it should even be eliminated? What happens when one powerful nation thinks it has the right to rule another less powerful nation or that its might gives it the right to exploit the resources of another nation? These are practical examples of the outgrowth of inner beliefs, either affirming diversity and unity or embracing beliefs that can easily lead to destructive conflict.

Peace education becomes more relevant when people are willing to explore their inner beliefs and how those beliefs are manifested in action. This can be a difficult process for the individual, and it can have political implications. In some settings this elicitive process can be seen as political meddling in the lives of the people or as an attempt to impose a foreign ideology on an indigenous set of traditions. Even when international conventions embrace, or even be founded upon, some widely accepted inner beliefs, that does not ensure acceptance. Many people believe that the international system of laws, regulations and conventions is just a part of the agenda of the "other," an instrument of domination or threats to one's freedom. Therefore, it seems to me, that the preferred starting point needs to be our inner beliefs rather than the stated propositions of an external body, whether the United Nations, an international convention like the Convention on the Rights of the Child or a religious institution.

Frame of reference

This chapter looks at peace, conflict and peace education from the reference point of the individual and the affinity groups that influence the person's identity. Each affirmation of belief begins with "I" or "We" – revealing a clear point of reference as the person within the context. I am not attempting to describe a set of universal human needs, such as Abraham Maslow's hierarchy of needs, or create a conceptual analysis of conflict or culture. My goal is to provide to the development worker or peace education practitioner a framework, centred on the person, for exploring and understanding the person and the contexts where peace education programmes are implemented.

Affirmations

I am using this term to express inner beliefs that can shape the characteristic behaviour of individuals and groups. These inner beliefs are foundational in that they become a base on which peace education programmes can be supported. I recognise that there is a distinct difference between an affirmation of what one believes and the manifestation of that belief in practice. However, as inner beliefs are articulated as affirmations, they create a framework to explore particular practices.

This chapter presents twelve affirmations. Each one is captured by a brief three-to-five word phrase that expresses an inner belief as a simple concept. Then the affirmation is explained and supported by reference to religion, culture, reason or convention. Because WV is a Christian NGO, particular focus is given to rooting each affirmation of belief in the Judeo-Christian tradition. However, references are also made to teachings of Islam, Buddhism, Hinduism, Baha'i, Confucianism, and both traditional wisdom and international conventions.

There is a question of universality to these affirmations that I cannot fully address. Each of these affirmations of belief finds some support from all types of societies, cultures and religions. Simply stated, there seems to be a universality to the affirmations, but this is not a distributive universality which would imply unanimous support. The elicitive process that has been employed to generate these affirmations is rooted initially in one particular tradition and then linked to other traditions. Is it possible, in this case, to move from the particular to the general? I believe that is premature at this stage. What I propose is that in each context where peace education programming is developed, an elicitive process is needed to explore and bring to the surface those inner beliefs of the people that have a direct impact on peace formation. That means that in contexts around the world, eliciting a comparable set of inner beliefs will form a foundation for developing peace education approaches appropriate to that context. In time this may lead to affirmation of many common inner beliefs that are universal in scope and foundational to peace education.

This chapter introduces two diagrams to assist in picturing these twelve affirmations. The first diagram looks through the lens of relationships. In each sphere of relationships there is brokenness, but each sphere also provides a venue for building peace, including through peace education. The second diagram focuses on the person within his or her own context. It is the dynamic of internal processes within each person within a context of influences and forces from the environment in which that person lives. The diagram creates an image of the dynamic of change, the potential of each person, and the impact of choices. Neither image alone fully captures the twelve affirmations, but when both diagrams are taken together there are overlapping layers of insight that demonstrate the coherence of these affirmations.

The concluding section of the chapter suggests areas for further reflection, application and exploration of the role of inner beliefs in reference to peace education and the broader arena of peacebuilding.

TWELVE AFFIRMATIONS FROM INNER BELIEFS

The following twelve affirmations provide a basic foundation for peace education among children and adults.[5]

1.   *I am somebody . . . and so are you*

I believe that every girl and boy, woman and man has value and dignity that are an innate aspect of being a human person. There is equality not in abilities, but in value and rights. Within the Abrahamic religions of Judaism, Christianity and Islam this concept is rooted in the first chapter of the Book of Genesis. In the creation story the Creator-creature relationship is established and the concept of humankind as the preeminent creature is declared.

> Then God said, "Let us make humankind in our image, according to our likeness; and let them have dominion over the fish of the sea, and over the birds of the air, and over the cattle, and over all the world animals of the earth, and over every creeping thing that creeps upon the earth."
> So God created humankind in his image,
>   in the image of God he created them;
>   male and female he created them. (Gen. 1:26–27)

Theologians speak of the *imago Dei,* the image of God. This concept gives high dignity to humans, is an act of grace from the Creator to the creature and distinguishes humans from all other animals, plants or mechanistic parts of the universe. In Christian theology this concept is so foundational that the incarnation of God in Jesus Christ in human flesh would have been impossible without the creation of people in the *imago Dei.* With this high view of humanity, it was then conceivable that God could take on humanity in the person of Jesus without compromising divinity.

The affirmation "I am somebody . . . and so are you" means that every person should be treated with dignity. I believe that there is an equality of value in all human beings and that such equality is not to be compromised because of gender, ethnicity, religion, age, intelligence, physical characteristics, variety of abilities, family heritage or any other distinguishing factor. In fact, one of the striking observations of this text is that the image of God is linked to gender, so that the image of God is a reflection of both maleness and femaleness.

The United Nations has given recognition to this essential equality of persons in the Universal Declaration of Human Rights. Article 1 states, "All human beings are born free and equal in dignity and rights. They are endowed with reason and conscience and should act towards one another in a spirit of brotherhood."[6]

When the government radio in Rwanda in 1994 called Tutsi people "cockroaches," it was grossly inflammatory language that denied human dignity to Tutsi people.[7] It was a way for Hutu extremists to say, "We are somebody. . . . You are nobody. You are worse than nobody. You are vermin and deserve to be destroyed." The denial of dignity and equality is one of the first steps towards destructive conflict and violence.

A greatly honoured national document is the Declaration of Independence of the United States of America. The document states, "We hold these truths to be self-evident, that all men are created equal, that they are endowed by their Creator with certain unalienable rights, that among these are life, liberty and the pursuit of happiness." While this is a stirring statement of equality, it must be noted that those who wrote it were all white males. The rights of women were not included in that statement of equality. In addition, that "equality" did not challenge the institution of slavery. In the draft developed by Thomas Jefferson there was a section on slavery. However, the focus was on blaming the cruel institution on the British king and condemning the king for trying to use slaves for insurrection against the colonists. In the final document Native Americans are referred to as "merciless Indian savages." The failure to apply the belief in equality eventually contributed to destructive conflicts within the United States at the levels of institutional and economic conflicts, civil war, political struggles, and civil rights and women's rights campaigns.

Similarly, when males in any culture think of women as less in value or primarily useful for their ability as labourers, their necessity for producing children or as objects of pleasure, this is the path towards domination and domestic abuse. Furthermore, if society sees children primarily as instruments for labour and means of income, objects of sexual pleasure or available fighters for the military, the path towards destructive conflict and suffering is evident.

In school, at home or in play, children can learn to treat all people with dignity. Calling people by the names that they prefer rather than "name calling" is a vital way to affirm worth. This is a beginning point in peace education. The Convention on the Rights of the Child has included this as a right in Article 7.1, stating, "The child shall be registered immediately after birth and shall have the right from birth to a name."[8]

2.   *We are one*

It is not enough to be somebody. That could mean that one is alone. It is also important that we be linked to others. The core belief is that each of us is united to all the rest of us. I believe that all the people in the human family are one people. The human race is a vast family of equally valuable human beings. Whenever people travel away from their own family, clan, tribe, or nation, they discover that the people they meet are still like them in being a part of the human family.

One of the core ways to express this unity of humanity is the Golden Rule, an expression of the belief that all people are neighbours and members of one family. When it is practised by individuals and organisations, it can be a powerful means of conflict prevention.[9] In the Hebrew scriptures we read, "You shall not take vengeance or bear a grudge against any of your people, but you shall love your neighbor as yourself: I am the LORD" (Lev. 19:18). In a practical expression of this Jesus stated, "In everything do to others as you would have them do to you; for this is the law and the prophets" (Matt. 7:12). When we treat other people as we would want to be treated, we affirm that we are all one.

This belief in the unity of humanity is shared by religions around the world. The practice of that unity has a variety of expressions. In addition to Judaism and Christianity, Brian Lepard has pointed out key expressions of the Golden Rule from several religions:

- Hinduism in the Bhagavad Gita – its conception of "the oneness of man with his neighbours and with God"
- Buddhist scriptures – "let him who desires his own advantage not harm another"
- Confucius – "what he himself does not want, let him not do it to others"
- Islam – "preferring others above themselves" Qur'an 59.9
- Bahá'í – a seeker of truth "should not wish for others that which he doth not wish for himself"[10]

As I worked among the Nuer people of southern Sudan, I came to appreciate their concept of unity as expressed in the word *Naath*. They recognise themselves as one people with a shared responsibility to one another, and many of their customary laws flow from this essential belief in their shared unity.[11]
As we do peace education, we lay the foundation by teaching that every individual is to be respected and valued and that every individual is connected to one universal human family.

3.   We are different

I believe that we are one human family linked by our unity, but we are also a family with rich diversity. Philosophers and theologians through the ages have wrestled with the problem of the one and the many. There is diversity within the unity. This diversity can enrich our appreciation for one another, or it can be a basis for division and conflict. Whenever forced uniformity substitutes for unity, there is conflict. Whenever diversity is elevated to a level that disdains human unity, there can be anarchy or chaos. Therefore, it is important in peace education to teach both unity and diversity.

Each person is unique, with individual gifts, abilities, strengths and weaknesses. The human race carries a rich global diversity that includes gender, age, ethnicity, language, culture, size, colour, height, intellect, physical skills, emotional expressions, learning styles and the list goes on. It is important in peace education for each person to recognise his or her uniqueness and also the differences he or she has from others. But it is also vital to show respect for others and to be able to see how differences can actually enhance the beauty and the possibilities of our unity.

When children play games that require a variety of skills for a team to be effective, they can see the value of differences. When youth or adults work on common tasks that require different skills, they are able to experience the positive impact of being united around diversity. But if children and youth observe that some people are excluded because of their differences and their abilities ignored, whatever efforts are made in formal peace education may be unable to overcome the observed experiences of exclusion.

In 1 Corinthians the concept of unity and diversity is developed by comparison with the human body:

> Indeed, the body does not consist of one member but of many. If the foot would say, "Because I am not a hand, I do not belong to the body," that would not make it any less a part of the body. And if the ear would say, "Because I am not an eye, I do not belong to the body," that would not make it any less a part of the body. If the whole body were an eye, where would the hearing be? If the whole body were hearing, where would the sense of smell be? But as it is, God arranged the members in the body, each one of them, as he chose. If all were a single member, where would the body be? As it is, there are many members, yet one body. (1 Cor. 12:14–20)

The concept of unity that embraces diversity is vital for all human relationships. It applies to individual relationships with other individuals. It applies within the nuclear and extended families. It applies within communities and between communities. And it applies to states and the family of nations.

How an NGO handles its own internal diversity will teach a great deal to the community. If women are relegated to low-level jobs, or a particular ethnic, tribe or caste group has all the top leadership positions, or people connected with one political party seem favoured, the NGO can anticipate that conflicts will surface within the agency and within the community. The tension that exists in managing diversity cannot be eliminated. But when differences are respected and people have opportunities to use their varied abilities, this will contribute to a more peaceful and just community.

The Preamble of the Charter of the United Nations states that the members "reaffirm faith in fundamental human rights, in the dignity and worth of the human person, in the equal rights of men and women and of nations large and small." In this one statement there is the expression of both unity and diversity of persons and states with particular recognition given to gender differences and to small nations.

Finally, I want to point out the importance of simultaneously holding to all of the first three affirmations – equality, unity and diversity. If there is neglect or rejection of the belief in equality, then the affirmations of unity and diversity may be applied in ways that will lead to destructive conflict. For instance, one may say that people have an essential unity; however, if equality is ignored the differences between people may create a hierarchy of value. This loss of equality leads to a loss of genuine respect of differences and will inevitably lead to dominance by one side. This allows for a caste system, or class system or value judgements based on race, gender, religion or ethnicity. Whether we are talking about the legally segregated systems of the United States in the twentieth century, apartheid in South Africa, caste and class systems in a number of countries or governing systems that grant favourable status to a religious, political or ethnic group, all fail to practice genuine equality, unity and diversity. The minority or out-of-favour group will ultimately be forced into uniformity which generates destructive conflicts internally within people and externally between people and systems.

4.   *We need one another*

I believe that within the human community we need one another. We are interdependent. It is a simple and self-evident concept that everyone needs someone else and that we cannot live our lives alone. But this affirmation goes much further than our need for one other individual. We actually need everyone. There is a need for the larger community, and that need extends to every level of society. People need to be in community with one another. Local communities need neighbouring communities and the state. And all nations need all other nations. Today the globalisation process has extended this interdependent concept to a universal level. The Barcelona Declaration begins: "We live in a world in which isolation is no longer possible. We live in a time of unprecedented mobility of peoples and intermingling of cultures. We are all interdependent and share an inescapable responsibility for the well-being of the entire world."[12]

In the creation story of Genesis, God said, "It is not good that the man should be alone; I will make him a helper as his partner" (Gen. 2:18). This story teaches the concept of interdependence. The need for one another is a direct outworking of our diversity. Because there are different needs and abilities, the diverse gifts of the human family are able to complement one another. When people recognise their need for one another, it strengthens their tolerance and gives them incentives for building peaceful relationships.

Quite often, even in the midst of a "hot conflict," communities discover that certain trade activities continue. One community may have agricultural skills while another has developed trade routes and capacities to deliver nonagricultural supplies. Because traders and agriculturalists need each other, they may continue their economic exchanges while others from both groups are engaged in violent conflict. When the conflict escalates to the point of closing down most of the bridges that connect people, the crisis and pain are amplified to the point that they can hardly endure. If there is to be peace, some of the networks that demonstrate interdependence have to be reestablished. Conversely, when the networks of interdependence are very strong, peace incentives are high and conflict may be prevented or held to a low level.

It is possible for people to affirm the concept of interdependence but then only apply it in relationship to people of their own choosing. So people may be comfortable with an interdependent life within their own community but reject the concept that this needs to be applied between communities and in the global family of nations.

Some people accept the reality that this is a pluralistic world, but they compensate by trying to create what I call segmented pluralism. This is accomplished by creating homogeneous communities that experience interdependence among their own members but then separate themselves from others who are different. Communities are segmented or segregated from one another in a way that rejects or at least minimises interdependence across differences. This segmented pluralism creates a context for destructive conflict to develop and makes it difficult to build a culture of peace.

I grew up in the 1950s-60s in the southern part of the United States during the time of racial segregation. Within the white community there was broad acceptance of interdependence. But that was applied primarily to other whites. Generally speaking, whites did not feel they were interdependent with blacks or "coloureds" (the term used at that time). So this became a segmented pluralism, in which diversity with interdependence and equality was accepted within the white segment, but diversity without interdependence and without equality was the normative white community belief when it viewed the black community.

In parts of the world where there are conflicts between ethnic, religious or cultural communities, it is common to see these distinct communities develop strong internal interdependence and yet create barriers that keep intergroup relationships at a minimum. For peace to be built, these groups must discover ways to interact to the benefit of both communities through interdependence. Frequently a way can be found through economic relationships, mutual trade, employment of different skills or collaborative tasks of development. It can also become practical for children and youth within the educational system. Peace education that embraces equality, unity, diversity and interdependence can create a living model of peaceful interaction and interdependence that can break down barriers that the adult communities have built up.

Development agencies can incorporate peacebuilding in almost any sector of work. Microfinance institutions can link people together across natural barriers by the way they make lending decisions and form credit groups. Water projects can involve people in interdependent programmes that create mutual benefits. Children will grasp the values of peace if they see the interdependent relationships within the community being worked out in practical ways across differences. And then, when these basic beliefs are both taught *and* demonstrated, they may be incorporated into strong values that reinforce a culture of peace.

In contrast to segmented pluralism we need to develop interactive pluralism. While recognising that many families, clans and communities are formed as homogeneous communities, it is possible to practice interdependence across community differences. When communities intentionally interact with one another, particularly with those who are different from them, they discover their mutuality and can create an interdependence that builds peace.

Again I can illustrate interdependence from what I learned among the Nuer people of south Sudan. The Nuer are an "acephalous" society, meaning there is no head person or hierarchy within their traditional governance system. Therefore, the Nuer, in their most traditional system, have no paramount chief or king. The Nuer are a segmented society with each family or clan operating in an autonomous fashion. However, as I stated previously, the Nuer call themselves *Naath* (one people). So they have the concept of the one and the concept of the many. When the "one people" faces a threat from neighbouring groups, the segments unite to defend against the threat. As soon as the threat is gone, the group quickly reverts to life in smaller segments. Over many decades the Nuer, who live near the border areas with other tribes like the Dinka, the Anyua, the Murle and the Shilluk, learned to live in an interactive way with those who were different from them. When they had conflicts, commonly over grazing lands, water and cattle, there were traditional ways of solving those conflicts, restoring peace and reconciling.

However, for decades there has been a complex and highly destructive war in Sudan. One of the tactics of war, used by both the government of Sudan and the rebel groups fighting the government, has been to separate the tribes and keep them in conflict with one another. This continuing state of tension or conflict reinforces segmented pluralism and makes it very difficult to practice interactive pluralism. As a result, conflict flares up between the different tribes in a cycle of continuing destruction. It is broadly recognised that the eventual solution must be found in patterns of life that provide for interdependence and equality while affirming both unity and diversity.

Peace education must help people discover how they need one another. Children can discover this through games of co-operation, small tasks that require different skills, and discussions of how within the economic world we need one another to meet basic human needs for food, clothing and shelter. As children move toward youth and adulthood, they can extend this concept to the political spheres, which makes it possible to sustain a peaceful and just environment for living.

5.   We are interconnected with nature

The interdependence of people has a complementary belief in interdependence between people and the natural world. I believe that we need the natural world around us, and the natural world also needs us to care for it. We are interconnected. For people to live, they must have air, water, land, animal life and the resources that are found in the natural environment. For the environment to be sustained and kept in equilibrium humans need to care for the environment. When there is degradation of the environment, the consequences can be far-reaching and result in conflict between peoples, communities and states, as well as undercutting the capacity for physical life.

There is a range of beliefs in traditions and religions about exactly how humankind fits within the natural world. However, there is a broad acknowledgement that harmony, balance and interdependence between humankind and nature are vital for sustaining the world and its population.

Stephanie Kaza has written extensively about Buddhism and ecology. She writes:

> A first step in keeping peace with nature calls for contact with ecological suffering in the world today. One must meet directly the ravaged land of industrial clearcuts, the chemical soup of polluted

waters, the sprawling megacities filled with traffic and smog. In these places of life-threatening deterioration, peacemaking as a practice has real consequences for both human and nonhuman beings.[13]

Returning to the creation story of the Abrahamic faiths, it is evident that stewardship or care of creation is the mandate to humankind. In the two creation stories of Genesis 1 and 2 there are key words that need understanding. In the first chapter the man and woman are told by God to "be fruitful and multiply, and fill the earth and subdue it; and have dominion over the fish of the sea and over the birds of the air and over every living thing that moves upon the earth" (Gen. 1:28). The concept of dominion is quite different from domination. The second chapter, expanding the meaning through Hebrew parallelism, says, "The Lord God took the man and put him in the garden of Eden to till it and keep it" (Gen. 2:15). These religious texts make it clear that the creation belongs to God, who is the owner of all things. Our human responsibility is to live in harmony with one another and with nature and to function as stewards or caretakers of the natural world. When this is done, the natural world becomes a caretaker of humans as well.

This concept of mutuality between nature and humanity was expressed in the "Declaration for All Life on Earth" in Tokyo in September 2000 at a UNESCO designated Flagship Event for the International Year for the Culture of Peace. The declaration stated, "We shall create a world in which each person is aware that we are enabled to live through the blessings of nature, and lives in harmony with nature, showing gratitude for all animal, plant and other forms of life.[14]

In the work of peace education, children can experience, verbalise and practise this harmony between nature and humankind. In many contexts they will also be able to articulate the conflicts that erupt between people and nature. This includes natural disasters, such as earthquakes and volcanic eruptions, and also the blend of natural and human disasters, as when the environment is degraded by people through deforestation, which is then followed by rains, floods and erosion that escalate the conflict and the consequences. Teaching peace with the environment can be done through words, drawing pictures, acting out dramas and taking action, such as planting tree saplings.

After the great tsunami of 26 December 2004 in Asia, issues of peace with the environment have become more prominent. High levels of development along coastlines can create heightened vulnerability for massive numbers of people. Where mangroves had been destroyed so that shrimp farming and tourism could be expanded, the tsunami impact was greater because there was no longer any cushion for the powerful ocean surge. In Aceh, Indonesia, the loss of agricultural lands from the tidal wave and the loss of timber in the highlands to accommodate rapid reconstruction both threaten the future well-being of the people. Issues of global warming have come into the relief and development conversation as the seas rise and coastlines recede. In the United States the catastrophe that befell New Orleans, Louisiana, in August 2005 was exacerbated by the gradual destruction of wetlands in favour of urban economic development, the construction of a coastal city below sea level, and the failure to incorporate protective levees sufficient to hold out the flood waters from a major hurricane.

Children, youth and adults need to reflect on their inner beliefs about our environment. When we believe that we are interconnected with nature and must learn to live interdependently with the environment, this can reshape our daily lives and our approaches to development and public policy. If the land ultimately belongs to the Creator and the human mandate is one of stewardship and the common good, issues of land ownership arise. Land ownership is a root cause of many conflicts in the world.

6.   *We organise ourselves*

This affirmation that "we organise ourselves" moves us beyond the individual and into the reality of groupings, organisations and systems. We must go beyond inner peace for individuals, interpersonal peace in social relationships and environmental peace with the natural world. I believe that the human family at every level of society organises itself into groups and creates systems to enhance the organisational arrangements. Groups commit to values, develop corporate attitudes, make decisions and take action. Like individuals, groups can act in either constructive or destructive fashion. Sometimes they fight for their own self-interest, to gain power, to pursue greed or to act out grievances. At other times they fight for the well-being of the whole community, or the common good, and work for a just peace, wise governance and sustainable development.

It is important for children, youth and adults to apply peace education teachings to the groups within their contexts. This may start with understanding the family, nuclear and extended, as a governance system. In the family there are different roles, distribution of power and responsibilities, attitudes, values, skills, behaviours and consequences for actions. This is also true within the school, whether it is a single class meeting under a tree in the bush or a complex school system with headmasters, teachers, curricula, multiethnic communities and multiple religious faiths. The affirmation connects us to civil society organisations, religious institutions, economic systems and governance systems from the local to the national to international arenas.

Children can apply peace education to the groupings that are appropriate to their own age and situation. When there are civil conflicts in an area, children often have much more awareness of the engagement of groups in the conflict than adults may want to credit them with understanding.

In July 2002 a team of WV peacebuilding staff met with the development community in Pottuvil, Sri Lanka. We gave instructions on how to use a tool to map the groups within a community and to show the interrelationship of the groups within the conflict setting. One of the focus groups comprised children from 7 to 15 years of age. When they explained their mapping diagram to the community they showed an awareness of groups that amazed the adults. Their map included the Tamil and Sinhalese communities, and the Buddhist, Hindu, Muslim and Christian religious groups. They included the military forces of the government of Sri Lanka and the forces of the LTTE rebels. They had WV and several local NGOs mapped into the diagram. And they drew lines between the groups to show which ones had good relationships, which ones were in alliance, and which ones were in conflict or had significant tensions. But the biggest surprise was that they included in the map their understanding of the international players. They included India, with major influence as the regional power; the United States, which was supporting the government of Sri Lanka; and Canada, which was linked with the WV development programme. Canadian WV sponsors fund this particular Area Development Programme (ADP), and many of the children write letters to their sponsors in Canada. These children produced a surprisingly sophisticated analysis of the groups that were interacting within a highly charged conflict setting.[15]

Peace education needs to include an appropriate level of systems analysis and intergroup relationships according to the age of the participants and the freedom and security that exists within the setting for this type of learning. As group analysis is learned and applied, the applicability of peace to each setting will become more powerful. Very young children can talk about their family, draw the setting where meals are eaten, talk about roles and think about the way they organise themselves. For each age there are levels of organised life that are experienced and known by children, and this simple belief that "we organise ourselves" has peace implications.

There are many stories in the Hebrew and Christian scriptures that illustrate the role of groups in either stirring conflict or being instruments of peacebuilding. The story of the Tower of Babel shows how people who all spoke the same language wanted to organise themselves to "build ourselves a city, and a tower with its top in the heavens, and let us make a name for ourselves" (Gen. 11:4). On the one hand, this demonstrated how people can work together to accomplish large goals. But on the spiritual side it showed people of pride who wanted to show they could reach into heaven and even rival God.

Very detailed family conflicts are seen in the story of Isaac and Rebecca and their two sons, Jacob and Esau. There is scheming, lying, deception, anger, hatred and plans to commit murder. Finally, Jacob fled from Esau and lived in another land. After years of separation there is the remarkable story of the return of Jacob to the land of his ancestors and his process of reconciliation with his brother Esau (Gen. 25—33). John Paul Lederach does a beautiful job of writing about the mapping of the conflict and the process of reconciliation within this family system.[16] A similar study could focus on the story of Joseph, who was sold into bondage in Egypt by his jealous brothers. Yet finally, after many years, Joseph was able to apply his organisational skills to save Egypt from famine and to use his interpersonal skills to reconcile with his brothers and be restored to his father (Gen. 35—50).

One of the clearest illustrations of organisational arrangements used for peace-making is the story of Moses and his father-in-law, Jethro. After Moses had led the Hebrew people out of their captivity in Egypt, there was the challenge of building a nation for a formerly enslaved people. Moses initially established a pyramidal structure and functioned as the sole decision-maker over the people. He "sat as judge for the people, while the people stood around him from morning until evening" (Exod. 18:13). He explained that "when they have a dispute, they come to me and I decide between one person and another, and I make known to them the statutes and instructions of God" (Exod. 18:16).

Jethro observed the style of governance of Moses and recognised its problems. His counsel was this:

> "What you are doing is not good. You will surely wear yourself out, both you and these people with you. For the task is too heavy for you; you cannot do it alone. Now listen to me. I will give you counsel, and God be with you! You should represent the people before God, and you should bring their cases before God; teach them the statutes and instructions and make known to them the way they are to go and the things they are to do. You should also look for able men among all the people, men who fear God, are trustworthy, and hate dishonest gain; set such men over them as officers over thousands, hundreds, fifties and tens. Let them sit as judges for the people at all times; let them bring every important case to you, but decide every minor case themselves. So it will be easier for you, and they

will bear the burden with you. If you do this, and God so com-
mands you, then you will be able to endure, and all these people
will go to their home in peace." (Exod. 18:17–23)

In this brief story there is awareness about how poor governance systems
can stir weariness and conflict among people and between them and their leaders. Jethro indicates the value of having wise people with integrity in positions
of leadership, a distribution of roles and power, and an appellate system for
handling important cases. He also indicates that good governance benefits the
leaders and the people and enables the community to live in peace.

Many NGOs are engaged in supporting the development of civil society. If
the development process contributes to good governance, it will also strengthen
the values of peace. The way an NGO is organised within itself may contribute
to peace or stir discord. The same is true for the educational system, the market
systems, the land distribution systems and even family systems. We always
organise ourselves, but doing so does not always contribute to peace. Knowing
the inner beliefs of people in each context regarding the appropriate ways to
organise families, communities, businesses and government is vital and can be
explored in an elicitive process. The results can shape the design of peace education programmes.

7.   *I am a whole person*

I believe that we must take a holistic look at the person, the community and
the context where peace is to be built. Peace education contributes to a transformational process that engages the whole person in his or her whole context. The mind needs to be engaged in thoughts, concepts and visions of peace
along with the critical thinking processes that help one make wise decisions.
The emotions, the mind, the heart and the spirit must be engaged in making
commitments that are values based and ethically astute. The body must move
into action so that attitudes and values become deeds and behaviours. The
social and interpersonal context must be considered, because people need
networks of relationships with others, those who are similar to them and those
who are quite different. The culture provides language, custom, music, art
and religion to express the beauty of the vision, to lift people beyond the
mundane and the present reality and to empower them to transform destructive conflict into constructive creations. The society with its systems of governance, education and variety of civil society organisations is the one who
weaves the web of structures and organisations, norms and freedoms that
make a peaceful society practical. And the economic world provides means

for meeting the basic material needs of the whole community, satisfying the drive for productivity and fulfilment of passion and joy in creating, countering the danger of idleness and realising dreams and opportunities that go beyond basic needs.

Since peace links all spheres into a whole that benefits the entire community, peace education must seek to engage the whole person. The reality is that issues can be solved, peace agreements can be signed, and people can even start to make a new beginning after a destructive conflict. But, if people do not have sustainable livelihoods, or if the governance is corrupt, or if access to resources and their distribution is seen as unjust, the peace may crumble. The whole person must be considered within the whole context if peace is to be learned and practised.

One way to make this concept concrete is to engage children in communication games and dramas that demonstrate the role of nonverbal as well as verbal communication and actions. Body language can communicate joy, excitement, anger, fear or sadness. Each context has culturally appropriate ways to communicate: from eye contact, shaking hands, bowing, patting someone on the back, smiling, making clicking sounds with the tongue, among others. This approach to learning points out that we are whole people and that peace education must engage our minds, emotions, wills, spirits and bodies. In addition, if a role play incorporates people dealing with hunger, disease, a local bully, parents and teachers, or the marketplace, it moves from the individual and interpersonal relationship to the social context. The more we consider the whole person in his or her whole context, the more likely it will be that a peace education programme will contribute to building peace.

8.   I can contribute

I believe that every person has the potential to contribute something to the good of the community. There is a created or God-given capacity within all people that enables them to make constructive contributions to the rest of the human community.

When I was a young parent, we found a song that we frequently played and sang in our home. It was a children's song. One line said, "You are a promise, you are possibility, you are a great big bundle of potentiality." This ability to contribute includes the capacity to dream dreams and create visions for a better future. People have the ability to imagine a better world, a more peaceful, just and kind world. When children are asked to describe a world of peace or draw pictures that describe the world they want to build, they show remarkable creativity, imagination and practicality.

Peace education can make use of some of the concepts and methods of "appreciative inquiry"[17] to help children, youth and adults envision a better future. Consider the example of the WV ADP community in Pottuvil, Sri Lanka. This is a mixed community in the "uncleared" areas (the government of Sri Lanka was unable to clear the area of rebel fighters from the LTTE). Present during the day of meetings in March 2002 were Tamil and Sinhalese, Buddhists, Hindu, Muslim and Christian women and men, children, youth and adults. I asked them to imagine the world they wanted for their community and encouraged them to draw pictures of that future. One of the mixed groups asked a woman to explain the picture that the group had drawn. She pointed out rice paddies, fishing boats, schools, a post office, a temple, a mosque and a church, all which were linked as a symbol of co-operation; trees, roads and homes; and people from all groups moving freely together. Then she pointed out a beautiful woman in the centre of the picture. She said, "This woman is a minority woman. She has on her finest clothing and her most valued jewellery. She is walking in the majority area. It is midnight. And she is safe." In the midst of a country at war, this was one group's vision of peace.

Visions of peace and justice that are pictured and verbalised can serve as magnets to draw out peoples' best efforts. They provide a way to nurture the constructive self that is within and to unite individual efforts as communities work towards a better future.[18]

When people are in conflict, the peacemaker tries to connect the constructive side of one person to the constructive side of the other. Years ago my teacher, Hugh Halverstadt, said that we have a "fair fighter" and a "dirty fighter" that live inside each of us.[19] If the "fair fighter" in me can link up with the "fair fighter" in you, we have a reasonable chance of resolving our differences, reconciling our relationships and creating a peaceful way of living together.

Peace education needs to be built on the belief that all people, including children, can envision a more peaceful and just world and can be constructive agents for changes that will contribute to that better world. All people can develop values, attitudes and skills that help resolve conflicts and build peace. There is a positive role that everyone can play, every day, all the time. One of the statements that I frequently repeat is that "peace belongs to everyone, and peacebuilding takes everyone doing what he or she can."

9. *I can destroy*

I believe there is an opposing side to our potential for constructive contributions. We also have a destructive capacity. There is a broken reality to the world and within each person. I can build up, and I can tear down. I believe that acknowledging this is crucial in order for people to understand conflict. Within each person is a "dirty fighter." We can also say that there is a "little imperialist" inside each of us. We all have a drive to conquer others, to rule over them, to take what is not ours, to prove our power, to vent our anger or frustration on others, to "get even" with those who have wronged us and greedily to take whatever we lust after.

In conflict analysis we examine root causes through a "greed and grievance lens." In examining the political economy of war, greed for resources is a common cause and frequently points to key actors. The power of these actors expands as they organise themselves into groups with common greed or grievance agendas. At the root of this is the "dirty fighter" or "little imperialist" inside us who wants to link up with others acting out of the same motivation. This is as old as humankind and is illustrated in the greed for power and the longing for the knowledge of good and evil in the biblical story of the Fall (Gen. 3:1–7). In the Book of James this root cause analysis of conflict is stated in a crystal-clear fashion. James writes:

> Those conflicts and disputes among you, where do they come from?
> Do they not come from your cravings that are at war within you?
> You want something and do not have it; so you commit murder.
> And you covet something and cannot obtain it; so you engage in
> disputes and conflicts. (James 4:1–2)

As I have taught this concept of the dirty fighter in various countries, I frequently ask people to explain what an imperialist is. Almost always someone quickly identifies the imperialist nation or people that has had a profound effect on them in their context. Sometimes people identify a former colonial power, and sometimes it is a neighbouring state or a nearby ethnic or religious group. Always, the group identified is the "other." I have never had someone start off by admitting the imperialist is within himself or herself. However, when I suggest that each of us has a little imperialist inside, there is immediate agreement and frequently some uncomfortable laughter.

The sobering reality is that all peoples and groups have blended capability. They have the potential to make very constructive contributions towards the well-being of others, even to be heroic. But there is also the potential to be a saboteur of peace and justice and a willing participant in destructive and even violent behaviour. Individuals do not fall into only one camp – constructive or destructive. The potential for both resides in everyone and our attitudes and behaviours blend both capacities simultaneously. When peace education helps children and youth deal concretely with this reality, it can lessen the tendency to judge others and may help them gain some humility and perspective about themselves as well as others.

Reflect on this often told traditional story.

> An elder Cherokee Native American was teaching his grandchildren about life. He said to them, "A fight is going on inside me. . . . It is a terrible fight and it is between two wolves.
>
> "One wolf represents fear, anger, envy, sorrow, regret, greed, arrogance, self-pity, guilt, resentment, inferiority, lies, false pride, superiority and ego.
>
> "The other stands for joy, peace, love, hope, sharing, serenity, humility, kindness, benevolence, friendship, empathy, generosity, truth, compassion and faith.
>
> "This same fight is going on inside you, and inside every other person, too."
>
> The grandchildren thought about it for a minute, and then one child asked his grandfather, "Which wolf will win?"
>
> The old Cherokee replied, "The one you feed."

10. *I am responsible*

While our capabilities are a blend of constructive and destructive potential, I believe that the responsibility for what we decide to do rests solidly with each of us. Once we reach a stage or age of accountability, each person is responsible for his or her own choices in life.[20] Stephen Covey has pointed out that "the word *responsibility* is 'response–ability' – the ability to choose your response."[21]

This ability to choose a response and be accountable for one's choices applies both to individuals and to communities or groups. It is important in peace education for children, youth and adults to embrace responsibility for their attitudes, decisions and behaviours. Responsibility calls for action, just reactions. Those who react to events may be driven primarily by an emotive or reflexive response and may act out as the "dirty fighter" rather than the "fair fighter." However, those who take action in an emerging situation are more likely to make decisions formed around values and commitments. This is where character and skill combine. Skill training can provide decision-making and problem-solving tools for analysis of the situation, options, potential consequences and preferred results. Character that has been formed and tested over time helps a person make commitments that are values based for the well-being of all.

The biblical narrative of the Creation and the Fall indicates that both God and the serpent (representing evil) treated the man and the woman in the garden as responsible individuals. They could make their own choices and live with the consequences. The woman chose to eat the forbidden fruit, and she offered it to the man. He also chose to eat. When God confronted them, God held the woman, the man, and the serpent responsible and imposed serious consequences on each. When the man tried to blame the woman, and the woman tried to blame the serpent, God rejected their excuses and dealt with them as responsible for their choice (Gen. 3:1–20).

When one develops peace education approaches with children, it is important to include practical examples of being responsible. Internally, we must learn to resist the urges or drives of the "dirty fighter." As an example, it is common to desire to "get even" with a person who has caused us pain or suffering. We must also resist greed, being silent when we need to speak, speaking words that cause hurt or injury, jumping to conclusions prematurely, believing gossip and rumours without searching for the truth – and the list continues. Externally, we are responsible to speak and act for justice, mercy, truth and peace. It takes courage to stand with others for what is good and to stand against others who seek destruction. In Islam, the concept of jihad at its core is the holy struggle to do what is good. Mohammed Abu-Nimer writes, "In addition to the Qur'anic verses that indicate the possibility of peaceful and nonviolent jihad, various Islamic sects have argued that there are several levels of jihad and that the jihad against self-desires, temptations, and selfishness is the most difficult to achieve."[22]

"The Declaration on the Role of Religion in the Promotion of a Culture of Peace" states, "We are all individually and collectively responsible for the common good, including the well-being of future generations."[23]

His Holiness, the Dalai Lama, in his speech for the 1989 Nobel Peace Prize, said:

> Responsibility does not only lie with the leaders of our countries or with those who have been appointed or elected to do a particular job. It lies with each of us individually. What is important is that we each make a sincere effort to take seriously our responsibility for each other and for the natural environment.[24]

Responsibility rests with the antagonists in conflicts. But it also rests on each person who is nearby. Vachel Miller writes of the need to empower "positive bystandership":

In situations of potential violence, bystanders can also affirm the dignity of potential victims and thus prevent the perpetrator from assuming that others agree complicitly with his actions. By bearing witness to the humanity of potential victims and advocating for non-violence, bystanders can delegitimise the use of force – whether on school playgrounds or in international relations. Peace education curricula might be strengthened by including dialogue about this concept and providing students with practice in being a positive bystander to conflict in their immediate contexts. An emphasis on positive bystandership would complement attention to bullying in school. The problem of bullying in schools is an immediate issue for children, and a discussion of bullying would naturally lead to concern for being a positive bystander in instances of peer violence.[25]

Teaching, training and acting as engaged bystanders is a way to say "I am responsible" rather than "It is not my problem." Embracing responsibility is a stance of power and empowerment. Many conflicts continue unimpeded because people choose not to get involved constructively, instead allowing the destructive cycles to "run their course." However, when intervention comes early, many conflicts can be cut short and adversaries can be assisted to resist the "dirty fighter" within and strengthen the "fair fighter." This brings hope for resolution of issues and reconciliation of strained or broken relationships.

Finally, it is good to acknowledge at this point that communities and groups also bear responsibility for their attitudes, decisions, behaviours and the resulting consequences. When communities or organisations take a stance for peace and justice, it may have a more powerful impact than the statements or actions of individuals. Doing so can also help others find the courage to act constructively. Similarly, if communities or groups act out of their destructive side, the negative consequences are also multiplied. Institutional and systemic injustices are the organised expressions of individual injustice. The more organised and systemic the destructive behaviours, the more difficult it is to intervene and restrain the impact. Children and youth can understand this basic concept when they draw on their own experiences with bullies on a playground or a gang of intimidators. They can also understand the necessity for engaging the broader community, which has sufficient power and influence to counter the bully or the gang. This can range from involving individual teachers, a schoolmaster, parents, community elders and leaders to involving community police. When key segments of a community say "We am responsible," and unite their wisdom and efforts, very significant changes can be made for the well-being of the whole community. Change can start with a single child and spread to an entire community.

In the Pottuvil ADP in Sri Lanka a few children decided in 2002 that they would no longer be just bystanders concerning the problem of illicit alcohol. In one village nearly 100 per cent of the men had an alcohol problem, and there were many illegal alcohol sellers. The consumption of alcohol was causing poor nutrition and wasted money, and domestic violence was widespread and severe. The children decided to organise themselves, appeal to their parents to stop drinking, put pressure on the police to raid the illicit traders and try to convince some sellers to change to a different business. This process culminated in a parade that involved more than 10,000 people marching through the pouring rain. The police responded to the children's campaign and broke up more than 200 illicit alcohol businesses. Months later the use of illicit alcohol was down dramatically, and domestic violence was reduced.[26] This simple story illustrates how children can be agents of change when violence is affecting their world.

11.   I am spiritual and moral

People are physical, mental, emotional and social beings. But they are also spiritual and moral beings. The internal spiritual life of each person, whether or not it is reflected in a religious expression, is a vital part of human nature. The spiritual brings heart and mind together. Furthermore, in every cultural and religious expression there is a sense of awareness and connectedness to a higher power, a spiritual reality external to the individual; in many cases this higher power can mean a universe of spirits or even a universal God.

It is spiritual strength that can empower people to act in a responsible fashion to build peace and resist destructive conflict. Spiritual development, which can be encouraged and nurtured in peace education, also provides resiliency so people can endure the turbulence of conflict and maintain a degree of personal balance and well-being even though their external world may be chaotic. The development of inner peace is vital for the work of outer peace.

Peace education can include times for silence, reflection, use of the imagination and prayer. In fact, if peace education fails to provide space for people to develop their inner life of the spirit, then the "hidden message" will be that peace in the world has no connection with peace within people. For many people around the world, it is impossible to conceive of peace without the involvement of God. Practitioners or adherents of traditional religions and major religions need to have freedom to reflect on their heroes or models of peace and justice; meditate on their scriptures and sayings; gain the support of their sacred communities; and see that their attitudes, decisions and actions for peace and justice are undergirded and supported by their religious life.

The spiritual dimension is also key in dealing with the healing of trauma caused by conflict. War-affected children and youth are wounded in their spirits. Many have been terribly violated in their bodies, minds and emotions. The healing process can never be complete, and emotional and spiritual scars will last throughout life. However, it is possible to experience substantial healing. Many broken people can become positive contributors to peace and justice. The path of healing may be very long and have many setbacks. But certainly it must include the nurturing of the inner spiritual life in conjunction with the nurturing of a safe, accepting and encouraging community environment where there is protection from abuse and opportunities for growth.

We are not only spiritual, but we are also moral beings. We all have concepts of right and wrong, good and bad, appropriate and inappropriate. Moral development, according to Kohlberg,[27] develops in stages throughout childhood, youth and adulthood. Moral development is influenced by the type of environment that is created and by the way a child experiences limits, tests boundaries, faces consequences and develops skills in decision-making and values formation.

Mavis and James Olesen have written about the importance of incorporating moral development into the peace education process:

> Violent responses may seem simple, clear and quick. Peaceful responses seem complicated, fuzzy and time consuming. Because of this reality, education in general and peace education in particular have to help students understand and desire to practise the morality and ethics of peace. Students must realise that the moral choices have consequences. They need to understand that the values each persons adopts will play a role, however small, in creating a society.[28]

Sensitising the conscience to make moral and ethical decisions is a key part of the development of children, youth and adults all through life. What is recognised in religion and tradition is that people have a conscience and they make moral choices. In the Christian scriptures we read: "What the law requires is written on their hearts, to which their own conscience also bears witness; and their conflicting thoughts will accuse or perhaps excuse them" (Rom. 2:15).

The presence of a conscience, which may range from overly sensitive to indifferent, does not mean that a person will always choose what is good. There is an inner battle that goes on within a person concerning many choices that are to be made. Paul, an apostle of Jesus, wrote about this inner struggle. Most of us identify readily with his words:

> For I do not do the good I want, but the evil I do not want is what I do. . . . So I find it to be a law that when I want to do what is good, evil lies close at hand. For I delight in the law of God in my inmost self, but I see in my members another law at war with the law of my mind, making me captive to the law of sin that dwells in my members. Wretched man that I am! (Rom. 7:19, 21–24)

Moral development and nurturing an informed conscience are vital for peace. But beyond that, there must be moral courage in order to follow through on decisions that are made with the skills of critical thinking and filtered with ethical and moral testing.

Beyond the morality and spirituality of individuals is the role of groups and organisations making moral stands and functioning as a corporate conscience for the community and the state. This is an extension of morality from the individual to the community. When communities wrestle with their moral positions, they need to bring the skills of critical thinking to the table. The potential influence of organised groups is great. Therefore, there is a multiplier effect for moral courage expressed by groups. In addition, the group members can reinforce one another and stir up the courage to stand for what they believe is right and good. When peace education helps groups to make moral decisions and take morally supported stances on issues, it contributes to the development of moral courage.

In 1999 I participated in an exchange visit of Nuer and Dinka chiefs and leaders as a confidence-building step leading up to a major peace conference in southern Sudan. The two tribes had been at war for eight years and had caused terrible and mutual destruction of life and property. The eight Nuer members of the delegation shored up their courage to go to Dinkaland to test if their Dinka counterparts would receive them in peace and not kill them. When we arrived, we were greeted not with hostility but with cheering crowds, rebel soldiers providing protection and a bull sacrificed to indicate a desire to cut off everyone from a history of conflict and to start on a path of peace.

As the Dinka discussed the second half of the exchange visit, when they would travel to Nuerland, they realised that the risks were very great. Their perception of Nuerland was that near anarchy reigned, and it was uncertain if any one leader could provide protection for them. One Dinka chief said, "The

Nuer have disarmed us with their courage to come. Now we must get the courage to go back with them."

Late into the night the Dinka talked together. They told each other stories of what their ancestors had done for peace, the risks they had taken. They faced the fact that some had died in the process. They stirred up each other's courage to go.

Simultaneously, the Nuer talked among themselves, considering ways to reassure the Dinka that they would be safe. The Nuer decided that they would offer to leave one or even several members of their group behind in Dinkaland. Then, if the Dinka were killed in Nuerland, the Nuer who remained behind could also be put to death.

When the Nuer shared their plan the next morning, the Dinka said it was not necessary. They had stirred up the courage of the group and had decided to go to Nuerland with the Nuer chiefs and without leaving any Nuer hostages behind. When they arrived in Nuerland, they also were greeted with great celebration and the sacrifice of a bull.

Within two weeks this moral courage exhibited by a few Nuer and Dinka gave courage to both communities, who instructed their representatives to proceed to the village of Wunlit for the peace conference. At the end of the ten-day conference a covenant of peace was signed that ended eight years of war. Looking back on the events, one of the most critical stages was the way that the small communities of Nuer and Dinka participating in the exchange visits had stirred up one another's moral courage to test the security and prove that peace could be established.[29]

With inner spiritual strength, a trained moral and ethical conscience and a community that can fortify moral courage, it is possible for individuals and communities to make significant contributions towards peace. When peace education engages all three of these and provides opportunities and space for their development, it contributes to a transformational process.

12.   *I can change*

The final affirmation that is foundational to peace education is the belief that people can change. This is a core concept in religion and in tradition, as well as self-evident in experience. As children grow towards adulthood, every society believes that they can and will change. The whole process of education and development is built on the concept of change. When change is intentional, it creates the possibility of shaping the changes that are made.

However, change is not inherently good. Change carries potential for good or ill. It is provisional in its nature, and change takes place in the context of a temporal reality. First, I consider the potential for good or ill and then reflect on the provisional and temporal aspects of change within people.

It is common for people to develop hardened views of others that no longer allow for the possibility of change. One might say, "He has always been like that. You'll never change him." In the United States people might put it this way, "You can't teach an old dog new tricks." All of us have known people who have become very set in their ways; it seems as though they will never change. We have habits that are deeply ingrained in our lives, and we know that it is difficult for us to break habits. But habitual patterns, although difficult to modify, do not contradict the core belief that "I can change."

Change can be either progressive or regressive. It is possible for a person who has been caring, honest, kind and a contributor to society to change in a negative way. Sometimes external events, coercion or becoming a victim of violence brings about the change. The Lord's Resistance Army (LRA) has abducted teenage boys and girls in the Acholi region of Uganda for years. The LRA forces the children to commit atrocities until finally they become different people who are capable of terrible violence and abuse.

In another setting a seemingly honest businesswoman can find that the lure of money and power can reshape her whole life. In many conflict settings it is greed for resources and power that is at the root of much destruction. Such greed can bring change to a person.

In some cases the inner spiritual resources and moral courage that may be in the process of being formed can be overwhelmed by the events that occur. In other cases people are enticed by their own inner desires and choose a destructive path. This is the sobering side of the belief that one can change.

The positive side of change is that people can be transformed from destructive patterns to constructive ones. Sometimes this comes from inner choices that are made by the person. Sometimes there are external pressures to change, or consequences force a reassessment of behaviour, or a community influences a person to change. The reasons for change are too complex to know fully the dynamics that bring it about. But many external and internal influences can bring about significant change for the better.

In May 2002 I attended a town gathering in Sierra Leone to celebrate the opening of their rehabilitated market and court centre. The war had ended. Throughout the country WV was facilitating a programme in which thousands of former combatants and war-affected youth were meeting in small groups to form community, work through trauma recovery, learn about reintegration into society and make a new start. Some of those former combatants had been a part of the work crew that rebuilt the market. During the ceremonial opening a man stood and spoke to the gathered crowd. He confessed that he and the others had been a part of the destruction during the war. He thanked the community for giving them a chance to make a new start. And he said rebuilding the market and court centre had put him on a new path of bringing good to the community rather than destruction. The community cheered, clapped and welcomed the man and his former soldiers back into their relationships.

During the ceremony in Sierra Leone, I was asked to give the keynote address. I selected words from the Book of Ephesians in the Christian scripture. The text says, "Thieves must give up stealing; rather let them labor and work honestly with their own hands, so as to have something to share with the needy" (Eph. 4:28). This sacred text shows that people have the potential to make radical changes. Rather than steal from others, it is time to use your own skills and produce a good product. And then, rather than spending all the profits on yourself, let the former thief now share with those who are in need. So the one who destroys society by stealing can change and become a productive citizen and contributor to others in need. I applied this text in Sierra Leone to the marketplace celebration. Those who had fought, killed and destroyed had made a radical change. They had rebuilt what had been torn down, and they had contributed to the well-being of the whole town. The town had also changed. Rather than condemning and rejecting the ex-combatants, the townspeople had extended forgiveness and gave them an opportunity to make amends and to demonstrate their change of heart. Then the town welcomed them back into the community as full participants.

These illustrations only show people changing in one direction. However, over the years of one's life, many changes can take place. Some are constructive and some are destructive. This is the provisional or temporary nature of change. A change may be genuine, but it may last only for a period of time. Positive change must be reinforced. However, even when constructive changes are reinforced over many years, forming depth of character, a person doesn't reach perfection; there is no guarantee that destructive changes will not occur. This provisional reality, when reflected upon, can contribute to personal humility and to sober analysis as one works for peace but faces the struggle of the human experience.

Finally, the reality of change also raises the issue of the temporal versus the eternal. A human life is contained within a limited time span. Death and the shadow of death are parts of the changing human experience. Violent conflict brings death and destruction prematurely and can generate cycles of destructive conflict. However, when people change constructively, they embrace life for themselves and others and can contribute to more peaceful, just and life-giving communities.

What is key for children in peace education is that they understand that they themselves can change, that other people can change, and that even organised groups can change. Peace processes need to keep the door open for combatants to become peacemakers. But peace education must also be realistic. It should alert people to the possibility that some of those who start on a path of peace and justice may turn away and follow their own agenda, seeking their own interests rather than the interests of the community as a whole. When people and systems turn violent, great human suffering, injury, trauma and death occur. When people and systems turn towards peace, communities are enhanced.

I frequently tell people, "Remember, it is never too late for people to join the reconciliation process." This is a way to keep alive the hope that people can change for the better. It is also a way to keep ourselves honest, so that we do not close a final door of condemnation on others. Finally, it is a way to stimulate thinking about what can be done to help bring people into a peace process or create a constructive role for bystanders to play rather than assuming they will remain neutral or passive. Providing creative roles for people gives them the opportunity to make moral choices, take responsibility for themselves, act out

Figure 7–1. A matrix of the twelve affirmations

Affirmations from inner beliefs	Core values	Relation-ships	Dynamic change
1. I am somebody.	Equality	x	
2. We are one.	Unity	x	
3. We are different.	Diversity	x	
4. We need one another.	Interdependence	x	
5. We are interconnected with nature.	Ecology/environment	x	
6. We organise ourselves.	Organisational/institutional	x	
7. I am a whole person.	Holistic		x
8. I can contribute.	Constructive		x
9. I can destroy.	Imperial		x
10. I am responsible.	Responsible		x
11. I am spiritual and moral.	Spiritual/moral	x	x
12. I can change.	Potential/provisional/temporal		x

of their "fair fighter" side and change progressively and constructively in ways that contribute to a just and sustainable peace.

EXPRESSING THE TWELVE AFFIRMATIONS

Figure 7–1 lists the twelve affirmations of beliefs and the corresponding core values that are expressed. In addition, this matrix indicates a primary (x) presence of each affirmation through two lenses: relationships and dynamic change.

Diagram #1: Spheres of Conflict and Peace – A Relational Framework

Figure 7–2 provides a relational framework for affirmations dealing with the self, others, groups, nature and the spiritual. It shows the following areas:

Me – This is the sphere of the self. It includes one's relationship with self and involves such issues as identity, sense of equality with others, pride, self-worth, shame, guilt, honour, confession and forgiveness, emotions, will, trauma and healing. Whether or not a person has a growing sense of inner peace has a profound impact on his or her ability to contribute to others in a constructive way.

We – This is the sphere of close interpersonal relationships, particularly with family, friends, and near neighbours. It is the set of relationships with which we are most intimately connected. In this sphere people usually expect to be loved and accepted, and it is in this circle of relationships that people hope to find safety and protection. However, when these expectations are disappointed, this sphere of relationships can be a place of deep and lasting pain and suffering. When destructive conflict is experienced in the family, with close friends, or within the natural web of relationships with neighbours or members of extended family or clan, there is a loss of one's core place of living and vulnerability escalates. Therefore, building peace within the family system and within the network of friends and neighbours is basic to building a sustainable community of peace.

They – This sphere relates to the "other" and extends interpersonal relationships to inter-communal relationships. It includes relationships with other people and other communities who are quite different from us and different from our closest community of relationships. Differences can easily become the focus, whether ethnicity, race, language, culture, class, gender, nationality, economic status, power, religion or political views. Building constructive relationships across differences and developing a deep appreciation of the richness of diversity is

Figure 7–2. Spheres of conflict and peace

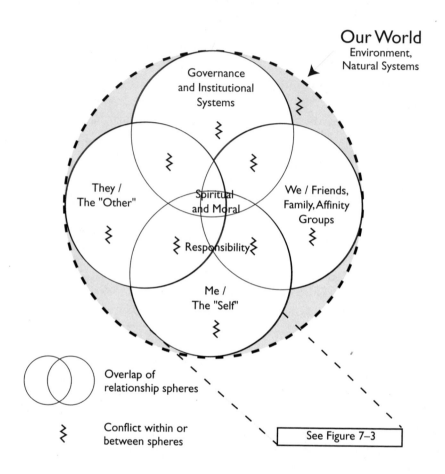

foundational to building inter-communal peace. In peace education it is important to go beyond tolerance of differences and gain an appreciation of differences.

Our world – The human relationship with the environment is the focus of this sphere. This recognises the interdependent relationship between humanity and the natural world of water, air, land and its natural resources, animals and plants. Both an environmental ecology and human ecology contribute to peace. When the natural environment is placed under stress or portions of it are destroyed, it can be a root cause of destructive conflict. In addition, in many conflicts around the world, a major driving force is greed for natural resources and a willingness to sacrifice the well-being of people, the environment, and governance systems in the process of obtaining the desired resources. In contrast, as the human family cares for the natural environment, then the natural world provides for the human family.

Spiritual and moral – Spiritual and moral capacities exist within people. Moral capacity means that people can make choices between good and bad, appropriate and inappropriate, right and wrong. Each person continuously develops his or her own standards and also must interact with community standards within each context. Organisations and institutions, including governments, also have a moral climate that can be viewed as the character of the organisation, which is revealed by its behaviour. Within most legal frameworks both individuals and groups can be held accountable for their actions. In peace education, children, youth and adults need to be nourished in defining their values in relationship with others and assisted in strengthening the moral courage to stand for values that build just and peaceful communities.

People also have a spiritual capacity that can take many forms and expressions. Sometimes this shows itself in the organised framework of a particular religion – Christianity, Islam, Buddhism or traditional religions. At other times this spiritual capacity is primarily seen as an awareness of a higher power or of spirits or as a deeply personal or communal relationship with God. There are times when spiritual pursuits greatly strengthen people's capacity to contribute constructively to peace. There are also times when the power of the spiritual is strongly tilted towards the destructive. Peace education is not a form of religious education. However, peace education must take seriously the spiritual and the moral capacities of people and provide ways for strengthening constructive spiritual resources and building moral courage for the work of peace.

Governance and institutional systems – This final sphere in Figure 7–2 displays the organising capacity of people to employ relationships to live together and accomplish various tasks. Each organisation contains human networks of relationships, both formal and informal. In addition, organisations develop their own systems and structures which try to control or determine how people will relate to one another and how tasks will be accomplished. Every organisation has its own types of dysfunction which can contribute to destructive conflict both within the organisation or within the community where the organisation functions. One of the simplest forms of organisations is the family system, either nuclear or extended. Roles are defined, relationships are built, tasks are accomplished. The family system can be a venue of very destructive conflict, including domestic violence, or it can be an environment where peace is built and values that support a just and peaceful community are transmitted. Peace education needs to help children begin to think about the simple ways people organise in the family, in the school and in the community. This lays a foundation for children eventually to be engaged in the process of strengthening good governance or effective organisational patterns in the workplace and the community.

Overlapping spheres – As is evident in the diagram, all spheres of this relational framework overlap. In one sense, every destructive conflict or constructive peacebuilding process is affected by a nested set of relationships. The whole person is a combination of all of these relationships. A person's relationship with himself or herself has an impact on the relationship with friends, family and near neighbours. That set of relationships affects relationships with those who are different, the "other." All relationships are in the context of the natural environment, and everyone is a member of various organisational systems. The formation of a moral core, the strengthening of moral courage and the connectedness to the spiritual all influence the other sets of relationships. Therefore, as peace education is done, whether formally or informally, it has the capacity to affect all of these relational spheres and spread its influence within the community.

Diagram #2: Dynamic model: Persons in context

Figure 7–3 provides a dynamic model for affirmations that focus on the whole person, the ability to be both constructive and destructive, the responsibility to make choices with moral courage and the dynamic of continuing change. This model reinforces the relational framework in dealing with the whole person in context and also in recognising the role of the spiritual and moral in making responsible choices.

Figure 7–3 shows the following:

External contexts – People and communities are always found in a particular context. There is a physical environment, an economic environment, a governance system and a network of people, communities, cultures and relationships. The beliefs within the people and the world view that are prevalent is part of the context. The context is always dynamic, whether the changes are slow or rapid. All aspects of the relational framework are present in the context. The person is an individual transformation system. The external context provides input to the person and brings many forces to bear on the person. Then the person must deal with his or her inner beliefs, the outer pressures and the context in charting a course in life. The output from this personal transformation process has an impact on the external context.

Person – This represents the whole person – body, mind, emotions, will and spirit. Peace education seeks to engage the whole person. It is not enough to

Figure 7–3. Dynamic model: Persons in context

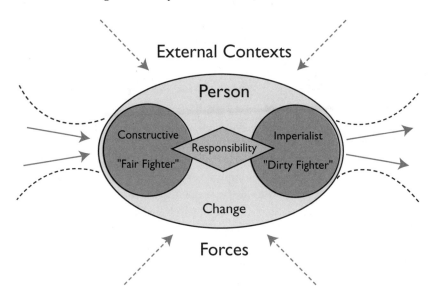

engage the mind and focus exclusively on content. That is why peace educators speak of knowledge, values/attitudes, skills and behaviours. Body language communicates even more powerfully than verbal language because it is a communication of the whole person. Conflict affects the whole person, and therefore peace must address the whole person.

Constructive – Within each person is an ability to be constructive and to contribute constructively and even heroically to others. This may be called the "fair fighter" within us. This potential to fight fair exists with all people, even those who show little evidence of it in their present or past behaviour. The "fair fighter" strives to benefit the whole community while taking seriously his or her own needs and value, works for constructive resolution of divisive issues, shows respect for diversity and appreciates the value of every person. Peace education seeks to strengthen the "fair fighter" within each person.

Imperial – Within each person is an ability to be destructive, to seek to rule over others. The imperialist is known for attempting to impose hegemony or control over others, particularly over nations or groups of people. But each person has a "little imperialist" within. The "dirty fighter" strives to benefit himself or herself at the expense of others. This may range from the use of violence, manipulation of information, deception, or withholding oneself or one's abilities from constructive peace and justice processes. The "dirty fighter" may be very active in the fight or may fight using passive aggressive behaviours. Peace education seeks to constrain the "dirty fighter" within each person. This may be done by a growing awareness of the potential to be destructive and a growing commitment to make choices to fight fair. The "dirty fighter" may also be constrained by the community through systems and patterns of accountability.

Responsible – Each person is responsible. For children, this is a developmental process of learning to bear responsibility and developing the ability to respond appropriately to various situations and challenges. Figure 7–3 depicts the struggle that ensues as the "fair fighter" and the "dirty fighter" offer conflicting options, forcing the person to make choices. This responsibility to choose is then informed by the spiritual and moral capacity of the person and engages the will as the person decides whether he or she has the moral courage to make some tough decisions. The concept of responsibility also implies that a person has the ability to act in many situations rather than only responding. Peace education engages people in understanding situations and making choices for action that keep destructive conflicts from developing and move current conflicts towards constructive resolution.

Change – Finally, this diagram recognises the reality of change. Change takes place continuously for everyone. There is developmental change that takes place from birth until death. The reality of death means that all change is limited by the time span of one's life, and all suffering, trauma, disease, and limitations are a shadow of the death that is to come. For many children who live in the midst of destructive conflicts, death, injury, trauma and the attendant types of suffering are common aspects of life. Peace education takes place in this reality and must find ways to deal honestly with the temporal nature of life. This temporal aspect of life is also a reminder that all changes that take place within the person are provisional rather than permanent. One may make choices for a period of years that tend to strengthen the "dirty fighter" within. However, it is still possible to change and move towards the constructive. Similarly, a person may be known as a "fair fighter" and an example to others of constructive behaviour and peaceful living. But that same person can then change in a negative way, make choices that are primarily self-centred and become a hindrance to justice and peace. Finally, change implies potential. Every person has the potential for positive and constructive change and growth. Peace education is built on a belief in the potentiality of each person. We teach peace because we believe that every child, every young person and every adult has the potential to change for the better and to contribute to a just and peaceful community.

RECOMMENDATIONS FOR APPLICATION
AND FURTHER EXPLORATION

The following areas raise questions and arenas for application of these concepts and for further exploration.

Global versus contextual – These affirmations from inner beliefs are an attempt to identify areas that have a trans-cultural relevance. This must be tested. In each local context and cultural setting the application of the affirmations will vary. As an example, the affirmation "We organise ourselves" does not specify *how* people organise themselves. In each culture families, clans, communities and governing systems organise themselves in dramatically different ways. This can be seen in family structures, roles of parents and children, gender roles and extended family networks of clans and tribes. Societies have a rich variety of governance systems. Among acephalous societies, like the Nuer of Sudan, there is no head person above the family level. They have a decentralised system of "custodians" with varying roles according to spheres of responsibility.[30] The original systems of the past have been modified by colonial rule and the introduction of chiefs by the British colonial system of indirect rule. In addition, the last few decades of conflict have made military structures dominant.[31] In contrast to acephalous societies are those with chiefs, paramount chiefs, kings, democratic systems and hierarchical structures. The apogee of hierarchical systems was the god-king model of ancient kingdoms and is still evident in the present-day Siem Reap, Cambodia, represented in graphic display by Angkor Wat temple of the twelfth century Khmer empire.

Religion specific – This chapter has drawn from a variety of religious teachings and beliefs. However, the faith drawn from most frequently is the Judeo-Christian tradition and the scriptures of that faith. Further study is needed to see how these affirmations from inner beliefs relate to a number of religions. It would be very valuable in a multifaith context to explore the teachings of each religion present in that setting. Rather than just pursuing a general understanding of each religion, these twelve affirmations could be used as a framework for the exploration. Religious leaders and adherents could be interviewed to see how they understand each of these affirmations through the lens of their religion. Religious texts and documents that provide teaching on these beliefs could be gathered, and those sayings could be incorporated in a peace education programme. Furthermore, the affirmations could become a basis for multifaith dialogue and discussion and to assist in mutual understanding and respect.

Culture specific – Culture incorporates religion but is far broader. Within each culture there are traditional teachings, patterns, proverbs, sayings and practices. Songs, symbols, art and language can provide insights into the belief systems of the culture. Each of these affirmations elicited from inner beliefs can be used as a way to explore a particular culture and discover its beliefs. A compilation of songs, proverbs and even games can be incorporated into a peace curriculum as part of the process to make it relevant to its context.

International and national conventions and laws – International conventions, like the Convention on the Rights of the Child, the Charter of the United Nations and the major conventions on human rights, codify many of these inner beliefs. This is a worthy area for continued research and exploration. This chapter makes reference to several of those documents. For some people lodging these beliefs in international documents is very helpful and carries weight when the affirmations are taught in a local context. In addition, many national documents incorporate these same beliefs in various forms. For any NGO, whether international or local, developing a peace education programme for its own context, it is advisable to research some of the core documents of that country and use quotations and references from the national context in the peace education curriculum. By using the twelve affirmations as a framework, a search can be made. National constitutions, laws, international conventions signed by the national government, resolutions of the legislative branch of government, rulings of the judiciary, or speeches of national founders, heroes and leaders are good sources of documentation. In addition, consider the national anthem; popular songs; children's stories; works of well known artists, sculptors, and poets; and even national monuments with their inscriptions. Once again, this helps to root the peace education curriculum within the context of the people and culture and the inner beliefs that are prevalent in that setting.

Interface with specific peace education curricula – These twelve affirmations are not a curriculum, but they can be used as a tool to examine and strengthen a curriculum chosen or developed for a particular context. These beliefs lay a foundation for understanding conflict and the dynamics of building peace in the inner person, peace between people and communities, peace with the environment, peace with the spiritual world and moral values and peace in the world of institutions and systems. As a tool, it is possible to take these twelve affirmations and create a matrix to elicit from the people and community what they carry as inner beliefs that directly affect peace and peace education. Focus group interviews could surface the beliefs along with stories and illustrations of how these beliefs are manifest in the life of the community. Once this is done, the beliefs articulated in that context can be used to test curricula to ensure that they are incorporated into the peace education programme. If there are any inner beliefs that were not included in the modules of a peace education programme, then supplementary learning activities can be added to the modules to strengthen the curriculum. The purpose of this chapter is to press us to examine our underlying beliefs that shape the values which need to be reflected in a particular curriculum or in peace education activities applied to a particular context.

Development programme implications – An integrated multi-sectoral programme of development, as found in many WV ADPs, always has a curriculum, even if it is not consciously understood or has not yet been articulated or documented. The processes used for the development programme, when done well, can help build a more peaceful and just community.[32] WV has articulated this in its research and has endorsed an approach that focuses on five strategic processes that can facilitate the integration of peacebuilding with transformational development.[33]

Development processes communicate a message to the community and are built on the inner beliefs and chosen values of the staff and organisation. When development processes contribute to a more peaceful and just community, that is also an informal type of peace education.

Consider the following illustration. Suppose that an ADP chooses to emphasise self-help groups (SHG) as a development methodology. The SHGs are intentionally organised across ethnic, economic or religious lines. The SHGs use participatory methods to make decisions, select their leaders and plan their activities. Several different SHGs are linked together in a coalition so that they can leverage their capacity to accomplish more.

How can this common illustration contribute to peace? In the WV framework for integrating peacebuilding with development, this example uses three of the five strategic processes: (1) creating a culture of good governance, (2) transforming persons, and (3) working in coalitions across boundaries. The SHG, by its design, teaches people how to create a responsive and inclusive governance system for a small group of people. When the SHGs are intentionally organised across ethnic, economic or religious lines, they provide opportunities for people to learn to live with their differences, make changes in their attitudes and begin to weave a pattern of shared experiences. The linking of several SHGs so that they become a coalition greatly strengthens their potential for impact, and it also gives the members increased incentives to protect a peaceful community that is bringing benefits to many. The strategic use of these development processes contributes to a more peaceful community without organising a single "peace project." It is integrated into development.

But we can go deeper than just exploring the development processes used. We need to ask, What are our inner beliefs that drive us towards using those processes? This is where the twelve affirmations apply. Consider the underlying beliefs that support this example of employing SHGs as a promising practice for peace. What does this example suggest we believe? It suggests at least the following:

- I am somebody . . . and so are you – we can work together as mutually and equally valuable people
- We are one – our unity is demonstrated by working as one SHG
- We are different – diversity can be valued and respected and can generate strength through combined abilities
- We need one another – one person alone accomplishes little and has unmet needs, but together we can accomplish much and meet one another's needs
- We organise ourselves – forming a SHG and linking with others in a coalition multiplies the good that we can accomplish
- I can contribute – each person has something to offer to others, and a SHG allows people to be full participants
- I am responsible – organising a SHG is a response to a perceived need, and joining the SHG is an assumption of personal responsibility to help it succeed
- I can change – within a diverse SHG and coalition I may have to face some of my prejudices and with the support of the group make changes in my attitudes and behaviours

Based on this one illustration of development practice I have illustrated eight of the twelve affirmations that have been discussed in this chapter. The message is straightforward. Our inner beliefs can shape our values and behaviours and lay a foundation for peace and peace education. Development staff can explore these twelve affirmations and examine their current programmes to see how these beliefs are being manifested in their context. When raised to a conscious and intentional level in the minds of an NGO staff team or with community leaders, these affirmations of inner beliefs can turn the entire programme of development into an informal peace education programme. Then, when a peace education programme is designed with a particular curriculum and taught in either a community-based or school-based setting, the formalised process of peace education will be undergirded by the methodologies and beliefs that drive the integrated multi-sectoral programme of development.

CONCLUSION

I believe that WV is practising peace education beyond its current profession. It is more common in life for one's practice to fall short of the standards we profess for ourselves. But in peace education we have not previously organised our thinking and beliefs clearly enough to be able to say that we have an approach. I am confident that most of our staff, if asked directly, would say that we do not have an approach or a philosophy for peace education. As a result, we have had a hidden curriculum. It has even been hidden from us. So in many ways this has been a process of clarifying our inner beliefs and our core values so that they intentionally undergird the peace education programmes that we conduct.

Our previously unarticulated philosophy of peace education has been formed by our core values as an organisation, our beliefs and philosophy about development and responding to emergencies, our commitment to engaging in advocacy for a more just society and our mission to follow Jesus in service to the poor with a special focus on children. What I have tried to do in this chapter is to identify and articulate inner beliefs that undergird our approaches to conflict and peace, to root those inner beliefs in the Judeo-Christian sacred scriptures, to relate them to the multi-faith context of our world, and to give them a global connection with international conventions and agreements.

It is my hope that this book will provide new tools and resources that give substantive guidance to any NGO leadership team seeking to embrace peace education as one of the programmes in its community. These affirmations from inner beliefs provide a framework that can be explored in a variety of cultural contexts. Chapters by Randall Salm and Robert Krech provide insight into the experiences and programmes that WV offices around the world have developed to employ peace education within the development context. These chapters enable learnings from one context to be known and applied in contexts across the World Vision Partnership. They also establish connections in multiple national offices, creating the opportunity for the formation of a dynamic network of peace education practitioners. Vachel Miller's chapters provide an overview and analysis of key curricula that are currently in use in a number of places around the world. With the insights from his analysis, it is possible for an NGO to choose one of these, or combine modules from several of them, to know the strengths and weaknesses of a particular curriculum and to supplement materials and activities that can enhance the curriculum for the local context. Mavis and James Olesen provide insight into the pedagogical principles and practices that need to be grasped and applied as we continue to keep our focus on children and develop programmes that are age appropriate, developmentally sensitive and holistic in approach. Heather MacLeod addresses the painful realities that so many children face as they live in situations of domestic violence or families devastated by HIV/AIDS, serve as soldiers in the midst of war, suffer as victims of conflict and deal with trauma as they try to recover and develop. Millions of children grow up in post-conflict or latent context settings that have less obvious but equally damaging forms of structural violence. Peace education programmes cannot assume that the context will provide relative stability, well-trained teachers, interactive learning environments or reasonable teacher-student ratios in the schools. Allen Harder opened this book with an Introduction that focused on nurturing a culture of peace and describing the mandate of peace education. His final contribution is a case study of Cambodia, found in Appendix 2. This case shows how to take the lessons of this book and apply them to a particular context in the development of an appropriate programme of peace education. For the reader, this is the journey . . . grasping the mandate, integrating the concepts and applying them to a particular context in designing a peace education programme that contributes towards and nourishes a culture of peace.

WV national offices around the world have specialised in community-based development with a high value on formal, non-formal and informal learning structures. So the challenge is great and the opportunity is before us. In a multitude of ways the children have been leading us. And they will continue to do so. This book is just an opening chapter of one NGO's journey into peace education. May these early steps along the way be used to encourage the WV community and many other NGOs to believe that we can all make significant contributions to peace education, to the strengthening of a culture of peace and to the development of more peaceful and just communities around the world.

NOTES

[1] John Paul Lederach, *Building Peace: Sustainable Reconciliation in Divided Societies* (Washington, DC: USIP Press, 1998); idem, *Preparing for Peace: Conflict Transformation across Cultures* (Syracuse, NY: Syracuse Univ. Press, 1995), 55–62.

[2] William Lowrey, "Passing the Peace," in *Land of Promise,* ed. Andrew Wheeler (Nairobi, Kenya: Paulines Publications Africa, 1997).

[3] Ian M. Harris and Mary Lee Morrison, *Peace Education,* 2nd ed. (Jefferson, NC: McFarland and Company, 2003), 9.

[4] Brian D. Leopard, *Rethinking Humanitarian Intervention* (University Park: Pennsylvania State Univ. Press, 2002), 39–40.

[5] Rob Kresch, in Chapter 2 of this book, describes the policy framework within WV that gives a home to peace education as an element of transformational development. He also describes how WV seeks to integrate peacebuilding and child protection within that framework.

[6] United Nations, Universal Declaration of Human Rights, 10 December 1948.

[7] Abram de Swaan, "The Social Construction of Hate: Modern Instruments at the Service of Genocide."

[8] Convention on the Rights of the Child, 30 November 1989.

[9] Bill Lowrey, "The Golden Rule as Conflict Prevention," *Global Future: A World Vision Journal of Human Development* (2005), 25.

[10] Brian D. Lepard, *Rethinking Humanitarian Intervention,* (University Park: Pennsylvania State Univ. Press, 2002), 50–52.

[11] William Lowrey, "Passing the Peace . . . People to People: The Role of Religion in an Indigenous Peace Process among the Nuer People of Sudan" (dissertation, The Union Institute and University, Cincinnati, Ohio, 1996), 127–28.

[12] UNESCO, "Declaration on the Role of Religion in the Promotion of a Culture of Peace," Statement 1, 18 December 1994, Barcelona.

[13] Stephanie Karza, "Keeping Peace with Nature," in *Buddhist Peacework: Creating Cultures of Peace*, ed. David W. Chappell (Somerville, MA: Wisdom Publications, 1999), 82.

[14] "Declaration for All Life on Earth," 30 September 2000, Nippon Budokan, Tokyo. Available on the UNESCO website.

[15] A four-person team of WV staff from Myanmar, Indonesia and the United States visited this ADP in July 2002 as part of the field exercise in training staff to do conflict analysis and tracking of indicators of peacebuilding within transformational development.

[16] John Paul Lederach, *The Journey toward Reconciliation* (Scottdale, PA: Herald Press, 1999), 17–26.

[17] Jane Magruder Watkins and Bernard J. Mohr, *Appreciative Inquiry: Change at the Speed of Imagination* (San Francisco: Jossey-Bass/Pfeiffer, 2001).

[18] Cynthia Sampson, Mohammed Abu-Nimer, Claudia Liebler, and Diana Whitney, eds., *Positive Approaches to Peacebuilding: A Resource for Innovators* (Washington, DC: Pact Publications, 2003).

[19] Hugh Halverstadt, D. Min. course in conflict management, McCormick Theological Seminary, 1980.

[20] Certainly there are widely recognised exceptions related to mental and physical health when persons are not held accountable for their actions. This is true not only in international law; it is also found in customary laws within tribal contexts.

[21] Stephen R. Covey, *The Seven Habits of Highly Effective People* (London: Simon and Schuster UK, 1989), 71.

[22] Mohammed Abu-Nimer, *Nonviolence and Peace Building in Islam: Theory and Practice* (Gainesville: Univ. Press of Florida, 2003), 62.

[23] UNESCO, "Declaration on the Role of Religion in the Promotion of a Culture of Peace," Statement 8, 18 December 1994, Barcelona.

[24] Dalai Lama, "The Nobel Peace Prize Lecture, Oslo, Norway," in Chappell, *Buddhist Peacework,* 211.

[25] Vachel Miller, "Peace Education Curriculum Analysis," draft chapter for the WV Peace Education Consultation, 2003, 29.

[26] Keith Bodner, with Bill Lowrey, *Paths to Peace: The Journey of God's People toward Wholeness* (Monrovia, CA: World Vision International, 2002), 28–30. Story by G. D. Niles with Nelathi De Soysa.

[27] Lawrence Kohlberg, "Moral Stages and Moralization: The Cognitive-Developmental Approach," chapter 2 in *Essays on Moral Development,* vol. 2, *The Psychology of Moral Development* (San Francisco: Harper and Row, 1984), 170–206.

[28] Mavis Olesen and James Olesen, "Teaching for Peace" (Chapter 5 in this volume).

[29] Bill Lowrey, personal experience and observation, February 1999, Thiet, Leer, Wunlit, south Sudan.

[30] Wal Duany, *Neither Palaces nor Prisons: The Constitution of Order among the Nuer* (Ph.D. dissertation, Indiana University, 1992).

[31] Lowrey, *Passing the Peace . . . People to People.*

[32] WV Peacebuilding has developed a training module for integrating peacebuilding and development. It makes use of the do no harm/local capacities for peace framework and additional conflict-analysis tools to assess the context. A two-year research process identified five strategic development processes that form a framework for integrating peacebuilding with development. Tools are used that enable communities to conduct their own assessments of their development programmes and to analyse how they are contributing to peacebuilding. Focus-group discussions explore the strategic processes and the extent to which they are being practised in the community. This approach to integrating peacebuilding in development functions as an informal peace education mechanism.

[33] "Strategic Processes/Indicators/Tools for Integrating Disaster Mitigation, Peacebuilding, and Response to HIV/AIDS in Transformational Development," WV Core Documents, Transformational Development, 2002. The five strategic processes are (1) creating a culture of good governance; (2) transforming persons; (3) working in coalitions across boundaries; (4) enhancing community capacities; and (5) developing sustainable livelihoods with just distribution of resources.

Appendix 1

Unpacking peace education

Vachel W. Miller and Robert Krech

WHAT IS PEACE EDUCATION?

For the purpose of this publication it is preferable to define peace education both in conceptual and programmatic terms. This facilitates the design of programmes in which both the potential and limitations of peace education are clear. Peace education is well suited to address some conflict dynamics, but it is not appropriate to address all the causes of conflict experienced by a community. Before defining peace education the two components concepts need to be clarified.

Peace is a preferred condition in which people and communities value and use effective mechanisms to resolve conflicts without violence, there is a presence of mutually beneficial and respectful networks of relationships at all levels of society and across all differences, and there is an environment in which people create and sustain institutions which honour truth and beauty, show mercy, practise justice and contribute to the common good (WV operational definition).

Education or learning is fundamental to being human. We are constantly learning in all aspects of our lives for our whole lives. *Learning* involves activities, processes and experiences that enable change in individuals and groups – whether by formal or informal means, whether intended or unintended, and whether direct or indirect. *Teaching* involves creating, facilitating and guiding the learning process. *Education* is structured and deliberate activities, processes and experiences that create change in knowledge, attitudes, values, skills, habits and behaviour.

This paper was a final product of the Peace Education Consultation (PEC), September 2003, held in Siem Reap, Cambodia. Revised and updated by Allen Harder, 2005.

Education can be both positive and negative in purpose and outcome. The purpose and outcome may not correspond with each other, as what is learned may not be what is intended. Education, at times, can directly or indirectly contribute to underlying causes of conflict. Also, when education does not address issues of conflict, it may further support violence. Ideally, education seeks to equip and empower people for effective engagement with their world, engagement that contributes to their own well-being and that of others.

Peace education is the learning and teaching that nurtures the knowledge, attitudes, values, skills, habits and behaviours that enable people to engage actively with conflict and violence and build a peaceful world for children and adults. It makes certain assumptions:

- In addition to seeking to facilitate engaging the world, peace education takes violent behaviour as the central problem and peaceful behaviour as the central desired outcome.
- Everyone has the capacity for participation in violence and destructive conflict and participation in peace and peaceful conflict transformation.
- Knowledge, attitudes, values, skills and habits are important to why people either participate in violent conflict or participate in peace.
- When individuals are nurtured in appropriate knowledge, attitudes, values, skills, habits and behaviours, they are equipped for peaceful relationships and empowered to engage critically with violence and people in conflict.

At a pedagogical level, peace education incorporates many of the best practices found in quality education. Quality education promotes relationships of care, respect and collaboration. In this way peace education shares the goals of quality education. Yet peace education involves more than the formation of peaceful learning environments. Peace education works for change at multiple levels, enabling learners to build peace within the self, family, peer group, community and world (for example, culture or structures).

The broad nature of peace education provides space for many different kinds of initiatives, yet what all peace education programmes have in common is a holistic effort to nurture the knowledge, attitudes, values, skills, habits and behaviours that enable people to engage with conflict and violence, build positive relationships and nurture a healthy community for peace.

PEACE EDUCATION AND PEACEBUILDING: WHAT'S THE DIFFERENCE?

Peacebuilding can be defined as programmes and activities that address the causes of conflict and the grievances of the past, that promote long-term stability and justice and that have peace-enhancing outcomes. Sustained processes of peacebuilding steadily rebuild or restore networks of interpersonal relationships, contribute toward just systems and continually work with the interaction of truth and mercy, justice and peace (WV operational definition).

Peacebuilding as currently understood within the broader peace and conflict literature fits well with WV's definition. It is both *structure-oriented* and *actor-oriented* in its approaches, and it serves both to prevent violence and to end violence, transform conflict and build peace. The structure-oriented approach is concerned with those political, social and economic conditions of human insecurity that are important causes of conflict. Peacebuilding interventions often seek to make governance systems more transparent and responsive, open economic opportunities and widen possibilities of participation in social arenas such as schooling or health care. The actor-oriented approach is concerned with the relationships and interpersonal dynamics between individuals and groups. Actor-oriented interventions usually involve conflict-resolution processes such as negotiation or mediation, or dialogue for reconciliation. Peace education is an actor-oriented approach within the larger sphere of peacebuilding, addressing the knowledge, attitudes, values, skills, habits, behaviours and in general the capacities of individuals or groups for more peaceful behaviour and relationships. Peace education, however, is not well suited to create direct changes to the structural conditions underlying conflict. As such, peace education contributes to peacebuilding. It is likely that peace education would be complemented by structure-oriented interventions and other actor-oriented interventions that might not be considered explicit peace education programming to address the complex causes of conflict and violence to build peace. For example, while peace education could affect the attitudes, perspectives, and behaviours of two groups in conflict with each other, peace education would not be likely to change directly the underlying economic or political issues that are contributing to their conflict. It might, however, address these issues in an initiative to raise awareness of their impact on peace and conflict in a long-term strategy to change policy.

WHAT DOES PEACE EDUCATION LOOK LIKE?

Peace education is an umbrella concept. Many different activities – such as teaching conflict-resolution skills or providing psychosocial assistance – are rightfully considered elements of peace education, even though by themselves they are not peace education. Peace education takes whatever tools, methods or approaches are conducive to teaching peace. A peace education programme is more than such individual elements. For WV, a peace education programme involves a holistic effort to nurture human capacities for peaceful living and the

Figure A1–1. Educational initiatives for learning to live together

Educational Initiative	Nature of learning goals
Peace education	Conflict resolution, peace, reconciliation, tolerance, respect for human rights, civic participation…
Education for mutual understanding	Social cohesion, respect for diversity, inclusive national identity…
Multicultural/intercultural education	Tolerance, respect for diversity, anti-racism, non-discrimination…
Human rights education	Respect for human rights and responsibilities, rights of women, children and minorities, tolerance, non-discrimination, prevention of bullying, civic participation…
Life skills/health education	Preventive health, HIV/AIDS prevention, prevention of substance abuse, respect for the health rights of others, respectful relationships…
Citizenship education	Active and responsible participation in civic/political life, democracy, respect for human rights, tolerance…
Education for sustainable development	Environmental sustainability, respect for the rights and welfare of all…
Humanitarian education	Respect for humanitarian norms, humanitarian acts, non-discrimination…
Values education	Internalisation of values of peace, respect and concern for others…

prevention of violence. As such, a WV peace education programme will reflect, to the extent prudent and possible, the following principles:

As a process, peace education:
- *responds* to the contextual nature of conflict and violence, particularly as experienced in the lives of children and helps create a culture of peace
- *respects* children as agents of transformation, enabling their participation in social analysis and action
- *equips* children with tools to protect themselves and others from violence
- *engages* schools, families and other actors in children's lives in order to transform environments that harm children
- *integrates* a critical awareness of gender in curricular choices and pedagogical practices

- *strengthens* relationships of caring, mutuality and trust
- *builds* the inner/spiritual resources for living in harmony and hope
- *nurtures* the healing of broken relationships with self, family, God, others and the environment

As a philosophy, peace education:
- *respects* human capacity, unity, diversity, equality and interdependence
- *affirms* responsibility for constructive engagement with conflict
- *bears witness* to injustice and violations of human dignity at all levels of society
- *advocates* for the possibility of change at the local, national and international levels

Education initiatives can also be categorised by the types of goals they set out to achieve.[1] Even though the different interest areas reflect a different starting point, they clearly have overlapping goals, as illustrated in Figure A1–1.

The flower diagram (Figure A1–2) on the following page summarises the principal features of peace education discussed in this section. The foundational pieces make peace education unique among other peacebuilding and conflict resolution interventions. The philosophy is the "attitude" behind the key features of what makes peace education what it is, although these are shared by other approaches to peace. Examples of peace education programmes or interventions are on the flower petals.

NOTE

[1] This section is taken from Margaret Sinclair, "Learning to Live Together: Building Skills, Values and Attitudes for the Twenty-First Century" (Geneva: UNESCO International Bureau of Education, 2004), 22.

Figure A1-2. A peace education sector diagram

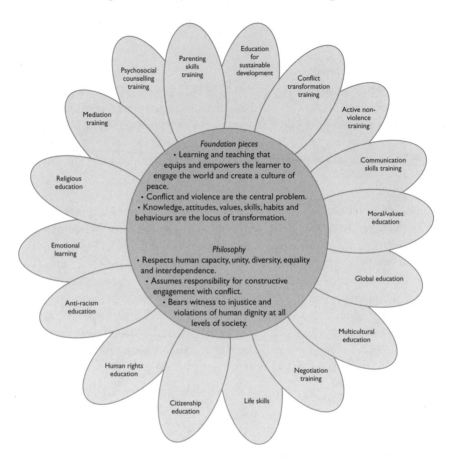

Appendix 2

Putting peace education to work in the context of Cambodia in the shadow of Angkor Wat

A Case Study

Allen Harder

The World Vision Peace Education Consultation, held in Siem Reap, Cambodia, in September 2003, included a field day at a World Heritage Site, the ancient Angkor Wat temple complex. The field trip was designed to facilitate an encounter with the realities of Cambodia. The senses would be deeply engaged: listening to the story of the Cambodian genocide and hearing Cambodians tell of their hope for restoration; marvelling at the magnificence of Cambodian antiquity, emotionally grappling with the poverty of the people and their suffering; touching the ancient stones; smelling the rich tropical rainforest; and being cooled in its breezy canopy of trees after the humid heat of open spaces. Encountering history as a part of the context constituted a new element in developing a holistic peace education concept and strategy.

ENCOUNTERING ANTIQUITY, HISTORY, GENOCIDE AND RECOVERY[1]

Angkor Wat itself is the most magnificent (and latest) of a vast complex of temples built between 800 and 1250. It represents the peak of Khmer splendour, when its kingdom spread throughout Indochina and down to the Malay territories. "Uncovering" these temples began in the mid-1800s with French explorers. When it came to light that their architecture, planning and artwork is of world-class quality, and that the Khmer kingdom represented a pinnacle in agricultural management and urban planning, modern Cambodians discovered a source of meaning and pride which would become pivotal in their emerging identity as a nation.

The genocide of the Khmer Rouge period (1975–79) sapped the nation of its strength, values and sense of self-worth. The Angkor Wat complex lay near the centre of the Khmer Rouge power base during the time of Vietnam's occupation of Cambodia (1979–89), where it struggled to regain power. Until the final capitulation of the Khmer Rouge forces in 1999, many areas around Angkor Wat were unsafe due to hidden landmines. Since then, the continued pillage of ancient artifacts by unscrupulous art merchants has threatened to deprive Cambodians of their rich heritage and identity.

After exploring the Bayon temple, which commemorates the great Cambodian king Jayavarman VII, ancient Cambodian life and military victories, we proceeded to the Ta Prom temple, characterised by the old-growth forest intertwining with the ruins. We were invited to find "seats" in an open space in the temple ruins to hear the story of an elderly Cambodian war survivor who had dedicated his life to sweeping in the temple. He told of his suffering under the Khmer Rouge and his dedication to service to the temple as an expression of his religious beliefs and as his contribution to the restoration of Cambodia. We then moved to another section of the temple complex, gathering under a Banyan tree – a sacred tree for Buddhists because the Gautama Buddha liked to teach his followers under a Banyan tree – to hear the reflections of young Cambodians.

An overview of contemporary Cambodia "second generation" society, those who did not experience the conflict directly, revealed a troubling insight into the impact of cultural genocide. Today's children experience second-generational trauma, which includes domestic violence, rape and sexual abuse, trafficking of drugs and people, and many other symptoms. Many Cambodians reflect on the degradation of Cambodian culture and values/morals. Even though Cambodia is not actively engaged in war, this generation is facing many problems that prevent the building of real peace in society. Those who were raised under Khmer Rouge patterns of influencing and controlling by threat and violence have brought this same pattern into their families and communities. Violence is becoming a normalised part of daily life, rather than being based in personal experience of civil war.

Group discussion revealed the need to understand the source, or root cause, of the high level of violence modelled in families, communities and society, as well as the high level of acceptance of violence, in order to understand its effects. The impact at the community level includes distrust and the self-focused survival instinct that has become a dominant paradigm for thinking and living. It is also the source of deep corruption and factionalism at all levels, as groups are normally formed through common opposition to an issue/group rather than commonalities, leading to segregation.

The group also heard the positive side about Cambodian society – the resilience of the people and the positivism/hope of the current generation that change will take place. People are resourceful in struggling through issues, and the ready laughter of Cambodians gives them strength to continue in the most difficult of situations. Cambodian people need to connect with their recent history, which has deliberately been kept hidden from the current generation in a mistaken attempt to move forward. Youth are relatively unaware of the Khmer Rouge history, even though they are struggling with its legacy. The result of being separated from the historical basis for positive Cambodian social norms is a normative of violence for these youth – their own peers and traumatised adults become their role models.

Many believe that issues of injustice and the failure to try former Khmer Rouge soldiers also affects Cambodians' difficulty in moving forward. The government has instilled the fear that opening the door to international tribunals will lead to war; many high-level government officials are implicated. Culture and religion support values that seek to save face and avoid confrontation. "Escape" is sought in the "forgive and forget" concept. There is a belief that judgement will be meted out in the afterlife – for Christians – or in the reincarnated life – the Buddhist concept of karma.

Systemic and institutional injustices threaten progress towards peace. The powerful in government are able to make the necessary changes to bring about peace but are reluctant to do so. Even as peace education aims to educate the powerless, the victims, the current generation cannot be safeguarded from conflict through peace education because normally victims do not even receive recognition that their rights have been violated, let alone experience justice. Even if justice is received, there is little to address the need for healing and for societal support of victims' needs. This highlights the need for advocacy for the rights and needs of victims and the need to make an impact at the institutional level when considering peace education and peacebuilding.

GENERATING PEACE EDUCATION PROPOSALS
IN THE SHADOW OF ANGKOR WAT

After lunch we proceeded to the main temple complex, Angkor Wat itself. But rather than pursuing "tourist" objectives, we were led to a grove of trees near the outer wall. The assignment: to put to work the rich inputs received in the morning towards designing a peace education initiative for a fictitious Cambodian Area Development Programme (ADP). A number of assessment questions was posed to help guide the planning.[2] We were given the profile of a typical ADP in a Cambodian village, highlighting issues conducive to violence present in the community (domestic violence, tension due to presence of former Khmer Rouge soldiers and demilitarised government soldiers, low school attendance, frequent possession of small arms by villagers, high level of children with disabilities, landmines, weak or nonexistent civil society, corruption of local officials, occasional communal disputes).

As this was a learning exercise, it was stressed that this session was to be more reflective in nature than output oriented – WV Cambodia would not expect any ready-made project designs coming out of this session. In the plenary feedback session three viable options were presented:

- Create a peace education activity to revitalise culture through art, theatre, music, storytelling and dance – a one-to-two-year programme bringing community together, building trust and serving as an entry point for future peacebuilding programmes in community.
- Identify problems; identify teachers and key community actors; focus on improving education and gender balance in schools, and on cultural renewal; gain trust and then treat issues such as domestic violence using renewed traditional concepts. Build relationships initially in order to address larger issues.
- Look at several entry points, shifting focus away from economic needs as the heart of the survival mode and instead providing community training to teach co-operation and bring about a more communal outlook. Also, provide conflict-resolution education and training about water and irrigation issues, and thus introduce peace education elements.

This exercise illustrated well the steps in a programmatic approach to peace education that began emerging throughout the consultation.

The debate around the inclusiveness or exclusiveness of peacebuilding, peace education, advocacy and child-protection interventions was stretched and sharpened through encountering Cambodia and Cambodians in their reality at Angkor Wat. The complexity of designing an appropriate strategy in a postwar recovery phase of a programme could not be avoided.

The Angkor Wat Day brought to light some important lessons:

- History must be taken into account where peace education is being contemplated, both as a source of identity, self-esteem and values and as the soil in which current problems are rooted.

- Meeting the need for justice for both the victims of past violence and the current victims of secondary violence requires an advocacy approach. The challenge is to incorporate this need into peace education.
- The collective suffering of a people in a postwar community requires a multilevel response, including peace education and peacebuilding interventions.
- Peace education is more than teaching conflict-resolution and transformational skills; it must address the issues of identity, social change, personal empowerment, strengthening positive cultural myths and symbols, and creating a nurturing social context for youth to become agents of peace.
- We need to experience the context with all our senses to become attuned to issues and nuances of the conflict when considering peace education.

The Angkor Wat Day did what a day in a seminar room could not do: experiencing the Cambodian context with all our senses. Participants became attuned to issues and nuances that left an emotional impact while stimulating the mind and demanded a response.

In the shade of Angkor Wat and the post–Khmer Rouge context the consultation participants were able to celebrate the transition of Cambodia to a post-conflict situation as well as address the challenge of carrying out education for reconciliation and healing in their own national contexts.

GENERATING A PEACE EDUCATION INITIATIVE POST CONSULTATION[3]

After the consultation, WV Cambodia management and peacebuilding staff discussed possibilities for developing a peace education programme as an integrated component in our long-term, community-based ADPs. We hired a consultant to conduct participatory assessment of youth (including minority ethnic groups and disabled children), teachers and adults in a WV target community. The results of this assessment were analysed, and, in light of a number of articles from the consultation, the peacebuilding staff drafted an outline of a peace education programme/curriculum. The Peacebuilding Unit and the Gender and Development Unit then collaborated to hire and supervise a consultant to develop a draft peace education curriculum for non-formal children's clubs based on the assessment results and to further child participation processes in a number of target communities. The curriculum consistently drew on traditional and current cultural and societal factors and norms in Cambodia. The Peacebuilding Unit and the Gender and Development Unit worked together to revise the draft curriculum and to produce a number of Cambodian-style visual aids (including the published storybook *Who Is Responsible for Violence*). Two ADPs were selected to pilot the peace education curriculum in 2005.

The curriculum is designed for an eight-month programme. It includes modules on understanding ourselves and our emotions, diversity, gender, healthy relationships, good fun/bad fun, conflict resolution and peacebuilding – with a special focus on value transformation and empowerment. The final month and a half of the programme gives youth a chance to become peace activists in their own communities on issues of peace and violence which affect them (such as crime, inter-family violence, ethnic diversity, domestic violence, gangs, sexual violence). Youth themselves determined activities with the support of a WV mentor. WV Cambodia has piloted the curriculum in three children's clubs in two districts; it is currently revising the Khmer and English versions of the curriculum. A third ADP implemented the revised curriculum in June 2005. In March 2005 the Peace Road Clubs participated in a national children's forum as part of the U.N. Study on Violence against Children. Some club members were thrilled to have the opportunity to share their perspectives with high-level government, NGO and U.N. agency staff at the national consultation.

In addition to this programme WV Cambodia has contributed significant time, expertise and funds to a collaborative project co-ordinated by Tearfund to develop two sets of Safe Children Karaoke Videos, with corresponding secular and Christian training materials. These materials will be utilised by NGOs, religious groups and other agencies throughout Cambodia. Finally, WV Cambodia is currently selecting an ADP to participate as a designated Hub of Learning for the three-year WV regional peacebuilding initiative, entitled "Empowering Children as Peacebuilders." Peace education has become a strategic programming focus for WV Cambodia, which is providing a new vision for how youth and children can be important agents of transformation in their own families and communities.

As part of organisational restructuring, WV Cambodia has also recently created a Peace and Justice programme department, implementing about 10 projects addressing sex tourism, sexual abuse of children, worst forms of child labour, gender-based violence, child protection, peace education and peacebuilding.

NOTES

[1] This section was written with significant input from Bill Forbes and Cecile Archie.

[2] The questions related to (1) foundation, principles, context; (2) tools, methods, pedagogy; and (3) WV implementing, integrating, doing.

[3] This section was prepared by Bill Forbes, WV Cambodia's Peace and Justice program manager (June 2005).

Appendix 3

Peace education resource packet

Randall Salm

The objective of this annotated bibliography is to develop a functional and varied list of effective peace education resources for use by WV field personnel. This list of resources includes a wide variety of materials for developing, implementing and evaluating peace education programmes in many cultural, social and political contexts. It also partially addresses a few other topics that indirectly relate to peace education programme development, such as children in war, structural violence, country conflict assessments and peace agreements. When possible, the citation includes title, author, publisher, how the resource can be accessed, language, a short summary of contents and whether the material is more theoretical or practical in nature. While most materials are in English and Spanish, a few are in French, Chinese or Arabic. An effort was made to identify as many free resources as possible, but some materials for sale are also included due to their value.

GENERAL RESOURCES

AMELY, Lyons, France
http://amely.ifrance.com/amely/
This organisation provides mediation training and support for school and community mediation programmes. It is led by several university professors. In French.

Association of Conflict Resolution (ACR), Washington, DC
http://www.acrnet.org/
The ACR is a professional organisation dedicated to enhancing the practise and public understanding of conflict resolution. The ACR was launched in January

2001, when the Academy of Family Mediators (AFM), the Conflict Resolution Education Network (CREnet), and the Society for Professionals in Dispute Resolution (SPIDR) merged into one organisation. CREnet had a large conflict-resolution-in-education component – previously it was the National Association of Mediation in Education. ACR has many groups working on standards and materials in different areas of conflict resolution.

The Education Section provides resources and support in the fields of peace and conflict resolution in pre-kindergarten to 12th grade, plus higher education. The Community Section supports community-based dispute resolution through community mediation and dispute resolution; public education and training; community involvement in conflict-resolution processes; and prevention and early intervention. Its material is both theoretical and practical.

The ACR library contains a number of resource lists under the following headings:

- Conflict Resolution Education Resources—Preschool–Grade 3
- Conflict Resolution Education Resources—Grades K–6
- Conflict Resolution Education Resources—Grades 6–8
- Conflict Resolution Education Resources—Grades 7–12
- Conflict Resolution Education Resources—Higher Education
- General Conflict Resolution Education Resources
- What Is Conflict Resolution Education?
- Recommended Guidelines for Effective CR Education Programs in K–12
- Teaching Students to Be Peacemakers
- Implementing a Peer Mediation Program
- Does It Work? The Case for Conflict Resolution Education in Our Nation's Schools

Boys Town Press, Boys Town, Nebraska
http://www.girlsandboystown.org/btpress

This organisation sells a wide variety of materials on child development, self-control, anger management, conflict resolution, communication skills, positive discipline, co-operation activities, and coping and other social skills. Most materials are interactive and fun; a few are more theoretical.

Canadian Centers for Teaching Peace, Okotoks, Alberta, Canada
http://www.peace.ca/

This website is a portal to a number of peace education centres in Canada, with all the resources that they provide. Many conferences and seminars are available, with new events posted frequently. The Information Resources section contains an annotated bibliography of a large number of diverse books on peace and conflict resolution as well as several peace education videos.

Childs Work/Childs Play, Plainview, NY

http://www.childswork.com

This organisation sells a wide variety of materials on child development, self-control, anger management, conflict resolution, communication skills, positive discipline, co-operation activities, and other social skills. Most materials are interactive and fun for use directly by kids; some are more theoretical.

Community Boards, San Francisco, CA

http://www.communityboards.org/

Community Boards presented its school-based conflict-resolution programme in 1982 with the Conflict Manager Program, a peer mediation model. Many other resources for classroom and school-wide use followed: classroom curricula, videos and posters, technical assistance and consultation, training and workshops. Today, its comprehensive Whole School Approach to Conflict Resolution encompasses mediation for youth and for adults, conflict-resolution education classroom lessons and curriculum modules, classroom management, skill building for parents and creating community partnerships. The material addresses both theory and practice.

In 2004 Community Boards redesigned its Conflict Manager Program training manuals into comprehensive planning and implementation guides. Written for those with no prior training experience, they were redesigned to improve and maximise the training experience. The curriculum is research based and has been proven effective in reducing violence. Community Boards sells a small number of comprehensive materials containing programme planning and learning activities. For elementary students there is a peace education curriculum and mediation materials. There are separate mediation programme materials for middle and high schools. There is also a conflict-resolution curriculum for grades 6 to 12 that addresses conflict dynamics and analysis, communication, culture, emotions and problem solving.

Conflict Research Consortium, Boulder, CO

http://www.Colorado.edu/conflict/peace/

This is an excellent site with free materials on many topics related to conflict analysis and resolution; it is literally an online clearing house. It contains materials designed to help people deal better with difficult, long-lasting and resolution-resistant conflicts. Some of the materials are theoretical, addressing the nature of conflicts and conflict processes. Other materials are practical, discussing typical conflict problems and potential solutions. While the practical material draws upon theory, it is largely based on practical experience and is designed to provide solutions to particular problems. Key programme features include:

- free online access to over 1,000 pages of full-text materials
- over 30 theoretical essays which explain conflict theory underlying practical material
- analyses of 100 common conflict problems
- discussions of 194 strategies for limiting conflict problems
- summaries of 222 articles and books
- carefully indexed links to more than 200 other high-quality, web-accessible resources

Conflict Transformation Program (CTP), Eastern Mennonite University

http://www.emu.edu/ctp/ctp.html

The CTP promotes peacebuilder development and strengthens the peacebuilding capacities of institutions. The programme builds upon the Mennonite commitment towards non-violence, witness, service and peacebuilding, and on extensive Mennonite experience in disaster response, humanitarian relief, restorative justice and socioeconomic development. The programme encourages the building of a just peace at all levels of society, especially in situations of violent conflict. The CTP believes that conflict transformation approaches must address root causes of conflict, must be developed strategically and must promote healing of relationships. The CTP website has many free theoretical and practical articles, links to related organisations in the Philippines and in Ghana, and a list of networking websites.

Cooperative Learning Center (CLC), University of Minnesota

http://www.co-operation.org/

The CLC, a research and training centre, promotes the development of co-operative social relationships and skills, especially in children, through education. The CLC has reviewed more than 800 studies and has contributed more than 80 research studies on student-to-student interaction and learning. Training includes instructors from preschool through college in all subject areas, available in North America and around the world. CLC has been a part of the College of Education at the University of Minnesota for over 20 years, being primarily the work of Roger and David Johnson. Co-operative learning is a relationship in a group of students that requires positive interdependence (a sense of sink or swim together), individual accountability (each of us has to contribute and learn), interpersonal skills (communication, trust, leadership, decision-making and conflict resolution) and face-to-face interaction and processing (reflecting on how well the team is functioning and how to function even better). The website contains a number of essays on theory and practice. A list of materials can be found under the Books and Supplies link and purchased through Interaction Book Company in Edina, Minnesota. The CLC offers 24 different books on theory and practice and 7 videos and cassettes.

Courage to Change, Newburgh, NY
Phone: 800–440–4003
Courage to Change is a small publishing company that markets a variety of books, videos and other educational materials that address social development and common psychological problems. Topics addressed in their catalog include self-esteem, feelings and emotional development, life skills, character development, conflict resolution, diversity, bullying, anger management, counselling, attention deficit disorder, cognitive therapy, depression, addictions, treatment planning and more. The materials address both theory and practice.

Creative Response to Conflict (CRC), Nyack, NY
http://www.crc-ny.org
CRC empowers children and adults by teaching them the skills needed to find non-violent and creative solutions to conflict. CRC seeks to reduce violence in homes, schools and communities by offering conflict-resolution workshops in co-operation, communication, affirmation, bias awareness, mediation and creative problem solving. CRC was founded in 1972. Experienced CRC staff provide specially designed programmes for people of all ages to practise new ways of examining conflict and developing solutions. Participants learn the skills essential to the peaceful resolution of conflict. The founding branch of CRC is located in Nyack, New York. CRC has more than thirty network branches and affiliates around the globe. CRC conducts thousands of workshops each year, building on the Quaker tradition of peaceful living. For more information, contact Creative Response to Conflict, Box 271, Nyack, NY 10960. Phone: 845–353–1796. Email: ccrcnyack@aol.com

Education for Peace (EFP), Sarajevo, Bosnia
http://www.efpinternational.org/
The EFP programme is sponsored by the International Education for Peace Institute. It seeks to resolve conflicts peacefully and create violence-free environments in schools, families and communities; build inter-ethnic harmony,

democracy and a culture of peace; assist traumatised children and adults; and share best practices. The EFP curriculum attempts to integrate peace into the public school curriculum with a set of core themes that transcend and unify the various subjects. While addressing themes such as inter-ethnic harmony, human rights and democratic decision-making processes, the programme gives particular attention to issues of world view, human nature, individual and collective development and the causes of violence and war. This approach supports a culture of peace and healing.

EFP's Conflict-Free Conflict Resolution model has been used in a number of contexts, including marriage, family and business, as well as in the EFP programme in 100 schools in Bosnia and Herzegovina, serving about 80,000 students and 10,000 teachers. The programme is focused on the values which promote conflict resolution and the ways in which those values may be activated to guide everyday behaviour.

Educators for Social Responsibility (ESR), Cambridge, MA
http://www.esrnational.org/

ESR helps educators create safe, caring, respectful and productive learning environments through the development of social skills, emotional competencies and character in young people. The Resolving Conflict Creatively Program is a well evaluated, K–8 programme in character education and social and emotional learning used in 400 U.S. schools. The programme is a comprehensive, multi-year strategy for preventing violence and creating caring and peaceable learning communities.

ESR also sells theoretical and practical materials:

- early childhood peace education (ages 3 to 7)
- elementary peace education (grades K–8): the Resolving Conflict Creatively Program, peace education literature programme, social and character education, family and bully-prevention activities, and a mediation programme
- Middle school level (grade 6–8): materials shared with elementary or high schools
- High schools: social-skill materials, and peer mediation and discipline programmes
- After-school peace education programmes

Finally, ESR, together with Lesley University, offers a master's degree in education with specialisation in conflict resolution and peaceable schools.

INCORE, Londonderry, Northern Ireland

http://www.incore.ulster.ac.uk/home/

INCORE is sponsored by the University of Ulster and the United Nations University. INCORE has a variety of information including country guides for regional conflicts; many recent peace agreements; and an information bank that contains lists of academic peace education programmes, peace studies resources and other resources.

Institute for Conflict Analysis and Resolution (ICAR), Fairfax, VA

http://www.gmu.edu/departments/ICAR/

ICAR is a doctorate and master's programme addressing deep-rooted conflicts in the United States and internationally. It is located at George Mason University and conducts research on the nature of social conflict and facilitates conflict-resolution processes at many levels. Co-located with ICAR is the *Peace and Conflict Studies Journal*, available online at http://www.gmu.edu/academic/pcs/. This journal addresses global social change, non-violence and peace movements, among other things.

International Storytelling Center, Jonesborough, TN

http://www.storytellingcenter.net/

The Interactive Storytelling Center creatively uses storytelling for many purposes, including conflict prevention and resolution. Under the Resources link it has a link to Building Peace One Story at a Time. Storytellers recognise the value of storytelling as a tool for reconciling differences and building peaceful relationships. One can take advantage of the ethical underpinning of a story to defuse harmful narratives. Folk tales and literary stories allow people to examine attitudes and prejudices on a symbolic level, employing ancient archetypes to focus on similarities rather than differences. Personal and family narratives allow people to see the world through the eyes of another person. The International Storytelling Center promotes the use of storytelling for peace and has several resources to assist interested people.

Living Values Education (LVE), United Nations, New York

http://www.livingvalues.net/about/index.html

The LVE programme is a partnership among educators around the world. It is supported by UNESCO, the Spanish Committee of UNICEF, the Brahma Kumaris and UNICEF. LVE is part of the global movement for a culture of peace in the framework of the International Decade for a Culture of Peace and Non-violence for the Children of the World.

This innovative global character-education programme offers a wide variety of experiential activities and practical methodologies that enables children and youth to explore and develop twelve universal values. In addition to programmes for classrooms and parent groups, LVE offers special materials for street children and children affected by war and earthquakes. Implemented in 74 countries at over 7,000 sites, educators implementing LVE report positive changes in teacher-student and student-student relationships inside and outside the classroom. Educators note an increase in respect, caring, co-operation, motivation and the ability to solve peer conflicts on the part of the students. Aggressive behaviours decline as positive social skills and respect increase. The LVE programme helps educators create safe, caring, values-based atmospheres for quality learning. More information on LVE can be found on its website in Chinese, French, Spanish and English.

Online Journal of Peace and Conflict Resolution, Washington, DC

http://www.trinstitute.org/ojpcr/

The *Online Journal of Peace and Conflict Resolution* seeks the reduction or elimination of destructive conflict. It is a free source of information to aid anyone trying to work towards a less violent and more co-operative world. Each edition of the journal typically has articles on peace education theory and practice, representing peace education efforts in many parts of the world. A search feature enables readers to identify relevant articles.

Peace and Justice Studies Association (PJSA), San Francisco, CA

http://www.peacejusticestudies.org/index.php

The PJSA is a non-profit organisation that was formed in 2001 as a result of a merger of the Consortium on Peace Research, Education and Development and the Peace Studies Association. Both organisations provided leadership in the fields of peace, conflict and justice studies. The PJSA is dedicated to exploring alternatives to violence and sharing visions and strategies for social justice and social change. The PJSA works to create a just and peaceful world through the promotion of peace studies within universities, colleges and K–12 grade levels; the forging of alliances in order to enhance work on peace, conflict and non-violence; and the creation and nurturing of alternatives to structures of inequality and injustice, war and violence through education, research and action. Three times a year the PJSA publishes the *Peace Chronicle*, year, which covers a variety of topics related to peace. It is available online. The Summer 2001 issue specifically addressed peace education.

Peace Education Foundation (PEF), Miami, FL
http://www.peace-ed.org/

The PEF is a non-profit educational organisation founded in 1980. The PEF's mission is to educate children and adults in the dynamics of conflict and to promote peacemaking skills in homes, schools and communities. It provides educational materials, training and innovative programmes that strive to make non-violent conflict resolution a lifestyle. The PEF offers grade-level specific, classroom-tested curricula for Pre–K through grade 12, as well as training and implementation assistance. The PEF model seeks to teach social competency and conflict-resolution skills and create a school environment based on trust, caring and respect. While each curriculum is presented in a developmentally appropriate format, the PEF curricula as a whole have a unified scope and sequence of content and skills. These curricula are being used in more than 20,000 schools around the world. There are two white papers that describe the philosophy, programme, curriculum and processes: "About the Peace Education Foundation" and "FAQ: Research, References and Other Vital Information."

The PEF sells a wide variety of materials, including curriculum, student materials, posters and videos. The four most popular books are offered in English, Spanish and French. The PEF also sells materials for family conflict resolution, bus drivers and in-school discipline programmes.

Peace Museum, Chicago, IL
http://www.peacemuseum.org/

The Peace Museum is actively dedicated to exploring creative, non-violent solutions to social issues through education, community involvement, and exhibitions chronicling local, national and international efforts to attain peace. The museum has a collection of more than 10,000 artifacts related to peace; they focus on individual peacemakers and artists, the horrors of war, Central America, domestic violence, human rights, prisons and women's leadership. Thirteen rental exhibits are available and travel to many cities throughout the United States and internationally. A peace curriculum is also available.

Peace Pledge Union, Cambridge, England
http://www.ppu.org.uk/

This website brings together resources of interest to pupils, teachers and parents to challenge the culture of violence and support peace and non-violence. Under the heading Study and Teaching Resources, it has considerable information online, including material on peace activists, non-violence and pacifism, conscientious objection, peace actions during various wars and reference documents.

Program in Dispute Resolution, NOVA University, Ft. Lauderdale, FL
http://shss.nova.edu/pcccp/

Among the many projects within this programme is the Project on Creativity and Culture in Conflict and Peacebuilding (PCCCP). It seeks to promote the role of cultural production, narratives and creativity in conflict-resolution and peacebuilding processes. The PCCCP addresses the role of cultural production and narratives through oral testimony, popular expressive traditions, literature, public folklore, mass media, photography, theatre, music, mural painting, and more.

Tampere Peace Research Institute, University of Tampere, Finland
http://www.uta.fi/laitokset/tapri/links.html

Most of this website is in Finnish, but the links identify, in English, a number of peace programmes throughout Europe, including Italy, Germany, Sweden, Denmark, Belgium and Ireland.

UNESCO, England
http://www3.unesco.org/iycp/

UNESCO has a large number of activities and resources in support of a culture of peace. Many of these are described in its brochure "Mainstreaming the Culture of Peace," available in English, French, Spanish, Arabic, Russian and Chinese. Below are the main programme areas of UNESCO, with the specific projects of each area:

- culture of peace through education: non-violence education, cultural and linguistic diversity in education, early childhood and family education, and the Associated Schools project
- respect for human rights: human rights, peace and human rights education, and International Decade of the World's Indigenous People
- equality between women and men: gender mainstreaming, women and a culture of peace, and gender equality and development
- democratic participation: management of social transformation programme; and human rights, democracy, peace and tolerance
- understanding, tolerance and solidarity: intercultural dialogue, dialogue among civilizations, tolerance programme, and fight against discrimination and racism
- participatory communication and free flow of information and knowledge: freedom of expression and democracy, ethical issues in communication, and media education.

- international peace and security: UNESCO water portal; ethics at UNESCO; education in emergency, crisis and reconstruction; and human security

UNHCR Peace Education Program, Geneva, Switzerland

http://www.ineesite.org/standards
http://www.ineesite.org/about/TTLMBKLT.pdf

UNHCR peace education is a component of the UNHCR Life Skills curriculum. Peace education programs in emergencies frequently include focusing on promoting tolerance, preventing violent behaviours and providing young people with conflict-management skills. UNHCR understands the delicate nature of starting peace education programmes in armed conflicts, due to feelings and attitudes about "peace" or "reconciliation" during or after the fighting. The UNHCR peace education program is based on the Living Values programme, a comprehensive values-education programme co-ordinated by the United Nations. Also available is a "Minimum Standards for Emergency Education" to complement the SPHERE manual and a "Technical Kit for Emergency Education" that includes peace education curricula.

The UNHCR peace education programme curriculum has been designed for use in resource-poor environments with multiple groups. The package contains guidebooks for teachers, teacher trainers and community workshop facilitators. The materials for the school-based programme are designed to guide novice teachers with a well-designed lesson framework and detailed instructions for activities. The main curriculum guides are supplemented by a rich collection of culturally appropriate resource materials, including posters, role-play scenarios and proverb cards. The resource guide explains the underlying theory, constructive classroom management and appropriate discipline. The INEE website provides guidelines for peace education programme development by clarifying effective strategies, identifying the concepts to be taught and suggesting critical values, skills and knowledge for peaceful interactions.

UNICEF, New York, NY

http://www.unicef.org/lifeskills/index_violence_peace.html

The best description of UNICEF's peace education work is the working paper "Peace Education in UNICEF," available at http://www.unicef.org/lifeskills/PeaceEducationUNICEF.pdf, written by Susan Fountain in 1999. It mainly addresses theory and programme development within the UNICEF framework, addressing activities within and outside of schools, elements of effective peace education programmes, participatory methodology and programme evaluation. UNICEF does not seem to have any additional information available online.

The UNICEF manual "Education for Conflict Reduction" focuses on issues of interpersonal conflict with the goal of developing culturally appropriate conflict-resolution skills in children. This manual has many activities covering a variety of key peace education topics. In the introductory sessions participants are asked to brainstorm their own ideas about the knowledge, skills and attitudes that should be included in peace education. At the end of each activity participants are encouraged to consider whether or not that activity would be appropriate in their own cultural context. At the end of the training, participants identify their priorities and select peace education lessons for their own settings. There is a concluding section on programme design.

World Health Organization, Geneva, Switzerland
http://www.who.int/en/

This website provides, in English and French, information on the World Health Organization's Life Skills education programme, which addresses a wide variety of health and social skills, including psychosocial skills, personal and social development, social problems and human rights. WHO identified five basic areas of life skills that are universally relevant for peace education: decision-making and problem-solving; creative thinking and critical thinking; communication and interpersonal skills; self-awareness and empathy; and coping with emotions and stress. In general, the term *life skills* refers to psychosocial skills.

Two free online documents from WHO's Information Series on School Health describe life skills in general: "Skills for Health. Skills-based Health Education including Life Skills: An Important Component of a Child-Friendly/Health-Promoting School" (Document 9) and "Creating an Environment for Emotional and Social Well-Being" (Document 10). It is possible that local WHO country offices may have developed additional educational materials or curriculum on life skills.

WRITTEN MATERIALS

Anger Management Student Workshop. Newburgh, NY: Courage to Change. Phone: 800–440–4003.
Workshop kit includes video, student handouts and teacher's guide. Kits are available for elementary, middle school and high-school levels. Helps kids identify

anger triggers and appropriate ways to channel anger. Cost for each about $140; cost for all three kits about $410. Practical.

Arcos, M. T., and P. Heyck. *Con Paz en la Escuela.* Bogotá: Ministerio de Justicia y del Derecho, 1998.
In Spanish, this book presents the Ministry of Justice's school mediation programme that was widely developed in Colombia. It explains its philosophical base, which focuses on social relations and personal and ethical development. It contains a number of activities for assessment and self-evaluation as well as developing curriculum, mediation and justice and peace programmes.

Aguilera Reija, B., et al. *Educación Intercultural: análisis y resolución de conflictos.* 2nd ed. Colectivo AMANI. Madrid: Editorial Popular, 1994.
In Spanish, this book provides a model for developing an intercultural education programme, addressing such issues as group formation, perceptions, interdependence and planning for change. It includes 58 activities for promoting intercultural peace. Theoretical and practical.

Ardizzone, L. "Generating Peace: A Study of Nonformal Youth Organizations." *Peace and Change* 28, no.3 (July 2003). Boston: Blackwell Publishing.
This article documents a study of youth participation in six different peace organisations in New York City in 2000–2001. It examines the problem of interpersonal and structural violence and why some youth become active in peace efforts and promotion of social responsibility. Theoretical.

Barak, G. *Violence and Nonviolence: Pathways to Understanding.* Thousand Oaks, CA: Sage Publications, 2003.
Designed as a text for university courses on violence this book examines most forms of violence, from verbal abuse to genocide. In the context of recovery and non-violence, Barak addresses peace and conflict studies, legal rights, social justice and non-violence movements. Employing an interdisciplinary framework, Barak emphasises the importance of culture, media, sexuality, gender and social structure in developing a comprehensive theory for recovery and non-violence. Contents include reciprocal violence and non-violence; case studies on violence and recovery; and summaries of mutuality, altruistic humanism, positive peacemaking and resiliency models of non-violence. Theoretical.

Bartel, B. C. *Let's Talk: Communication Skills and Conflict Transformation.* Newton, KS: Faith and Life Press, 1999.

Baxter, P. "The UNHCR Peace Education Program: Skills for Life." *Forced Migration Review* 11. Oxford: Oxford Univ., 2001.
Online http://www.fmreview.org/FMRpdfs/FMR11/fmr11.11.pdf
This article provides a three-page summary of the UNHCR peace education program with its application in Kenyan refugee camps.

Berman, S. *Children's Social Consciousness and the Development of Social Responsibility.* Albany, NY: State Univ. of New York Press, 1997.

Bickmore, K. "Education for Peacebuilding Citizenship: A Proposal for Teaching and Learning in the Context of Fragile Peace." *Canadian Issues/Thèmes Canadiens.* September 2002.

Bigelow, B., and B. Peterson. *Rethinking Globalization, Teaching for Justice in an Unjust World.* Milwaukee, WI: Rethinking Schools, 2002.

Boulding, E. *Building a Global Civic Culture: Education for an Interdependent World.* Syracuse, NY: Syracuse Univ. Press, 1990.

Boulding, E., and F. Mayer. *Cultures of Peace: The Hidden Side of History.* Syracuse NY: Syracuse Univ. Press, 2000.

Boutros-Ghali, B. "An Agenda for Peace." In *United Nations, Divided World: The UN's Roles in International Relations*, edited by A. Roberts and B. Kingsbury. Oxford: Clarendon Press, 1995.

Boyden, J., and G. Mann. *Children's Risk, Resilience and Coping in Extreme Situations.* A background paper to the Consultation on Children in Adversity, Oxford, 2000.

Briggs F., and R. Hawkins. *Child Protection: A Guide for Teachers and Child Care Professionals.* St Leonards, Australia: Allen and Ulwin, 1997.

Bush, K., and D. Saltarelli. *The Two Faces of Education in Ethnic Conflict: Towards a Peacebuilding Education for Children.* Florence, Italy: UNICEF Innocenti Research Center, 2000.

Carpenter, S., and W.J. D. Kennedy. *Managing Public Disputes: A Practical Guide to Handling Conflict and Reaching Agreements.* San Francisco: Jossey Bass, 1988.

This book provides extensive information on how to deal with public or inter-group conflict, including analysis, interventions, facilitating interactions and reaching agreement.

Cousins, L., and J. Jennings. *The Positive Behavior Handbook: The Complete Guide to Promoting Positive Behavior in Your School.* London: PFP Publishing, 2003.

Creating Peaceful Individuals. Mennonite Central Committee and World Vision Cambodia. Phnom Penh. No date.

Diamond, Louise. *The Peace Book: 108 Simple Ways to Create a More Peaceful World.* Berkeley, CA: Conari Press, 2001.
There are many simple and practical group activities in each section. Sections include inner peace, peace with family and friends, peace for children, peace at work, peace and public affairs, peace and co-existence, peace and reconciliation, peace and social change, peace and non-violence, world peace, peace and environment, peace and spirit, and the peace revolution.

Doucet, I. *Buscando la Paz en el Mundo: manual de recursos para la transformación del conflicto.* (In English, Resource Pack for Conflict Transformation.) Bogotá: Ediciones Clara – Semilla, 1998.
In Spanish, this book provides thorough explanations of most issues related to conflict transformation, which seeks to go beyond normal conflict-resolution goals to address the root causes of conflict and build systems that promote peaceful social interaction. The first section explains the causes and dynamics of conflict, key components of peace and various methods for transforming conflict into sustainable peace. The second part provides activities for skill development in conflict analysis, communication, negotiation, third-party intervention and sustaining peace processes after an agreement. The last part details how to manage the various types of workshops for skill development, conflict resolution and coalition building.

DuNann, D., and D. Leighton. *Introduction Chapter to Structural Violence* Draft. Online: http://www.psych.ubc.ca/~dleighton/svintro.html 1999

Elliott, H., ed. *Children and Peacebuilding: Experiences and Perspectives.* World Vision Discussion Papers. Melbourne, Australia: World Vision Australia, 2001.

Evans, J. "Children as Zones of Peace: Working with Young Children Affected by Armed Violence", The Consultative Group on Early Childhood Care and Development. *Coordinators' Notebook,* no. 19.
Online: http://www.ecdgroup.com/download/cc119aci.pdf
The contents of the manual include the situation facing children living in armed violence, the impact on children, developing appropriate interventions, principles for working with children affected by organised violence, early childhood programming guidelines, specific activities for young children and looking towards the future.

Fahey, J., and R. Armstrong, eds. *A Peace Reader: Essential Readings on War, Justice, Nonviolence and World Order.* Mahwah, NJ: Paulist Press, 1992.

Faith Based NGOS and International Peace Building. Washington, DC: U.S. Institute for Peace, 2001.

Fisas, V. *Cultura de Paz y Gestión de Conflictos.* Paris: Icaria, Antrazyt and UNESCO, 2001.
In Spanish, this book explores peace, violence, conflict, war, management of humanitarian crisis, post-conflict reconstruction, disarmament, and a global community based on ethics and a culture of peace. Regarding conflict resolution, it describes negotiation, mediation, two-track diplomacy and conflict transformation. It summarises the UNESCO Culture of Peace programme and its many different initiatives. Theoretical and programme development.

Fountain, S. *Education for Conflict Resolution: A Training for Trainers Manual.* New York: UNICEF, 1997.

———. *Peace Education in UNICEF.* Draft. UNICEF Staff Working Papers. New York: UNICEF, 1999.

Fullan, M. *Leading in a Culture of Change.* San Francisco: Jossey-Bass, 2001.

Galtung, J., ed. *Peace, War, and Defense – Essays in Peace Research.* Copenhagen: Christian Ejlers, 1976.

Garbarino, J. *Lost Boys: Why Our Sons Turn Violent and How We Can Save Them.* Garden City, NY: Anchor Press, 2000.

Guinan, K. *Peace Quest: Journey with Purpose – Nurturing Peace within the Self, Relationships, Society, and the Planet.* Kind Regards LLC, Blair NE. 2002 (order from http://www.celebratingpeace.com).

————. *Go with Peace: Enriching the Lives of Children through the Pursuit of Peace for All.* Kind Regards LLC, Blair NE. 2005. (order from http:// www.celebratingpeace.com). These two books by Kelly Guinan provide up to 200 activities for peace education organised under the themes of (1) Peace for Me, (2) Peace for Us, (3) Peace for Everyone, (4) Peace for the Planet, and (5) Practicing Peace. Excellent for trainers and teachers.

Halperin, D., ed. *To Live Together: Shaping New Attitudes to Peace through education.* Paris: UNESCO, no date.

Harris, I., and A. Callendar. "Comparative Study of Peace Education Approaches and Their Effectiveness." *NAMTA Journal* 20, no. 2 (1995).

Harris, I., and M. Morrison. 2nd ed. *Peace education.* Jefferson, NC: McFarland and Co, 2002.
The book begins with a discussion of the concepts of peace and peace educa- tion. It then considers religious and historical concepts of war, peace and peace education; describes how peace education can move people to work for social change and look for alternatives to violence; and discusses ways to begin imple- menting peace education in schools and other community settings. It addresses sensitive issues in peace education, key concepts and topics, important biologi- cal and cultural factors, and barriers facing those who teach peace. It provides the "how" of peace education by examining optimal pedagogy and practices. It includes a good annotated bibliography of peace education resources. Both theoretical and practical.

Holsti, K. *Peace and War: Armed Conflicts and International Order 1648– 1989.* Cambridge: Cambridge Univ. Press, 1991.

Hutchinson, F. P. *Educating beyond Violent Futures.* London: Routledge, 1996.

International and Cross-Cultural Negotiations and Dispute Resolution: A Re- source Manual. Boulder, CO: CDR Associates, 1993.

Isaac, A. *Education, Conflict, and Peacebuilding: A Diagnostic Tool.* Canadian International Development Agency's Peacebuilding Unit. Online: http:// www.acdi-cida.gc.ca/peace, under Themes/Education. 2002.

Jares, X. *Educación para la Paz: su teoría y su práctica.* 2nd ed. Madrid: Editorial Popular, 1999.
In Spanish, this book summarises the history of the peace education movement, including such programmes as the New School and Society of Nations, Montessori programme, Modern School, UNESCO's work and Peace Research models. It also provides an excellent model for developing a peace education programme that encompasses international understanding, human rights, multicultural education, disarmament, sustainable development and peaceful confrontation. Both theoretical and practical.

Keating, Tom, and W. Andy Knight, eds. *Building Sustainable Peace.* Calgary, Alberta: Univ. of Alberta Press, 2004.
Evolving around post-conflict peacebuilding, this collection presents an overview of the field of peace studies and offers fresh analytical tools which promote a critical reconceptualisation of peace and conflict, while also making specific reference to peacebuilding strategies employed in recent international conflicts.

Kreidler, W., and L. Furlong. *Adventures in Peacemaking: A Conflict Resolution Guide for School-age Programs.* Cambridge, MA: Educators for Social Responsibility, 1995.

Lederach, J. P. *Building Peace: Sustainable Reconciliation in Divided Societies.* Washington, DC: U.S. Institute for Peace, 1997.

Lederach, J. P., and M. Chupp. *Conflicto y Violencia: busquemos alternativas creativas.* Facilitator's Guide. Bogotá: Ediciones Clara – Semilla, 1995.
In Spanish, this is a leader's guide for training that uses participative techniques to build a strong sense of trust. Activities are Christian based and address non-violence, self-esteem and conflict styles, conflict analysis, communication skills and several forms of conflict resolution, such as negotiation and mediation. Both theoretical and practical.

Lee, E., et al. *Beyond Heroes and Holidays: A Practical Guide to K–12 Anti-racist, Multicultural Education and Staff Development.* Washington DC: Network of Educators on the Americas, 1998.

Martenz, A. *Character Building.* Newburgh, NY: Courage to Change. Phone: 800–440–4003.
This book provides 10 separate units dealing with various aspects of character development, such as relationships, self-discipline, honesty, citizenship,

responsibility and respect. Lessons use many learning formats, including role plays, discussions, art and reproducible activity sheets. For ages 11 to 15. Cost: about $25. Practical.

Meiners, C. *Learning to Get Along Early Education Series.* Newburgh, NY: Courage to Change. Phone: 800–440–4003.
This series teaches children aged 4 to 8 how to behave responsibly and respectfully towards themselves and other people. The six books address such topics as: when I feel afraid; understand and care; share and take turns; listen and learn; be polite and kind; join in and play. Each book is colorful and made to be read aloud, with discussions questions and additional games. Cost for each book, about $11; cost for the set of six books, about $65. Practical.

Mertz, G., and C. Miller Lieber. *Conflict in Context: Understanding Local to Global Society.* Cambridge, MA: Educators for Social Responsibility, 2001.

Miall, H., et al. *Contemporary Conflict Resolution: The Prevention, Management and Transformation of Deadly Conflicts.* Cambridge, UK: Polity Press, 1999.

Miller, V., and F. Affolter, eds. *Helping Children Outgrow War.* Washington, DC: Africa Bureau, U.S. Agency for International Development, 2002.

Moore, C. *The Mediation Process: Practical Strategies for Resolving Conflict.* San Francisco: Jossey-Bass, 1989.
This book provides detailed information on the nature and practice of mediation. It contains in-depth recommendations for assessment prior to bringing the parties together, leading the face-to-face interactions and reaching agreement. It addresses building trust and co-operation, identifying hidden interests and many other critical mediation issues. This information is applicable to many conflict-resolution efforts. Practical.

Nelson, J. *Positive Discipline.* New York: Ballantine Books, 1996.
This book provides a comprehensive model for teaching children self-discipline, responsibility, co-operation and problem solving. The contents provide useful tools for understanding children's behaviour, natural and logical consequences, using encouragement and regular meetings for setting rules and resolving problems.

O'Reilly, S. *The Contribution of Community Development to Peacebuilding: World Vision's Area Development Programmes.* Final report. Milton Keynes, UK: World Vision International, 1998.

Palomares, S., et al. *The Sharing Circle Handbook: Topics for Teaching Self-awareness, Communication and Social Skills.* Torrance, CA: Innerchoice Publishers, 1992.
This book provides information on Sharing Circle theory and practice. It describes how to set up and lead sharing circles, train student leaders and create discussion topics. It also provides a long list of discussion topics that help youth understand themselves and their feelings, relationships, school, communications and personal goals. Practical.

Panagtagbo sa kalinaw: A Basic Orientation Manual towards a Culture of Peace for Mindanao Communities. Mindinao: Catholic Relief Services, 1998.

Preventing Deadly Conflict: Final Report. Washington, DC: Carnegie Commission on Preventing Deadly Conflict, 1997.

Pritchard, M. *Life Steps: Building Character, Resiliency and Emotional Intelligence in Youth.* Newburgh, NY: Courage to Change. Phone: 800–440–4003.
This package contains 12 videos, each 25 minutes long, which address critical life skills for teens. Each video comes with a leader's guide. Topics include emotional intelligence, knowing who you are, self-control and taking charge, resiliency, empathy, caring and compassion, creative problem solving, getting along with others, building character, respect, responsibility, developing healthy relationships and doing your best. Each video costs about $75; set of 12 videos costs about $800. Practical.

Raviv, A., et al., eds. *How Children Understand War and Peace: A Call for International Peace Education.* San Francisco: Jossey-Bass Publishers, 1999.

Reardon, B. *Comprehensive Peace Education: Educating for Global Responsibility.* New York: Teachers College Press, 1988.

Repucci D., et al. *Preventing Child Abuse and Neglect through Parent Education.* Baltimore: Paul Brookes Publishing, 1997.

Rosandic, R. "Grappling with Peace Education in Serbia." *Peaceworks No. 33.* Washington, DC: U.S. Institute of Peace Press, 2000.

Rozenblum, S. *Mediación en la Escuela: resolución de conflictos en el ámbito educativo adolescente.* Buenos Aires: Grupo Editorial Aique, 1998.

In Spanish, this book provides a framework for understanding conflict and conflict resolution with youth, based on the author's Program for Alternative Conflict Resolution model. She addresses issues of change, programme implementation, conflict, negotiation, communication, conduct standards, perception, positions and interests, mediation and conflict de-escalation.

Salm, R. *La Solución de Conflictos en la Escuela.* Bogotá: Editorial Magisterio, 1998.
In Spanish, this book recommends teaching all children how to solve their own problems peacefully, through direct negotiation, while using mediation and peer review as secondary alternatives. It provides basic theory and 64 practical exercises for working with children on such topics as social relationships and norms; understanding conflict; communication; problem solving; self-esteem, affirmation and trust; respect and responsibility; tolerance and diversity; and cooperation and participation. There is also a guide for programme development in schools. Both theoretical and practical.

Salomon, G., and B. Nevo, eds. *Peace Education: Concept, Principles and Practices around the World.* Mahwah, NJ: Lawrence Erlbaum Associates, 2002.

Sandy, L., and R. Perkins. "The Nature of Peace and Its Implications for Peace Education." *Online Journal of Peace and Conflict Resolution* 4, no. 2 (2002):1–8.

Schilling, D., and S. Palomares. *Life Skills for Teens.* Newburgh, NY: Courage to Change. Phone: 800–440–4003.
This book contains 70 reproducible masters for life-skill activities for teenagers. Topics address managing anger, coping with fear, responsibility, understanding others, tolerance and achieving goals, among other things. Cost: about $30. Practical.

Schneider, Tod. *Transcending Violence.* Oregon: Trafford Publishing. Phone: 541–343–6813.
This book provides a novel exploration of the causes of violence, especially citing social learning theories and practice in everyday life. Based on this understanding of violence, the author proposes a number of pragmatic steps for reducing violence and living in peace.

Shapiro, L. *All Feelings Are OK: It's What You Do with Them That Counts.* Newburgh, NY: Courage to Change. Phone: 800–440–4003.

This comic workbook provides a fun way for children to learn about their feelings, needs and motivations. For ages 4 to 10. Cost: about $25.

Slavin, R. *Aprendizaje Cooperativo: teoria, investigación y practica.* Buenos Aires: Grupo Editor Aique, 1995.
Translated into Spanish from *Cooperative Learning: Theory, Research and Practice* (Allyn and Bacon, 1995), this book provides information on co-operative learning theory and practice. It provides practical guides on how to set up a co-operative learning classroom. It also describes potential academic and social outcomes of co-operative learning education methods. Both theoretical and practical.

Sinclair, Margaret. *Learning to Live Together: Building Skills, Values and Attitudes for the Twenty-First Century.* Geneva, UNESCO International Bureau of Education, 2004.
This study represents an attempt to interpret the aim of "learning to live together" as a synthesis of many related goals, such as education for peace, human rights, citizenship and health-preserving behaviours. It focuses specifically on the skills, values, attitudes and concepts needed for living together rather than "knowledge" objectives.

Sommers, M. *Children, Education, and War: Reaching Education for All Objectives in Countries Affected by Armed Conflict.* Conflict Prevention and Reconstruction Unit Working Paper no.1. Washington, DC: World Bank, 2002.

———. "Peace Education and Refugee Youth." In *Learning for a Future: Refugee Education in Developing Countries*, edited by J. Crisp. Geneva: UNHCR, 2001.

Stephan, W. G., and C. W. Stephan. *Improving Intergroup Relations.* Thousand Oaks, CA: Sage, 2001.

Stomfay-Stitz, A. *Peace Education in America, 1828–1990.* Geneva: UN Center for Human Rights, 1993.
The author presents the curriculum, writings and contributions of numerous peace educators in American schools, including Horace Mann, John Dewey, Fannie Fern Andrews, Edwin and Lucia Ames Mead, Jane Addams, Mortimer Adler, Albert Einstein and Robert Havighurst. Over 700 citations. Includes an extensive bibliography and a resource directory. Theoretical.

Tillman, D. *Living Values, An Educational Program: Living .Vvalues Activities for Children Ages 8–14.* Deerfield Beach, FL: Health Communications, 2000.

Trabajar para la Reconciliación: una guía de Caritas. Vatican City: Caritas International, 1999.
In Spanish, this book discusses reconciliation and conflict resolution from Christian and interdenominational perspectives. It provides a plan for programme development with fundamental activities for effective post-conflict reconciliation. It also summarises reconciliation experiences in 24 countries.

UNESCO Preliminary Consolidated Report to the United Nations on a Culture of Peace. Item 8.5. Code 1545EX/42. Paris: UNESCO, 1998.

UNICEF. *Children Affected by Armed Conflict: UNICEF Actions.* New York: UNICEF, 2002.

Varma, V., ed. *Violence in Children and Adolescents.* London: Jessica Kingsley Publishers, 1997.

Villa, J. D. *Estamos en Camino: talleres psicosociales para el desarrollo de las comunidades de paz.* Bogota: CINEP, 2000.
In Spanish, this book summarises peace education work in the Riosucio and Choco regions of Colombia. It contains 20 workshops addressing such topics as communication, community responsibility, conflict resolution, peacefully confronting armed groups, community decision-making, reinforcing the pre-war culture of peace, and relationships between leaders and the community. Its goal is to build a community of peace.

Weeks, Dudley. *The Eight Essential Steps to Conflict Resolution.* New York: Tarcher, 1992; *8 Pasos para Resolver Conflictos: mejore sus relaciones profesionales, familiares y sociales.* Buenos Aires: Editorial Javier Vergara, 1993.
In English and Spanish, this book explores popular but ineffective approaches to resolving problems and recommends an effective eight-step model for solving interpersonal problems. The recommended steps include creating the right environment; clarifying perceptions; note individual and shared needs; build positive, shared power; look to the future and learn from the past; generate options; develop individual pieces for building the ladder; and make mutually beneficial agreements.

ANIMATED FILM RESOURCES

Cultivating Peace in the 21st Century

The four films in *Cultivating Peace in the 21st Century* provide teachers with tools to engage high-school students in the search for a culture of peace in our homes, schools, neighbourhoods and global communities. The National Film Board of Canada films include:

- *Neighbours*: an Oscar-winning parable about two neighbours whose friendly relationship turns to hatred and who come to fatal blows over the ownership of a single flower located on the border between their properties. It is a great introduction to the causes of violence, presenting the fight for resources as an instigating factor in aggression, conflict and war (8 min).
- *Balablok*: an animated film caricaturing humanity's propensity to resort to violence rather than to reason. The whole arena of conflict is reduced to its simplest dimensions – cubes oppose spheres and violence transcends reason and understanding. No dialogue or commentary is necessary. Why they fight and what happens after the battle is a parody of sociocultural differences as the cause of conflict, violence and war (7 min).
- *View from the Summit*: a documentary about the 2001 Quebec Summit of the Americas. This video is designed to complement the *Cultivating Peace in the 21st Century* teaching resource for Grades 10–12. It includes ideas on how to incorporate the films into lessons, along with ready-to-copy student material and suggestions for evaluation. A free copy of the teaching resource, can be downloaded at http://www.cultivatingpeace.ca. This project was developed by Classroom Connections, a non-profit organisation dedicated to supporting public education in Canada (75 minutes, divided into five parts for classroom use).

The films can be ordered from the National Film Board of Canada (www.nfb.ca). Cdn$19.95.

Show Peace

The first three films in the Show Peace series have won 29 awards to date. These animated "shorts" without words provide good training material for conflict resolution with people from children to senior executives. Viewers can gain valuable insight into dealing creatively with disputes and anger at school, at home, in the workplace and in the community. Each videojacket contains a comprehensive bilingual (English and French) user's guide.

- *When the Dust Settles:* provides tools for conflict resolution. In this film two neighbouring gophers get caught up in slinging dirt, showing retaliation as a factor in escalating violence. This film succinctly illustrates how much can be lost, and how little won, by seeking revenge (7 min).
- *Dinner for Two:* Peace in the rain forest is disrupted when two chameleons get "stuck" in a battle for a bug, demonstrating retaliation as a factor in escalating violence, with catastrophic results. Luckily, a frog observing the fracas turns into exactly what they need – a mediator. *Dinner for Two* tackles conflict in lively, humorous and provocative ways. It shows that amidst the chaos that differences create, there are still paths to reconciliation (7 min).
- *Bully Dance:* about a bully who is himself a victim in his own home. The "stick people" in *Bully Dance* are imaginary, but this gritty tale is all too familiar. Like the dance beat pulsating throughout the film, the bully's intimidation of a smaller victim is unrelenting; no one stops the dance until serious harm is inflicted. While *Bully Dance* offers no simple solutions, it does compel viewers – teachers, parents and children – to take stock of their actions and to find ways to end peer abuse (10 min.).
- *Elbow Room:* You don't choose to sit next to someone who spurts ink on your face, talks loudly on the phone and plays irritating music, but in the workplace you have no choice. Or do you? This short animated film presents quirky characters who deftly "rewind" situations and start over when tensions get out of hand. *Elbow Room* is suitable for conflict-resolution training in the classroom and workplace, helping ensure that conflicts get resolved rather than escalate (8 min).

The films can be ordered from the National Film Board of Canada (www.nfb.ca). Cdn$49.95

UNICEF Cartoons for Children's Rights

Cartoons for Children's Rights is a UNICEF broadcast initiative that aims to inform people around the world about child rights. So far, the effort has forged partnerships with nearly 70 animation studios in 32 countries that have developed 30-second nonverbal public service announcements. UNICEF distributes the public service announcements to broadcasters for the cost of the tape. The spots have aired on more than 2,000 television stations globally. Some have won prestigious awards. In 1989 the U.N. General Assembly adopted the Convention on the Rights of the Child (CRC). This landmark treaty, now ratified by all but two countries on earth, spells out the rights of all children to health, to education, to an adequate standard of living, to leisure and play, to protection from exploitation, to express their own opinions and many more. All children have these rights. With its captivating images and cross-cultural appeal, animation is the perfect tool for informing children about their rights and society about its obligations, all over the world. Through *Cartoons for Children's Rights,* broadcasters can use their influence to help make the CRC relevant and important to the life of every child.

Two tapes are available from UNICEF. Tape 1, containing 29 spots, was distributed in 1998. These cartoons have reached an estimated viewing audience of more than one billion people. Tape 2, with an additional 37 spots, was released in mid 2005. It includes contributions from another 25 countries, covering the globe from Argentina to Armenia. Dozens of new characters have been created especially for the series. Hundreds of artists have participated – developing more than 45,000 drawings; they represent more than $3 million worth of donated time and talent. The public service announcements can be viewed at http://www.unicef.org/crcartoons/. They can also be ordered from the UNICEF website.

Contributors

Randall Salm has worked since 1987 on issues related to children in war and peace education, including documenting UNICEF's peace education experiences in Lebanon and Sri Lanka in 1991. He lived and worked in Colombia from 1995 to 2002, teaching conflict-resolution and peace skills to children, teachers and communities. He has recent experience with juvenile justice training and conciliation in court systems in Panama and Colombia, and currently works as an assistant dean at Northcentral Technical College in Wausau, Wisconsin, USA. He holds an MBA and a master's degree in conflict resolution.

Robert Krech has worked on and researched education and peace programs and policy for the last seven years in West and South Africa, South and East Asia, the Pacific and North America. As an independent consultant he has worked for NGOs, the World Bank, and is currently chief of party for a USAID-funded World Vision youth education project in Liberia. He holds a master's degree in education from the University of Toronto and specializes in comparative, international, and development education.

Vachel W. Miller, Ed.D., currently works with the Academy for Educational Development in Kampala, Uganda, as the research and policy specialist for a project on child labour and education. A graduate of the Center for International Education at the University of Massachusetts Amherst, his recent research has focused on indicators for peace-oriented learning environments. In prior work Miller co-edited a guidebook published by USAID for educational reconstruction in post-conflict settings entitled *Helping Children Outgrow War.* He has also been a staff member for a project focused on advancing healing and reconciliation in Rwanda. He lives with his family in Kampala, Uganda.

James Olesen and **Mavis Olesen** are retired educators from Regina, Saskatchewan (Canada). Jim, who holds a master's degree in education, is a retired high-school teacher and curriculum writer. He has finished writing a book about practical teaching methodologies around critical thinking skills and values education. Mavis, with a PhD in education, is an early childhood education expert and senior administrator. Both have experience in curriculum design and development in the province of Saskatchewan. They have worked within Aboriginal contexts in Canada and have done curriculum development in displaced peoples camps in Asia. They currently live in Regina, Saskatchewan, Canada.

Heather MacLeod, World Vision's international director of Child Protection and Children in Crisis, has applied her expertise in child protection, community and family structures and cultures of violence which confront children. Her work focuses on incorporating the needs of children facing violence in their environments into peace education, or conversely, how peace education can directly respond to their needs. Her past experience as a public health nurse in her home country of New Zealand provided her with a strong foundation for designing and managing projects for children affected by violence in many conflict situations, from the violence that children living in institutions in Romania faced to post-genocide Rwanda. Currently, she is responsible for the integration of the World Vision child-protection policy and practice. Her hands-on field experience in communities, combined with internal child protection policy development, provides her with a unique perspective to peace education. In addition to her official role, she is currently team manager for World Vision's Asia Tsunami Child and Family Protection group, based in Singapore.

Bill Lowrey is director of peacebuilding and reconciliation with World Vision International. He has led World Vision in integrating peacebuilding concepts and practices into emergency response, transformational development and advocacy ministries in its programs around the world and through regional peacebuilding networks. Lowrey received his PhD degree in 1996 in intercultural organizational behaviour and development from the Union Institute and University in Cincinnati, Ohio. His dissertation was a study of indigenous systems of peacemaking and conflict resolution among the Nuer people of Sudan. Based on his research, he developed and facilitated a peace process with the New Sudan Council of Churches that resulted in ending an eight-year war between the Dinka and Nuer peoples, the two largest tribes in southern Sudan. That initiative, known as the People-to-People peace process, was built around the inner beliefs and customary practices of the Nuer and Dinka people. In recognition of his work in Sudan he received the Peacemaker Award from the National Peace Foundation in Washington, DC, in June 2000 and the Peace Activist Award from the Tanenbaum Center for Interreligious Understanding in New York City in January 2001. Dr Lowrey lives with his wife, Linda, in Vienna, Virginia, USA; they have three adult children and three grandchildren.

Allen Harder has spent most of his working life in international community-development work. He has an MA in geography/international development from the University of Manitoba. He has extensive experience in senior programme leadership with the Mennonite Central Committee in post-conflict areas in Uganda, Cambodia, and Indonesia. Most recently, he worked with World Vision Indonesia for four years as senior peacebuilding and reconciliation advisor, where he led the peacebuilding unit to mainstream conflict assessment and peacebuilding strategies in emergency relief and community-development contexts. On behalf of the Asia Pacific PaxNet, he was instrumental in designing and organising the World Vision peace education consultation which spawned this book. He currently resides with his family in Abbotsford, British Columbia, Canada, where he does freelancing consultancy work.

Margaret Sinclair, a U.N. advocate of peace education, has spent many years in the U.N. system as an education planner, and promoter of education for refugees and other conflict-affected populations. Since 1987 she has worked with UNHCR's education programmes, and from 1993 to 1998 served as the senior education officer at UNHCR Headquarters in Geneva, where she helped initiate UNHCR's programme of peace and life-skills education for communities affected by conflict. After retirement in 1998 she has continued to undertake consultancies for UNHCR, UNESCO and other organisations concerned with education in emergencies. She resides in London, England.